The Turn of the Novel

THE TURN OF THE NOVEL

ALAN FRIEDMAN

NEW YORK OXFORD UNIVERSITY PRESS 1966

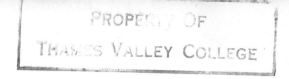

FOR LENORE

—ed ancor mi distilla
nel core il dolce che nacque da essa.

Acknowledgments

It is pleasant to be able to record my gratitude. At various stages in its preparation, this manuscript has been read by Frederick C. Crews, George P. Elliott, Richard Ellmann, John Paterson, Heinz Politzer, Robert Scholes, and Mark Schorer, from whose interest and responses I have drawn encouragement and profit. I want to thank Esther Baws, too, who undertook to type the final copy. My wife typed the earlier versions: she was at the typewriter two hours before our son was born; earlier, the idea of the book had been born with her help.

Acknowledgment is hereby gratefully made to Laurence Pollinger Limited, the Estate of the late Mrs. Frieda Lawrence, and The Viking Press, Inc., for permission to quote from *The Rainbow* by D. H. Lawrence, copyright 1915 by D. H. Lawrence, 1943 by Frieda Lawrence, all rights reserved, and from *Women in Love* by D. H. Lawrence, copyright 1920 by D. H. Lawrence, 1922, 1948, 1950 by Frieda Lawrence, all rights reserved.

Chapter 1, with minor changes, is reprinted by permission from *The Hudson Review*, Vol. XVII, No. 4 (Winter 1964-65). Copyright © 1965 by The Hudson Review, Inc.

Contents

INTRODUCTION

The main concern of this book is the development and transformation of the novel during the first part of the twentieth century. To understand the nature of that change, it is important to recognize that the course of fiction was altered not merely by radically new techniques, but by a new radical vision of experience. One of the purposes of this study is to explore the relation between the formal organization of experience in fiction and the ethical assumptions that guide the form.

The traditional premise about the design of experience which was profoundly, if variously, embodied in the eighteenth- and nineteenth-century novel, was the premise of a closed experience. That is to say, the novel traditionally rendered an expanding moral and emotional disturbance which promised all along to arrive, after its greatest climax, at an ending that would and could check that foregoing expansion. And so it did, more or less: first more, then less. But in the twentieth century a new assumption about the nature and the end of experience slowly came to dominate the form. My theme and argument in this book is the existence in the novel of a gradual historical shift from a closed form to an open form. In our century, I will show, the major tradition of the novel found energy by opposing a new premise to the old. Modern novelists turned to create experiences that promised from the outset, threatened all along,

and finally did indeed come to an end while remaining still unchecked—in extreme cases, still expanding. In the light of tradition,
that turn of the novel to an open form was a formal insult, but it
was more: it was a calculated assault on the "ends" of experience.

In the book that follows, I propose to trace that transition in modern English fiction; the seeds of change, however, were carried across
national and literary boundaries. Gide's *The Counterfeiters,* Verga's
early *The House by the Medlar Tree,* Kafka's *The Trial,* Mann's
The Magic Mountain—any of these might serve to illustrate the formal openness of experience in fiction. The change was widespread
and it was deliberate. In his *Journal of the Counterfeiters* Gide
writes:

> This novel will end sharply, not through exhaustion of the sub-
> ject, which must give the impression of inexhaustibility, but
> on the contrary through its expansion and by a sort of blurring
> of its outline. It must not be neatly rounded off, but rather
> disperse, disintegrate. . . .

In *The Trial* Franz Kafka comes to

> "A melancholy conclusion," said K. "It turns lying into a uni-
> versal principle." K. said that with finality, but it was not his
> final judgment. He was too tired to survey all the conclusions
> arising from the story. . . .

K. is still wondering at the end of *The Trial,* "Where was the Judge
whom he had never seen?" And at the end of *The Magic Mountain*
Thomas Mann gives us Hans Castorp's disappearance on the run
through the smoke of a world war, perhaps the only way, and certainly an open way, out of the novel's deliberate dialectic of recurrent impasse.

The roots of the change in the novel lie tangled deep in the modern experience. Causes in fields other than literature there doubtless
were—a confluence of psychological, philosophical, scientific, social,
economic, and political causes, analogues, and explanations—some,
if not all of them, bearing on each novel and every novelist. I think

it probably too soon to evaluate that confluence properly. But a shift in the literary vision of the ethical ends of experience has taken place. It may not be too soon to suggest that, whatever the causes, older assumptions about character, society, and career have already given place to newer ones; that self and world, sequence and consequence, if not in life at least in fiction, have been restructured; that, in short, we have been witnessing a mutation in the form of the novel which corresponds to a mutation in the ends of culture.

For endings are also ends. And that play on words is legitimate: life, culture, and the novel are processes; their ethical goals are revealed in the process which is their form. When, in the created experience we call the novel, "The End" consistently turns out to be another opening in experience, endlessness has become an end. The new form for the novel exposes not only heroes and antiheroes but readers, too, to an essentially unlimited experience. And when it does that most uncompromisingly, it gives us our special sense that in its vision of life something is intangibly but forcefully modern.

To show clearly the character of that transformation of the novel, I will try to point to a process that lies at the basis of fiction, that is, to an implicit structure that occurs as a process. That structure is a forward motion which can be distinguished from plot and which is more organic than plot to the existence of the novel as a literary form: experience. Now I think we are all prepared to acknowledge that the novel renders experience. We read a good novel because its experience is in some sense meaningful; as critics we ask, in what sense: what *is* the meaning of this experience? But throughout this work I am going to deal with experience itself as a meaning, as a shaping force lying behind and beneath other critical "meanings," more primitive and so more fundamental, less escapable, far more powerful in its meaningful impact on generations of readers. I am going to treat fictional experience as a process that must temporarily shape us while we are its readers. In order to talk about this primitive element in the novel, it has seemed advisable to give it a descriptive name. I call it a flux of experience. And to underline the point that fictional experience is not merely a process, but in all novels, as I shall observe later, a process with immediate—indeed, inexorable—ethical implications, I also call that same movement a stream of conscience: that is, a flux of moral experience. As I proceed, I hope to justify this peculiar usage.

Now it is probably easy to agree that experience is in some sense the basic "stuff" of fiction, but there may very well be doubt about the advisability or virtue of regarding it—or any flow or stream—as a form. One may especially wonder whether fictional experience can be analyzed into those clear and appropriate relationships that we require of a structure. But the doubt, I think, is unwarranted. The special genius of the novel as a genre is its ability to depict not only the exterior world of action, but the interior world of character—and one crucial thing more, the relation between them. In this respect, the distinction between Fielding and Richardson, for example, between stress on the organizing motion of plot and stress on the organizing motions of the heart, is only a relative one. Dr. Johnson is said to have observed that Fielding told his story by watching the face of the clock, Richardson by examining its inner workings; but the difference is a difference in emphasis and in degree, not in kind. In the novel, even in Fielding, the clock cannot keep time without the little inner wheels; and even in Richardson the little wheels must always move the hands. Time here is of the essence. It is the narrative interaction—that is, in time, in the storyteller's own good time—between the subjective and the objective worlds that creates what we call the novel. And it is there that I wish to focus an analysis of its organization of experience: on the interaction in time between the self and the world—not one, but *both* of which the novel as a genre, alone among literary genres, can transcribe with equal facility at precisely the forward-moving point of their intersection.

Experience, I will suggest, can be understood as a design. As long as we concentrate our attention to design only on such matters as plot and theme (the design of action and of thought: methods of imaginative organization more indigenous to the drama and the essay respectively, I submit), we inhibit our immediate response to the force and flow of fiction. We are probably all able to feel, but we will probably remain unable to describe or account for, a tide in the last two centuries of fiction: a change in the experiences that novels have rendered and in our experience of the novel. With respect to both the resolution of action and the resolution of themes, there is a single principal tradition of form for the novel from the beginning down to the present time (though exceptions exist: *Tristram Shandy,* for example). As in the drama, the main tensions and imbalances developed and elaborated up to the final crisis in the fiction are resolved after the crisis. Some such definition of form will work about as well for modern novels as for older ones. With respect, however, to the flux of experience—to the full, expanding interaction between the inner world and the outer world—the matter is otherwise. There are two traditions; and while they do overlap, there is an unmistakable shift, and a period of transition, in their relative power for shaping the novel. To see the change requires a change in our usual way of looking at novels, a shift in the focus of discussion to focus on their basis in experience. The slow but cumulative change is of critical significance. Earlier fiction attests chiefly and eloquently to the difficult necessity, the coherence and the dignity, of achieving a closed ethical experience in the course of life. Modern fiction attests chiefly and as eloquently to the reverse: an open experience.

A word about terms. The term "open" has already been made familiar as a term of literary criticism by Robert M. Adams in his admirable work *Strains of Discord: Studies in Literary Openness* (Ithaca, N.Y., 1958). However, since my approach to the novel differs from his, I am forced to use "open" in a sense different from his: though in another very familiar or "dictionary" sense of the word. (No other word will quite do to describe the movement away from the tightly knit pattern of the traditional experience in fiction. It seems best, accordingly, to state the difference in usage here and to follow it by a fuller discussion later in this book.) By "open,"

Adams means the deliberate and major nonresolution of meanings in a work. I use "open" to refer to an ending which does not contain or "close off" the rising pressure of conscience in a novel. That is, for Adams the total complex of meanings determines whether or not a work is closed. The determining issue for me is the specific underlying process by which fictional experience evolves and, in particular, the specific end of the process. The significant difference here is that one cannot say in Adams' terms (and he does not say) that the modern novel is "open"—i.e. predominantly unresolved in its major meanings. I hope to show (in my own terms), however, that the modern novel is a process of ethical experience which does not close: and that that is a major meaning.

A few words about my own terms. Since I was obliged to invent a descriptive name for a matter both moral and literary, I have on the whole preferred to choose a metaphoric and slightly playful one rather than still worse jargon: hence the "stream of conscience." For "stream," I employ whatever variety my context will allow—flux, current, swell—anything that will help keep visible this always half-vanishing but crucial fact of life in the novel: that its "structure" (as solid and stable a word as one can find) is in motion. It is always and only in motion. And that restless, energetic phenomenon can best be understood, not by denying its properties in an attempt to make it keep still for a minute, but by taking it for what it is, a flow, a journey, a process.

As for "conscience," I know of no simpler, more useful English word to describe the emotional and moral engagement of the reader in the experience of the novel. I do not think it will be difficult for readers and lovers of novels to distinguish "conscience" from "consciousness"—although the latter has become in recent years not simply a term more familiar, but a realm more familiar, to literary discourse. And indeed by my choice of words, "conscience" for "consciousness," I should like at least to suggest the reservations I feel about limiting discussions of modernity in the novel exclusively to matters of technique. Nevertheless, although after much searching of conscience I have been unable to find a better name for what I want to talk about in fiction, I frankly admit the limitations of the term.

Let me begin with limitations. By the "stream of conscience" in fiction I do not mean, for example, a flow of moral judgment, and I certainly do not intend to speak of a stream of choices between good and bad. I intend to speak of the full engagement between characters and their world, rendered for the reader as a process of their (and his) experience. By "stream of conscience" I mean to suggest *not* literally, but as clearly as I can, that the structural current of experience in a novel has, in its total organization, ethical implications. As a term, the "stream of conscience" provides a way of talking about those implications in the current of experience. It permits one to acknowledge that current as a moral form itself, a form that goes beyond (though it includes) the individual conscience of characters, a form that makes a moral statement of its own. Whereas the stream of consciousness, with rare exceptions, is used to refer to the modern novel alone, the stream of conscience will refer to the old novel as well as the new. Whereas the stream of consciousness in the novel is located *in* characters, the stream of conscience in the novel resides not exclusively in characters, but in the total experience of which they are a central part. The evolution of moral meaning in a novel—that gradual elaboration which asks for our imagination and receives our compassion, smiles, concern— is accomplished through and by means of character, but not merely in them. The stream of conscience will be used, then, to refer not simply to the moral process of behavior and awareness within characters, but to the total ethical process implicit *in the novel*—and hence in the reader. Moreover, I treat the process as a form. I offer a brief definition here: The stream of conscience in the novel is the structural flow of moral outcomes.

The outcomes I refer to are produced by the pressure of events. That pressure gives rise to an expansive movement from relative innocence to relative experience, a progress experienced within the novel by its characters, outside the novel by its readers. I hope to show that the flux of experience is the underlying structure of the novel; but I also want to show that the very same flux is its underlying ethical form. In other words, I want to deal with the novel structurally and ethically at the same time and in the same terms. Conscience in the novel is structural. I believe that it is its most important structure—that the ongoing process of conscience delineated by the arrangement of experience in any given novel is its fundamental imaginative organization. By regarding experience in both these ways at once, I hope to be able to demonstrate the existence of a progressive shift of design over the long course of the development of English fiction—design in both senses: formal pattern and ethical intention.

The Turn of the Novel

1

THE STREAM OF CONSCIENCE

Innocence in the novel is apt to be a slippery affair: let me quote from the most innocent fiction I know.

> A tall man of 29 rose from the sofa. He was rarther bent in the middle with very nice long legs fairish hair and blue eyes. Hullo Alf old boy he cried so you have got here all safe and no limbs broken.
>
> None thankyou Bernard replied Mr Salteena shaking hands and let me introduce Miss Monticue she is very pleased to come for this visit. Oh yes gasped Ethel blushing through her red ruge. Bernard looked at her keenly and turned a dark red.

The bashful specimen comes from *The Young Visiters,* misspelled and composed by Daisy Ashford at the age of nine.[1] Unquestionably, the book is some sort of masterpiece: it has a brilliantly managed, complex, and unified plot, a broad and sensitively rendered social milieu, a large number of astonishingly varied and vividly realized characters, a luxuriant surface of sensuous and material details integral to the psychological moment, technically admirable suspense and a firmly controlled point of view, incisive insight and deep irony, even a final fullness of meaning—all filtered through immature spelling and punctuation, and the immature, if not altogether innocent, mind of its author. Written at about the turn of the century and preserved in manuscript—penciled notebook—until

it was published in 1919, it constitutes not only a precocious unconscious parody but also a very reasonable facsimile of the genus Novel
for the first two centuries of its existence. Perhaps it deserves to be
honored as the last traditional novel, the *reductio ad absurdum*
which looks backward, as Joyce's looks forward. Forward or backward, nowhere else can we learn so easily what we want to know
about the genre as a whole. *The Young Visiters* reveals everything:
it is utterly defenseless.

> Well said Mr Salteena lapping up his turtle soup you have a
> very sumpshous house Bernard.
> His friend gave a weary smile and swolowed a few drops of
> sherry wine. It is fairly decent he replied with a bashful glance
> at Ethel after our repast I will show you over the premisis.
> Many thanks said Mr Salteena getting rarther flustered with
> his forks.
> You ourght to give a ball remarked Ethel you have such large
> compartments.
> Yes there is room enough sighed Bernard we might try a
> few steps and meanwhile I might get to know a few peaple.
> So you might responded Ethel giving him a speaking look.

As the excerpts suggest, Daisy Ashford's novel, like all novels, is
about morals, manners, marriage, and money; it gives us all of this
in movement. And its movement begins in innocence.

> . . . she ran out of the room with a very superior run throwing
> out her legs behind and her arms swinging in rithum.
> Well said the owner of the house she has a most idiotick run.
>
>   •   •   •
>
> Mr S. skipped upstairs to Rosalinds room. Good-bye Rosalind
> he said I shall be back soon and I hope I shall enjoy myself.
> I make no doubt of that sir said Rosalind with a blush as Mr
> Salteena silently put 2/6 on the dirty toilet cover.

Whose innocence? That of its tender author, age nine? Or of her
creature, Miss Ethel Monticue, age seventeen—"quite a young

girl" . . . "who did not really know at all how to go on at a visit," but seems used to "staying" with apparently anyone, Mr. Salteena or Bernard. When after barely thirty-six hours Mr. Salteena departs, leaving young Ethel in Bernard's hands, our child author has him remark solicitously

> I do hope Ethel will behave properly.
> Oh yes I expect she will said Bernard with a sigh.

And the very next time we see Bernard and Ethel

> I was thinking he said passionately what about going up to London for a weeks Gaierty.
> Who inquired Ethel in a low tone.

Clearly *both* heroine and author know what they are up to. And when Bernard and Ethel engage adjoining rooms at London's Gaierty Hotel, lingering doubt vanishes.

> The best shall be yours then said Bernard bowing gallantly and pointing to the biggest room.
> Ethel blushed at his speaking look. I shall be quite lost in that huge bed she added to hide her embarassment.
> Yes I expect you will said Bernard.

If Ethel Monticue is "innocent," the concept allows for a bit of sharp practice and may require some sharp definition.

To bring matters to a sharper, not to say glaring, focus, it may be useful to consider one of the least innocent fictions and one of the earliest English novels, John Cleland's classically dirty book, *Memoirs of a Woman of Pleasure* (originally published in 1749, just nine years after Richardson's first effort, *Pamela*). In the opening pages of her memoirs, Fanny Hill writes that her "foundation in virtue was no other than a total ignorance of vice, and the shy timidity general to our sex."[2] And although on page 125 she writes that experience "soon stripped me of all the remains of bashfulness and modesty," the intention of this sentence is clearly to remind us that even after one hundred salacious pages she still possesses some remnant of those qualities; after 161 pages, she manages to accept "a proposal which my candor and ingenuity [ingenuousness] gave me some repugnance to"; after 204 pages, she is still protesting, "I had not, however, so thoroughly renounced all innate shame as not to suffer great confusion at the state I saw myself in." And so on.

Now although Fanny Hill's protests, like the blushes of Ethel Monticue and the endless guarantees of Pamela ("don't be frightened—for—I hope—I hope, I am honest!"—Letter XXV), are never entirely credible, all three girls somehow manage to convey *nevertheless* a most unreasonably strong sense of innocence—their pure confusion perhaps about the impure stuff of their experience. Each girl, after all, is never entirely prepared for the next page. Admittedly, Fanny's case is special. Every new scene in *The Memoirs* exposes Fanny to a new "experience." The muck thickens; and it becomes Cleland's problem as a good pornographer to keep before the reader some (slowly crumbling) impression of Fanny's inner purity for purposes of titillation. And yet if we choose our words with greater care, we can say much the same thing about *Pamela* and *The Young Visiters*. No muck, less titillation; but each girl, as her innocence crumbles, is forever innocent of what the next chapter holds in store, unready—not quite ready—to interpret it when she arrives, unsure— not quite sure—of how to respond when it happens. Her innocence, if we may call it that, is the frame of mind on which the skein of action is wound.

There are differences of course. Ethel Monticue's innocence, confidently assumed by her author, is gradually and conclusively eroded by her story. Pamela Andrews' innocence must be circumstantially protested and re-propped so that Squire B— can assault it over and over again. But in both cases, innocence is the perspective which provides the necessary tension against which the events of experience may move. And the operation of that fundamental dynamism remains unchanged and essential—if subtler in its range of effects— elsewhere in fiction. Can we say everywhere?

Every central character must, in a sense relative to his story, be *relatively* innocent at the beginning of his book: that is, he must be more innocent earlier in the story than he is later in the story. On this agreement heroes and heroines shake hands: Moll Flanders with Molly Bloom, Joseph Andrews with Joe Christmas, Uncle Toby with Hans Castorp, Becky Sharp with Jane Eyre, Pip with Nick Carroway, Natty Bumpo with Bernard Profitendieu, and, for that matter, Lady Chatterley with Alice in Wonderland. To crash the world of fiction successfully, even a murderer, pervert, con-man, or whore must agree to respect at least one convention, the convention of his own innocence—Raskolnikov, Humbert Humbert, Felix Krull, Fanny Hill. The relative innocence of central characters is a truism; what is perhaps only barely less obvious is that "innocence" is a function of the organization of events, and may therefore serve as a very useful source for a theory of the dynamism—the motivation—of narrative form. At the outset of the form, even the most sophisticated of central characters must be innocent of what is going to come at him. Innocence in fiction establishes the crucial inner perspective because it is a pressure (as it were, "outward") to interpret freshly for the reader the outer, oncoming experience. The latter, outer experience, exerts a reciprocal pressure "inward" upon innocence (whether upon a great innocence or upon a presumed sophistication which proves inadequate, not quite adequate). The result, moment by moment from the character's point of view, is a continuous stream or series of responses—in perception, in action—which constitutes his gradual rendering of himself and his world. Now the intense energizing function of innocence in fiction helps to explain in part why so many great novels have had central characters of exceptionally great purity, simplicity, or harmlessness. But with an eye on structure, we can perhaps justifiably lay less stress on any specific traits of character. We can more generally and more usefully define the central subjective energy of the novel as an inward pressure not merely to engage with experience, but to interpret experience by responding to it.

For response, whether out of simplicity or subtlety, whether in action or feeling, constitutes interpretation.

> Ethel blushed at his speaking look. I shall be quite lost in that huge bed she added to hide her embarrassment.

We can, after all, imagine other responses than Ethel's blush; and other responses—if we or the author should insist on imagining them—would create other events, other characters, other stories; in short, another interpretation of experience.

> I screamed out, and fainted away. . . .
> When I recovered my senses, I found myself undressed and a-bed, in the arms of the sweet unrelenting murderer of my virginity. . . .   (Fanny Hill)

> . . . I sighed and screamed, and fainted away. . . . I knew nothing more of the matter, one fit following another, till about three hours after, as it proved to be, I found myself in bed, and Mrs. Jervis sitting upon one side . . . and no master, for the wicked wretch was gone. But I was so overjoyed, that I hardly could believe myself. . . .   (Pamela)

> It was only then that her still face showed the least emotion, a tear or two beginning to trickle down.
> "What are you crying for?" he coldly asked.
> "I was only thinking that I was born over there," murmured Tess.

Over the long course of a novel, the flux of such responses not only creates or defines character, as it obviously does, but does so through a process which we can isolate: with all the energy of their crumbling innocence, characters are obliged to interpret themselves as they interpret a changing experience.

That double interpretative process is the primary imaginative movement in the novel, a movement that is never merely cumulative, never piling experience on inexperience *merely* (as in some earlier narratives, Nashe's *The Unfortunate Traveller,* for example), but always moving from innocence to experience, from relative unreadiness to relative adequacy. The stream of responses, which is a stream of interpretation, is therefore a fundamental moral process in fiction.

Now it is precisely in the moment of not-quite-readiness ("I was only thinking that I was born over there") and under the threats and opportunities of experience, that responses are made, characters are created, interpretations are formed, and fictional events occur. In that incessantly recurring moment and in its necessary momentum toward sophistication may lie a clue to the relation between ethics and events in the novel. We may be able to trace a theory of single events which will allow us to see the full trajectory of such events in the fictional experience as both narrative structure and ethical form.

Let us consider for a moment the plight of those assaulted servant girls who hold open the doors through which English fiction enters so rudely—Defoe's Moll, Richardson's Pamela, Fielding's Fanny, and Cleland's Fanny. Four very different girls chased by four very different squires: a world of ropes, ponds, hedges, purses, employment agencies, mothers, captains, and justices of the peace. The pell-mell momentum of threat and opportunity, response and interpretation, grows increasingly tense. Squire A— tempts Moll with a silk purse and silken promises; Squire B— commands lackeys to spirit Pamela away and keep her in an isolated house; Squire C— has Fanny Goodwill bound on a horse and abducted as a "rebellious" wife; Squire D— has his procuress terrorize Fanny Hill with threats of debtors' prison before he generously pays her rent. Against such harsh and subtle assaults, what sort of chance does innocence stand?

In describing the existence of the novel as a genre, Mark Schorer has spoken of "the intersection of the stream of social history and the stream of soul. The intersection . . . provides the source of those generic tensions that make [the form] possible at all." [3] Can we go further and say that that same intersection provides the source of tension in each individual event by which any given novel achieves its existence? If we can, then we will at least be in a position to understand the remarkable resistance the soul puts up against social history, the sort of chance innocence does in fact stand against the harsh and subtle assaults of squires. But each individual squire immediately and loudly objects: by what authority, he demands, do we make a servant girl a soul and himself a fact of social history? Still, let us overrule him for a moment and side—tentatively—with the harassed girl. From her point of view, the encircling arms of the squire are embarrassingly twofold: the world of impersonal force (social, historical, physical, and natural) and the personal world of character. For squires, lackeys, and lovers, though "selves" like her own self, are from her point of view parts of her world, forces outside her soul with whom she must cope and to whom she must respond. (Our analysis is of course relative to an arbitrarily fixed center; and the moment the squire's protests become persuasive, we can—for his soul —simply reverse our procedure.)

Now in the moment of innocence, when the susceptible squire seizes her about the waist, each girl's responses may also be divided, conveniently, into a dilemma: how to feel about it and what to do about it. And both together inevitably constitute her "interpretation": perception and action. Moll Flanders is often content to count her blessings; Fanny Hill and Fanny Goodwill sometimes cry and kick against the aggressors; Pamela, "sadly vexed," usually contrives to let her affairs drift to the sexual brink. This running interpretation of the heroine's world—the current of small outcomes all along the way—generates its energy, it is true, through a limitlessly complex and dynamic interaction of self and world: the full inner and outer experience of fiction. But if we divide that experience—abstractly—into an onrushing double response of the self (insight and deeds) to the onrushing double trouble of the world (personal and impersonal), we have at least a coherent and consistent analysis that can account for any given event in terms of the tensions between individual innocence and the onslaught of history and society: blushes and wishes; captains and employment agencies. By including within the term "world" not only society and history but everything "not-self," we can even account for the circumstantial detail of events, the physical and natural texture: ropes, ponds, and hedges.

That double onrushing confrontation constitutes the full flux of experience in a novel. In turning now to the structure of events in fiction, I want to distinguish the formal development of experience from the development of what we commonly call plot. (The word *plot* is heavily and traditionally associated with "action"—we habitually distinguish plot from character as related but separable concepts. By now the association of plot with "what happens," and why it happens, is too strong to break.[4]) In what follows, I intend to place a more reasonable emphasis on the self in the experience we call the novel, and to restore focus on what in fact "happens" in fiction: interaction, rather than action.

If the fundamental unit of language is the word, and the fundamental unit of discursive prose is the assertion, it seems reasonable to suggest that the fundamental unit of fiction is the event. But what is a "single" event? We turn the page. The event isn't over: it may seem to be finished, but it has refused to sign a treaty over boundaries, refused to stay "single," even when the chapter closes on it. The event doesn't close: just as it has incorporated within itself smaller events, it contains within itself potentialities for further events which inexorably incorporate it, and it is alive only in the stream. By looking at events as an onrushing confrontation of tensions (between responses generated internally in character, externally in the world), we sacrifice something—the convenience of considering events as closed "units" in a separable "construction"—but we come closer to a dynamic and true sense of structure in the novel. For it is in some such way that we do read fiction: at some moments more aware of the force and flow of the stream; at other moments more aware of the single and particular event—we pause in acknowledgment, we know that it has occurred. If we can agree that the event is the fundamental unit of fiction, then we should agree to go further and say that the stream of events is the fundamental form of fiction.

The fundamental unit of fiction, "one" event, might perhaps at this point be formally defined as the dynamic confrontation of two pressures, self and world, which issues in any clear outcome—whether in perception or action or both, whether on the part of the self, the world, or both.[5] Several provisos and amplifications follow.

Of course the definition obliges us in the first place to choose arbitrarily, but not injudiciously, one character as the center or focus of any event and to regard that character as the continuous inward center for the duration of any sequence of events. If we regard as inward whatever parts of the narrative pertain to the character as a self—his perception, feeling, action, and so on—then *everything* else can be considered as outward, that is to say, as *that* character's world —including, most notably, other characters. The pressures exerted upon him by the world (in this relative analysis) can then include, for example, the pressures of other characters' perceptions, feelings, words, intentions, and actions; of social institutions and conventions; of physical and natural forces—soft chairs, open doors, bad weather, snapping twigs, falling rocks.

Now in the second place, it is in the nature of fiction as a stream or a process that any inner-and-outer happening which strikes us as an outcome will normally also be, with respect to the next event, an inception. That is, any new relation of the self to the world which we *call* an outcome either becomes *part* (if new stresses are introduced) or constitutes *all* of the two new pressures of self and world which produce the outcome of the next continuous event.

Third, thanks to a definition by now rapacious (inner *and* outer), all has become grist to our mill of events: everything from the discernible ripple of a single superficial incident to the strong but indistinguishable eddying of many incidents; even such stubbornly irreducible shoals and islands in fiction's flow as long landscapes or detailed interiors, summaries of the past or character analysis, expository meditation or the stream of consciousness; all of necessity become the background, the potential energy, inward or outward, for the succession of outcomes which establishes the stream.

Looked at in this way, therefore, an event is not only "what happens"—though, heaven knows, if we call it anything else, we are obligated to show what blessings will eventually flow from our sophistication. An event is a moment in the process which creates for us the inward self, a moment in the flux by which the self consciously copes with and interprets the world—other selves, social institutions, conventions, values, sometimes nature itself. But to say *that* is to say that the novel structures the specific and essentially moral process of which the human imagination is capable, structures it in the full substance of narrative.[6] By its obligatory attention to the perceiving self, the flux of experience in the novel is also obliged to create (even against the novelist's will) an ethical form in process. The stream of events may therefore (but not against our will) be studied as a process or flux of the conscience: we can grasp the perceiving self's attempts to grasp—to come to grips with, in perception and action—the assaults and offers of the surrounding world. Without changing the terms of our earlier definition of an event, but concentrating on the self's responses as developing and related interpretations, we can regard that peculiarly novelistic continuum, the inner-and-outer dialectics of the novel, event by event, under the aspect of an ethical form. We have already suggested that, with respect to structure, the fundamental form of fiction is the stream of events. With respect to meaning, it seems reasonable to suggest that the fundamental form of the novel is its stream of conscience.

That is what we read novels for: to share in creating the experience of one more world of selves, and one more, and one more. This may seem hardly a process of the conscience. But the novelist arranges in advance the rules of play (style and ethics; time and pace) and the reader, with all the energy of his imagination, plays the book as his experience. Instead of a "willing suspension of disbelief" before the unreality of the theater stage, the co-operative reader submits to (the novel produces) another kind of suspension, which we regularly call identification—a suspension of dissociation before the intrusion of personality. An "other" becomes our temporary self.

More precisely, others become our temporary selves, one after another, and we experience the fiction not from orchestra or balcony but from some center of the novel's world, through the temporary peephole of character, moving from innocence to experience on the subjective wedge that opens the future of narrative motion.

In that way the stream of events in the novel, just as we have described it, becomes the experience of the reader: the self and world in the novel become our self and surrounding world, so that the experience of reading a novel comes closer than does that of any other form of literature to our personal experience in time. The fundamental form of fiction in-forms the reader's self, and as a result consistent patterns of moral and emotional response in the novels of an era can and do take on the impact and authority of mythic information.

2

The Closed Novel and the Open Novel

The flux of experience—a process both inward and outward—is the novel's underlying form. Once one apprehends it as the crucial imaginative organization of fiction, it is possible to observe in its development during the history of the novel two opposed patterns for the process, two diverging myths[1] of experience. As the nineteenth century advanced into the twentieth, the novel began to offer not merely new techniques, but new patterns of information about the process of life. In so doing, the English novel moved gradually from a closed form of experience to an open form of experience, and it is on the existence and meaning of that historical transition that I wish to focus attention. I hope, as I proceed, to define it and to illustrate it.

The shift to which I refer was gradual, but it took place, I will suggest, with greatest velocity at about the turn of this century. And I think it reasonable to suggest further that the "open" pattern of the novel came into being because it reflected and conveyed a new attitude toward the process and goals of experience in life. It was not merely plot, or characterization, or technique, or point of view, or thought, or symbolic organization that changed; it was not a matter of irreconcilable meanings, conflicting themes, or difficult problems. The change in the novel took place at a more fundamental level than any of these; it left the novel "open" in another sense and in another respect, though in a respect that inevitably touched, now here, now

there, all these other matters. The process of experience which underlay the novel was itself disrupted and reorganized. The new flux of
experience insisted on a new vision of existence: it stressed an ethical
vision of continual expansion and virtually unrelieved openness in
the experience of life.

In this discussion of structure in the novel, a form conceived as in
motion and as a process, I am going to use "closed" or "open" to
refer to the full and final shaping of the flux of experience.[2] That
flux, I suggested in the opening chapter, can be regarded ethically. I
have called that ethical form—that is, the stream of moral outcomes
—a stream of conscience. By a closed novel, then, I mean a novel in
which that underlying ethical form, the stream of conscience, is
finally contained. By an open novel I mean a novel in which the
stream of conscience is finally not contained. And it is to the question of what "contained" means, and to the meaning of all these
terms[3] as they work themselves out in the fictional organization of
experience, that I now turn.

It is of course quite evident that both "flux" and "stream" of conscience are merely metaphors for the specific process by which moral
experience in the novel is expanded; but they are apt metaphors. In
the novel, any novel, the structural pattern of moral experience
grows broader and deeper as the tale proceeds. Each central "self"
moves through the process of events from a limited experience to a
wider one, from relative innocence to relative sophistication, from a
more-or-less contracted to a more fully expanded perception and interpretation. Tom Jones and Hans Castorp, Pip and Lord Jim, the
Vicar of Wakefield, Frankenstein, and Leopold Bloom undergo
much the same experience, *formally* speaking. To say that their experience grows "wider" or becomes "expanded" is to speak figuratively, of course. But by recourse to the preceding analysis of the
structure of events, it becomes possible to justify those terms with
some precision. We can show that Fielding takes great pains to convey the exact nature and degree of innocence with which his hero
enters the novel: Jones's limited "grasp" of experience—that very

grasp which his later history will find wanting. And we can show that Mann, Dickens, Conrad, Goldsmith, Mary Shelley, and Joyce take—must take—precisely the same strategic pains: all conveyed in terms of early events.[4] We can show, moreover, that the pressure of events modifies and alters that earlier innocent "grasp" through a process of responses and outcomes whose permutations are never merely cumulative, but which form an ever more complex and disturbing interpretation of experience in *that* book.

In the novel, then, the flux of experience considered morally—as a flux of conscience—is by its very nature expansive. But that implicit design, seemingly invariable, does vary. If it is looked at more closely, in terms of its continuous organization and its ending, two patterns—two traditions—can be distinguished.

The major tradition of the novel—more briefly, the traditional novel—nudges out of shape the innocent perceptions and expectations of its hero; in event after event he is buffeted, confused, and bedeviled through the buzzing, blooming confusion which is his history, until he achieves in the end—whether in fun or in grief, in defeat or decision—a new relation of the inward self to the outward world, which serves to contain the most distressing or disturbing of the preceding events. To put it more analytically, the major traditional pattern, or roughly that of the eighteenth and nineteenth centuries, postulates as its unspoken assumption about the shape of events that the climactic moments of widest moral expansion will be regularly followed by a limiting moral situation, a final re-organization of experience which restricts, either by narrowing or by moving in an opposed direction, the specific emotional and ethical expansion undergone in the climax. Briefly, in the traditional novel, experience is closed.

That is, it is closed by final events which constrict the climactic elaboration; and that deliberately controlled tapering after the preceding expansion of conscience gives the reader his sense of a "close." The novel's underlying formal impulse—elaboration and expansion—is checked and brought to rest. Nor is the closed ending "tacked on."

From the beginning and all along, events are arranged with the assumption of a closed ending in mind: and all the other techniques in the book—such techniques as tone, caricature, direct comment by the author—serve to reinforce the validity of the final ethical consolidation. The traditional stream of conscience—the structural flow of moral outcomes—no matter how boisterous or raging, is dammed; if it is allowed to flow through the ending at all, it escapes only through sluices.

In *Tom Jones,* for example,[5] the hero's rakish progress—from schoolboy pranks and affairs to a mock-Oedipal ordeal to prison and disgrace—concludes in the union of Tom and Sophia. The "innocence" of Tom—"that poor youth (however innocent)"—lies of course in "his own wantonness, wildness, and want of caution"; in that "goodness of heart and openness of temper [which] will by no means, alas! do [his] business in the world" (III, vii). Experience debases and refines him: ultimately his marriage resolves into a new "refinement" (XVIII, xii) the errors of his wild ways and oats, and the errors of his concealed birthright. And the refinement is structured by smaller outcomes all along the way: e.g. after sleeping with Mrs. Waters, who he will soon come to think is his own mother, he finds Sophia's muff left as her reminder and rebuke. The consolidated ending is envisaged by events and envisioned by the author— by all his assumptions about ethical and aesthetic form—in the recurrent see-saw construction, passion and penalty, imprudence and rebuke, by which Tom passes from innocence to sophistication.

The fact is obvious that the novel traditionally tends to conclude in marriage or death. But what I wish to call attention to is the equally evident fact that, traditionally, each final marriage or final death contains or "caps" each particular climactic expansion of conscience, that is, checks the preceding expansion and functions as a delimiting moral synthesis. (That this is *not* true of marriage and death in modern fiction even when one or the other is offered as a conclusion to the flux of conscience, I hope to show soon.) Now marriage is an expansion of a sort. It is so in the experience of the bride and groom, but not necessarily for the experience of the book. Tom Jones's marriage, finally uniting him with wisdom (his Sophia) dams and controls expanding error; Pamela's marriage (which as the subtitle assures us is "Virtue Rewarded") averts the further expansion of vice. And both are *formal* equivalents of Emma's marriage with Mr. Knightley, which banishes other errors and other vices—of judgment, of manipulation, of vanity. "Her own behavior had been so very improper! She was deeply ashamed, and a little afraid of his next look." But marriage with Mr. Knightley, like Mr. Knightley's advice, will restrain and contain Emma's improprieties.

> "You like it, my Emma, as little as I feared—I wish our opinions were the same. But in time they will be."

For it is the function of the conclusion to bring to rest not merely *an* expansion, but *the* expansion, to put to rest exactly those disturbances that have been raised to a pitch of complexity and intensity in the mounting climax. Only a whole novel and a whole conclusion can render that process fully.

> Mr. Rochester flung me behind him: the lunatic sprang and grappled his throat viciously, and laid her teeth to his cheek: they struggled. She was a big woman, in stature almost equalling her husband, and corpulent besides: she showed virile force in the contest. . . . At last he mastered her arms. . . . The operation was performed amidst the fiercest yells, and the most convulsive plunges. . . .
> "That is *my wife*," said he.
>
> .   .   .
>
> And now I thought: till now I had . . . watched event rush on event, disclosure open beyond disclosure; but *now, I thought*.
>
> .   .   .
>
> "He is stone-blind," he said at last. "Yes— he is stone-blind— is Mr. Edward [Rochester]."
>
> .   .   .
>
> "My seared vision! My crippled strength!" he murmured regretfully.
> I caressed, in order to soothe him.
>
> .   .   .

Then he stretched his hand out to be led. I took that dear hand, held it a moment to my lips, then let it pass round my shoulder: being so much lower of stature than he, I served both for his prop and guide. We entered the wood, and wended homeward.

Chapter XXXVIII

Conclusion

Reader, I married him. A quiet wedding we had. . . .

Now it seems reasonable (though heartless) to observe that Clarissa Harlowe's martyrdom is structurally and functionally parallel to Jane Eyre's or Pamela Andrews' marriages. Like anyone's marriage, Clarissa's Christian dying is an expansion of a sort, too. But her new breadth is a formal contraction of her experience. It reverses the previous eight volumes of expansion. It achieves (to recur to the definition I have given above) precisely a new relation of the inward self to the outward world, which serves to contain the most distressing or disturbing of the preceding events.

> She died blessing you all; and justified rather than condemned your severity to her. . . . I never saw, and never shall see, so blessed a *departure:* and no wonder; for I never heard of such a *preparation.* (IX, xxvi)

Anticipating a bit, we have only to compare Clarissa's death with, for example, the slow martyrdom of Joe Christmas in *Light in August* to see the structural and functional difference. Even in its last moments Joe Christmas's martyrdom effects no such reversal or reduction; it achieves no new relation of the inward self to the outward world which can contain the most distressing or disturbing of the preceding events; on the contrary, in a world of expanding dissolution and disorder (like Clarissa's), his death carries his fiction another step in the same, continuous direction. (And anticipating objections a bit, I hope to show that this same momentum is not merely a morbid vein in fiction: that the same form is entirely characteristic of modern novels in the lighthearted, optimistic, or comic vein; and is characteristically employed by modern novelists who offer to save and *order* their world.)

To return to the traditional ordering of the world of fiction, is it too unfeeling to say that Clarissa's saintly death functionally parallels, on its vaster scale, the small-scale and self-satisfied retirement from a life of distressing parish duties which concludes the Reverend Balwhidder's journal in Galt's *Annals of the Parish?* Galt eschews the usual endings. A thronged last sermon and the presentation of a silver server to a minister by his congregation conclude the book: they resolve a career in which, as the Reverend Balwhidder writes, "At the beginning of my ministry I was reviled and rejected." The total pattern—the conscientious struggles of the Reverend Balwhidder with his mildly corrupt parish, brought to an ending in peace with honor—bears the same formal stamp. Mackenzie's Man of Feeling, who, after a life of excruciating distress, expires with a much-delayed and much-needed confession of love on his white lips, takes good advantage of good form. Even Lewis's inexorable Monk, seized at the end by the Devil and carried aloft, learns to his amazement that his life has *not* been merely the moral expansion of his own diabolism, but a tissue of illusory temptations prepared by Satan and leading in fact—right then—to Hell; learns the hard way of the traditional structure of the traditional novel.

The Young Visiters too ends in marriage—three marriages, to be exact, and nineteen children. But the numerical explosion is a conscientious implosion. After six weeks in Egypt, "Ethel and Bernard returned from their Honymoon with a son . . ." (an outcome which, as we showed earlier, cannot be entirely unexpected). The Earl, a grasping con-man we have so far neglected to mention, "continued his merry life" until he married Lady Helena Herring, who "had very nice feet and plenty of money." And Mr. Salteena, Ethel's disappointed suitor, reluctantly married another girl and "found relief in prayer." The expanding and then narrowing flux of conscience as the pattern of the novel is a powerful assumption that underlies virtually the entire canon of English fiction from Defoe

and Richardson to Daisy Ashford and the early novels of the twentieth century. The novel's dynamic moral structure, novelists have
learned to their peril, had better be tapered to a "close." The form is
obligatory. Otherwise (as in due course we shall see) well-trained
readers are apt to mutter with dark prophecy and dire aesthetic dissatisfaction about the End of the Novel—that the end is unfinished
. . . but more . . . in effect, that the end is unfinished because no
finish was possible, that the end is a sign, the sign of a weakness, a
weakness in vision, the vision unreasonable, the reasons immoral,
the morals problematic, the problem ambiguity, ambiguity a failure,
the failure technique, the technique an evasion, the evasion of art,
the art of the novel: for the art of the novel is the art of life, and life
is short but the novel unending, the ending is novel, the novel is ending, and so on.

Now the assumption of a closed flux of experience has been normative, but not invariable. The contrary assumption about pattern
has all along held the charm of an attractive, opposed possibility.
Novels whose flux of experience resembles the open form that rises,
as I will suggest, to a position of major significance in the modern
novel were written from the beginning. It is certainly worthy of re-
flection that a few novels which were regarded in earlier centuries as
freaks or sports were composed in an open pattern; and have come
in our time, furthermore, to be considered both major aesthetic suc-
cesses, and also oddly in the modern key.[6]

Freaks and sports: as different from each other as they are, composed in two of the major keys of humor, nevertheless both *Tristram
Shandy* and *Jonathan Wild* derive a great measure of their wit and
satire from the opposed assumption (the "joke") that *in fact* moral
situations cannot—neither all along in the organization, nor finally—
ever be retrenched or integrated. For all the expansion, the inward
self can achieve no new, containing relation to the world. Through
(only through) the continuing inversion of irony, Jonathan Wild's
death by hanging was "as glorious as his life had been, . . . so truly

agreeable to it, that the latter must have been deplorably maimed and imperfect without the former." His execution was the "Completion of Glory" on the "Tree of Glory"; in his last moments he "applied his hands to the parson's pocket, and emptied it of his bottlescrew, which he carried out of the world in his hand." And the many wandering "selves" in the permutations and circles of Sterne's narrative are condemned by the subtler irony of indirection to persist (only barely) in widening efforts to escape from a comic purgatory that permits no exit. "L—d! said my mother, what is all this story about?—" Whether the last page was the intended conclusion or an accidental termination[7] hardly matters: the circles widen limitlessly. "A cock and a bull, said Yorick—And one of the best of its kind, I ever heard."

Comedy is one thing; *Wuthering Heights* and *Moby-Dick* were something else again. With almost incredible seriousness, both insisted on an explosive rather than an implosive structure. But *Moby-Dick,* the more uncompromising of the two, imagined an expansion of moral possibility projected to and even through the ending without a narrowing and integrating "stop" or containment. It was found not merely a freak, but an unacceptable one; forgotten . . . until its shape became our shape. (The importance to us of its expanding pattern should help to explain our superiority to earlier critics in discerning its merits. This is not to say that it is great because of its openness, but that when we returned to it, we found an impulse to a final moral openness that was virtually archetypal to modern fiction. Melville's *Pierre* has the same form, but it is not a great book.)

Wuthering Heights was not uncompromising. The centrifugal force of its moral savagery—seemingly unlimited, seemingly uncontained—was ultimately hemmed in (as Mark Schorer showed)[8] by the counterforce, the conventional force, of its narrators' viewpoints.

> [Heathcliff] looked at the opposite wall . . . with glittering, restless eyes, and with such eager interest that he stopped breathing during half a minute together.
>
> "Come now," I exclaimed, pushing some bread against his

hand, "eat and drink that, while it is hot: it has been waiting near an hour."

.   .   .

"I have not written my will yet; and how to leave my property I cannot determine. I wish I could annihilate it from the face of the earth."

"I would not talk so, Mr. Heathcliff," I interposed. "Let your will be a while: you'll be spared to repent of your many injustices yet. I never expected that your nerves would be disordered: they are, at present, marvellously so, however; and almost entirely through your own fault. The way you've passed these three last days might knock up a Titan. Do take some food, and some repose. You need only look at yourself in a glass to see how you require both. Your cheeks are hollow, and your eyes bloodshot, like a person starving with hunger and going blind with loss of sleep."

". . . as to repenting of my injustices, I've done no injustice, and I repent of nothing. I'm too happy; and yet I'm not happy enough. My soul's bliss kills my body, but does not satisfy itself."

"Happy, master?" I cried. "Strange happiness! If you would hear me without being angry, I might offer some advice that would make you happier."

"What is that?" he asked. "Give it."

"You are aware, Mr. Heathcliff," I said, "that from the time you were thirteen years old, you have lived a selfish unchristian life; and probably hardly had a Bible in your hands during all that period. You must have forgotten the contents of the Book. . . ."

The flux of experience was open; but Emily Brontë's sport, while stimulating, was watched closely within the text by umpires who adhered to the traditional rules of play; the novel was found acceptable.

Dickens toyed deliberately but warily with the open form. In *Bleak House* the two opposed patterns of conscience, open and closed, are played off against each other in the two plots as they intersect and pass each other. Lady Dedlock, whose life has been a deadlock, a fist clenched, is forced by the plot to reveal her moral transgression; the plot breaks open her conscience, Lord Dedlock's, and Tulkinghorn's, in a sudden and unchecked broadening of her emotional and moral responses in which she, Tulkinghorn, and Lord Dedlock are variously destroyed. In the counterplot, which literally surrounds the open form, the specific crises of Esther Summerson's climactic experience—her near escape from death by fever, even her near escape from marriage with her guardian—are finally "end-stopped," and this form barely contains the other opening form. (These crises are "end-stopped" by her healing marriage with a young man who is both doctor and savior.) It is an attempt, perhaps unsatisfying, to hold the line. The original conclusion of *Great Expectations* conceals another impulse toward a broad ending. The ending in which Pip marries Estella is of course narrow. But so was the first ending on its surface. For even there, Pip returns morally and emotionally to an appreciation of the solid virtues of Joe and Biddy—returns to his beginning—he even expiates by retiring into an unobtrusive commercial bachelorhood. To that extent the careful ending purports to integrate and contain a disturbingly broad moral situation. But Dickens vehemently refuses to give Biddy to Pip, an obvious ending which would certainly have narrowed the book (deplorably) and would have circumvented the ensuing fuss about whether Pip had any rights to Estella. The author's careful last assurances about the total uneventfulness of bachelor life were evidently not a narrow enough guarantee: readers demanded marriage with Estella. And perhaps they had a right to suspect that they were not being told the full story.

There are signs elsewhere, an inconsistent one in *Middlemarch,* for example. To place Dorothea's marriage to Ladislaw in perspective, one has only to compare it with the more powerful ending of *Daniel Deronda,* Gwendolen Harleth's staccato, "I shall live! I shall live!" Reiterated throughout the conclusion, Gwendolen's resolution to live (without Deronda's marital support) is intended to push back the terrifying expansion of insight and experience to which she has been exposed through earlier events. Dorothea's marriage, on the contrary, is a sudden expansion, a liberating last step: . . . arbitrarily and abruptly, it inverts our sense of the direction of earlier events, which seemed intended all along—quite as usual in nineteenth century fiction—toward a closed ending. "George Eliot's great novel *Middlemarch* is twisted at more than one point," David Daiches complains, "and especially in its conclusion, into a shape that is not the true shape of the vision of life that is being presented." [9]

The struggle between the more established pattern and the newer, less established possibility, between a finally contained experience and a finally unleashed experience, exists in the novels of Henry James, too. There it is a matter not of inconsistence, but of insistence; of characteristic Jamesian ambiguity on precisely this point: the moral interpretation of the seemingly closed ending. Significantly, there is no such problem in interpreting the conclusion of such an early work as *The American*. Christopher Newman's expanding experience reaches a clear limit; and it is contained. Not only unsuccessful in his suit for marriage, but finally incapable of the blackmail he threatens, his conscience and his experience narrow to a close together with the novel. Even his last impulse to interfere with the form is inhibited:

> "Their confidence . . . was in your remarkable good nature! You see they were right."
> Newman instinctively turned to see if the little paper was in fact consumed; but there was nothing left of it.

But James's own theoretical position may be taken as a warning of what is to come.

> Really, universally, relations stop nowhere, and the exquisite problem of the artist is eternally but to draw, by a geometry of his own, the circle within which they shall happily *appear* to do so.[10]

The italics are not mine: they are James's sleight of hand. Hand in hand with "relations" in his novels, the evolving stream of conscience also really stops nowhere; but James's pen moves quicker than the eye to make it happily appear to do so. Isabel Archer's rejection of the ardors offered—and the possibilities offered—by Caspar Goodwood; her return to the straitjacket of her marriage to Osmond: these *appear* the usual containing and capping of conscience after the crisis. But her return to Osmond is also, if not more so, the crest of a terrible and continuing expansion of her moral experience in the book; one that now implies a most painful continuation, one that really stops nowhere.

> "You must remember, after all, that he won't make you a scene!" said Henrietta with much intention.
> "He will, though," Isabel answered gravely. "It won't be the scene of a moment; it will be a scene of the rest of my life." (Chapter LIII)

Formally, the ending of *The Ambassadors* is penned in strict parallel. After he has absorbed all that Paris, Chad, and Mme de Vionnet can provide him with in the nature of moral experience, Lambert Strether's rejection of Maria Gostrey and his return to America constitute both a quick maneuver away from the prepared broad and broadening ending; and also something else: a clear-eyed renunciation which implies a continuing moral width and widening of its own. Kate and Densher's renunciation of Milly's bequest in *The Wings of the Dove* is a similar stroke by the master of appearances: "We shall never be again as we were."

What is ironically ambiguous in James is unambiguously ironic in Hardy.

> The century that began with Jane Austen's well-balanced heroines of strong will, who literally "will" themselves into normal behavior, rushes towards its end with the willful self-destructiveness of Hardy's heroines and heroes, who "will" themselves not into normality but into an obsession with guilt and penance.[11]

As the passage suggests, the difference from earlier fiction is not only psychological; it is structural. In the later Hardy we are spun around not only by an ending but by an organizing current of conscience all along. *Tess of the d'Urbervilles* virtually begins with the heroine's seduction. (How unlike the more traditional pattern, as in *Clarissa Harlowe!*) Hardy then goes on to make it deliberately and monumentally clear that the heroine's stream of experience cannot and will not finally be contained. (His last chapter, however, perhaps written by way of compromise with his audience, then attempts to wrench the book back into the conventional pattern and produces an aesthetic incongruity.) In *Jude the Obscure* the whirlwind of cruel probabilities, more extensive even than willful self-destructiveness, including cosmic indifference and an uncontrollable social destiny, is uncompromising: an unreversed, expanding experience to the last paragraph.

In Conrad, where we find clearly different heroes in a clearly different world, we find an oddly similar construction. In *Nostromo* experience is conceived as an explosive and irreversible process, finally unclosed and still expanding on a vast personal and national scale. In form, not content, the sailor Nostromo's experience is strikingly like that of the hay-trusser Henchard: a stream of events—obscurity, success, dignity, power, wealth, immoralism—that leads over the abyss into an orgy of self-destruction in a worsening world.

This is certainly *fin de siècle* gloom. But before anyone concludes that the open form is characteristic of the "tragic" novel, or perhaps characteristic only of pronounced pessimism or of the psychology of self-immolation, or perhaps the characteristic shape *only* of an experience which is finally corrupting, he ought to consider the case of E. M. Forster, in whose start-of-century novels the very same formal current is invariably employed to tell us about salvation and true happiness: the open stream of conscience of the first and second Mrs. Wilcox in *Howards End,* for example. And salvation again—a saving and final opening in experience—is the very unpessimistic intention of the very same pattern in D. H. Lawrence: *The Rainbow, Women in Love.* (Both books have been accused of not concluding at all: Ursula bypasses both marriage and death to end with the promise in a rainbow; Gerald's death by freezing brings about only increasing disturbances of conscience.)

I do not want to anticipate. The four novelists I am going to study would approve, I think, and novel-readers will not object, I hope, if I keep in suspense here the story of their efforts to change the course of fiction. For it is with Hardy that I propose to pause for an extended analysis of the turn of the novel. As I have been arguing, one might conceivably begin to study the change, since it is a gradual change, almost anywhere in middle or late nineteenth-century fiction. The novels of Dickens, or George Eliot, or Henry James, provide critical material for an investigation of the relative balance between shaping ethical assumptions. To concentrate, however, on that period in which the balance actually shifted, in which the subordinate formal impulse became the controlling formal impulse, one can most conveniently and economically follow the changes in a sequence of novelists from Thomas Hardy to D. H. Lawrence.

Though I do not want to spoil their plot (or their conspiracy, as one sometimes suspects), it is precisely because their plots include more than death or marriage that it may be harmless and useful to consider at this point just what happens to the old endings in the twentieth century. If, after the crisis of experience in her book, Emma's marriage—or Jane Eyre's, or Ethel Monticue's, or Pamela's—reorganizes and restricts the growing, the greatest, disturbances delineated in her book, Lucy's marriage in Forster's *A Room with a View* accomplishes the reverse. At the crisis, Lucy chooses the growing, the greatest, the most disturbing moral situation her book allows her in its delineation of disturbances: "Love is of the body; not the body, but of the body . . . she would gain something for the whole world. . . ." And this is precisely what Lady Chatterley chooses when she chooses to marry her gamekeeper: the broadest moral situation her book makes possible. The specific moral and emotional disturbances raised in the climax to a pitch of complexity and intensity are not put to rest: they are further expanded by the ending. Marriage, yes: but, in the new pattern of conscience, its emotional and ethical service to the fiction is reversed. And death serves the older and the newer novel with equal flexibility. In the inexorable rise of disorder, waste, and dissolution in Hawthorne's *The Scarlet Letter,* Dimmesdale's death serves to check the expansion. The death of Spandrell in Huxley's *Point Counter Point* only adds to the expanding disorder, waste, and dissolution. The death of Catherine in Hemingway's *A Farewell to Arms* does the same thing. Catherine's dying gives a final impetus to her fiction which is the very reverse of the impetus Clarissa's dying gives hers.

Can we say, then, and say it quite regardless of whether the novel is light or dark or speckled, that the expanding responses of the self through the time and world of modern fiction are finally uncontained? Can we say that final episodes which might in the past have delineated a containing reorganization of experience, no longer do so—morbidly hesitate to do so, cheerfully refuse to do so? To put it that way would not, of course, be to say that there are *no* final episodes, still less that there is *never* any reorganization of experience. It would be to say clearly that final episodes of reorganization (specifically) are simply absent; or *else* that the specific reorganization of emotional and moral experience which *is* delineated finally is one that holds the previous mounting disturbance (comic or otherwise) at an unreduced or even slightly intensified pitch. In short, it would be to say that the expanding flux of conscience in modern fiction is left finally open. It is "open" in one of three senses: finally uncontained, finally unreduced, or finally still expanding.

To put this structurally: in the underlying flux of experience, the unfolding of smaller structures (events) within the larger, gradually expanding design of conscience (the inwardly responsive moral relationships of people to each other, to society, to nature) finds no tapering relief and often no possible limit. Endlessness has become an end in itself.

Stephen Dedalus's brilliantly rhetorical departure

> Welcome, O life! I go to encounter for the millionth time the reality of experience and to forge in the smithy of my soul the uncreated conscience of my race

creates (and ironically recognizes the *need to create*) the new ending for the stream of conscience. That conclusion parallels (formally keeping its promise) Molly Bloom's nearly unlimited stream of consciousness which creates a certainly unlimited stream of conscience, "concluding" in her infinitely expanding and all-embracing Yes.

> and I thought well as well him as another and then I asked him with my eyes to ask again yes and then he asked me would I say yes to say yes my mountain flower and first I put my arms around him yes and drew him to me so he could feel my breasts all perfume yes and his heart was going like mad and yes I said yes I will Yes.

(I need hardly mention that to speak of an uncontained ending for conscience in *Finnegans Wake* is to put the case gently.)

Virginia Woolf ends *To the Lighthouse* this way:

> [Mr. Ramsay] rose and stood in the bow of the boat, very straight and tall, for all the world, James thought, as if he were saying, "There is no God," and Cam thought, as if he were leaping into space, and they both rose to follow him as he sprang. . . .
>
> .   .   .
>
> "He must have reached it," said Lily Briscoe aloud. . . . With a sudden intensity, as if she saw it clear for a second, she drew a line there in the centre. It was done; it was finished. Yes, she thought, laying down her brush in extreme fatigue, I have had my vision.

Apparently the novelist feels strongly the need to assert that she *has* ended. The final attainment of the lighthouse, there in the book's world, is no containment but actually an unstopped movement of still disturbed consciences. Yet Lily has had her vision. For the preposition in the title insists on the form—a trifle defensively—just as the wording of the ending does. It is doubtful whether even in extreme fatigue, Mrs. Aphra Behn, Jane Austen, Maria Edgeworth, the sisters Brontë, or careful Daisy Ashford would have conceived that she had "done" or "finished" with her "vision" and "drawn a line there" when she had at last envisioned a "leaping into space." Yet in another form, this is the vision of the end of experience in *Mrs. Dalloway:*

> What is this terror? what is this ecstasy? he thought to himself.
> What is it that fills me with extraordinary excitement?
>   It is Clarissa, he said.
>   For there she was.

The last two sentences put the merest in-drawn breath of a finish on the completed work. It isn't a limit: it is the hairbreadth of a border-line between the expanding responses of character and the boundary of their fictional world. Deliberately so; and deliberately conceived to convey, as a *way* of breaking off, "extraordinary excitement."

Aldous Huxley brings his *Antic Hay* to a close this way: "Shear-water sat on his stationary bicycle, pedalling unceasingly like a man in a nightmare"; a nightmarish vision followed by Myra Viveash's comment, "Tomorrow . . . will be as awful as to-day." And Huxley brings *Point Counter Point* to an end, *after* the explosive suicide of Spandrell under the eyes of the Lawrentian novelist, Mark Rampion, this way:

> And then suddenly there was no more music; only the scratch-ing of the needle on the revolving disc.
>
>   .   .   .
>
> That night [Burlap] and Beatrice . . . [sat] at opposite ends of the big old-fashioned bath. And what a romp they had!

Here we have opposite ends with a vengeance. For what Shearwa-ter's bicycle and Burlap's bath share with the vision of Clarissa Dalloway and the leap to the lighthouse, with Yes and the uncreated conscience, is the hitherto unfamiliar phenomenon of allowing the expansion of experience to end without a final constriction, emotional or moral—to be still unchecked on the last page.

But none of these endings—with possibly the exception of *To the Lighthouse*—is a mere gimmick pulled from a grab-bag of tricks, not a twist, not an incapacity, not a deception. The continual central impulse of each book, the meaning of its swell of conscience, demanded and received an open ending: indeed, it is the closed ending that might have distorted the book's vision and foiled its impulse. And yet the need to *suggest* a nonexistent containment (as in the case of Lily's line drawn in the center) persists.

> Gatsby believed in the green light, the orgiastic future that year by year recedes before us. It eluded us then, but that's no matter —tomorrow we will run faster, stretch out our arms farther. . . . And one fine morning—
> So we beat on, boats against the current, borne back ceaselessly into the past.

The narrator Nick Carroway's final sentence reflects his (and Fitzgerald's) need to put a containing limit on his experience, here ironic of course: since the experience of Gatsby (both the experience *by* Gatsby himself and the experience of Gatsby *by* the narrator) will really allow no such limit. The two motions, Gatsby's vainly into the future, Carroway's vainly into the past, are held together in the last sentence; the opposed currents of conscience locked there in an unrelieved tension.

No such tension, no containment which might distort the experience, no countercurrent at all, is imagined by Hemingway or permitted to his Lieutenant Henry after the death of Catherine in *A Farewell to Arms.*

> . . . it did not take her very long to die. . . . After a while I went out and left the hospital and walked back to the hotel in the rain.

Lieutenant Henry's every attempt at an inward resolution and reorganization of shattering events is simply shattered by Catherine's death, as all the preceding events had predicted it would be. It is instructive to see that at the conclusion of *The Old Man and the Sea,* Hemingway leaves his Old Man still sifting dreams on the seashore of still greater battles. The "meaning" has changed utterly of course, but what is peculiar is that the formal organization of each novel traces a limitless expansion of the developing relation of the

inward self to the outer world. Whether bitter (as in one case) or
bittersweet (as in the other), the particular stream is unreversed and
it is uncontained. For in the storm of the open experience, the winds
of fiction drive the crew—the reader and his heroes together—to the
sweet or the bitter end of the voyage, and there the exhausted crew
discovers that the wind is rising, that the barometer is falling, and
that the captain-author refuses to moor the ship. Battered by experience, compelled toward a wider and wider moral experience, central
selves in the modern novel achieve no restricting moral integration.
The openness is unrelieved.

Now I think it can be observed that when I speak of an "open
experience" I am not using the word "open" in the same sense that
Robert M. Adams uses it in his well-known investigation and defense of "literary openness." [12] For Adams, the structure of the modern novel is not distinctively or especially open. For example, of
D. H. Lawrence's novels, Adams writes:

> But the structure of [Lawrence's] novels is not, ordinarily, open
> to any notable degree. The narrative . . . achieves the modicum
> of resolution normal in the modern novel. (pp. 188 f.)

This is certainly quite correct—in Adams' terms—and the point
about Lawrence is important. It is not always seen, and it is worth
stressing, that Lawrence does largely resolve the meanings of his
books. (Adams defines the open form as "a structure of meanings,
intents, and emphases" which deliberately includes "a major unresolved conflict"—p. 13.) Yet Lawrence's novels, like modern novels
generally, in my terms are "open." They are open ethical experiences.
I am not here talking about a "structure of meanings" conceived
in terms of the conflict or resolution of major themes. I am talking
about a process. I am exploring a movement: the flux of conscience,
the progress from innocence to experience, with special attention on
the final arc of that continuous movement. My emphasis is on the
"goal" of experience; on the function of conclusion with respect to

course and climax. Logically, therefore, it is possible (and I hold that it is true in fact) that if modern novelists *were* to make special new consistent assumptions about the shaping character of the process of experience, they *might* (and they do) produce thematically "resolved" novels which are and *can be* resolved finally *only* by an openness in the stream of conscience. What sort of assumptions? If Lawrence in *The Rainbow,* for example (which we will examine closely later), were to conceive everywhere in his fiction the profound *need* for an opening in conscience—that is, in the process of emotional and moral relationships and responses; if he were to render the near impossibility of such an opening *all along;* if the climactic crisis mounted to the most intense *failure* to achieve an opening; yet if concluding events did render that opening *finally:* then of course his structure would be at last resolved in its "meanings"; and at the same time its flux of conscience would be open. His meanings *could* be resolved only by openness. (And those readers whose cherished and unyielding assumptions were thereby violated might—and did—cry with disappointment or fatigue that such a "goal" was *no* goal, such achievement failure, such finality confusion.) Yet Lawrence's assumptions are relatively bright.

To take a darker example of the unremitting assumption of an open experience, the one nearest to hand will do: *A Farewell to Arms.* Its themes "close"—but *not* the expanding experience. Major meanings are finally not in conflict, not particularly problematic or ambiguous: all is well resolved. And what the novel has everywhere assumed, fought to evade, and means terribly as it closes, is its utterly terrible openness: the stream unclosed, the process unreversed, the moral and emotional pressures uncontained. Lawrence is strenuously *un*-gloomy; but both he and Hemingway are *resolved* to end on openness. It is the stream of conscience, not the structure of meanings, which is open, since in each case the novelist conceives and provides no final events which limit the experience. Such a conception of experience or the meaning of experience is mythic, it is an "understructure"; perhaps distressing, certainly modern. Richardson and Field-

ing would not have done that; Dickens and the early Hardy could
not have done that.

One final point: by an open experience or an open current of conscience I do not mean merely an "ongoing" ending—a lot depends,
after all, on *how* life goes on. The last broad flow of Moll Flanders'
ever muddying stream of ever muddier conscience is decidedly
cleared, strongly tapered, and much reorganized to hold the book in.
Conscience, after its climactic tumult of expansion, is closed. But
Defoe makes it clear that life goes on. *This* way:

> In a word, we were now in very considerable circumstances,
> and every year increasing; for our new plantation grew upon
> our hands insensibly. . . . Thus all these difficulties were made
> easy, and we lived together with the greatest kindness and com-
> fort imaginable. We are now grown old; I am come back to
> England, . . . we are both of us in good heart and health . . .
> resolve[d] to spend the remainder of our years in sincere pen-
> itence for the wicked lives we have lived.

When Moll finally "goes on" she does so with a last-minute, unconvincing containment, as if Defoe were under compulsion to depict
that. As finally in *Sons and Lovers,* Paul Morel "goes on," but with a
last-minute, unconvincing[13] expansion, as if Lawrence were under
compulsion to depict that. Characters can, after all, "go on" finally
with a narrowed—shall we say, refined?—conscience (Fielding's
Jones); or can "go on" finally with a blunt conscience (Faulkner's
Jason); or come to an open ending in death explosively (Conrad's
plain Mr. Jones); or come to an open end on the edge of death, still
expatiating (Cary's Jimson).

Now it will be perceived that the preponderant weight of tradition
leans toward a well-closed final chapter. That is what critics and
readers for a very long time have probably meant by a "satisfying"
conclusion: not merely a well-contained action or a resolution of
themes, but the sense of a tapering experience. It will be the point
and effort of this book to show that that assumption comes under a
gradual and mounting attack by novelists—by practitioners of the art

of fiction—toward the end of the nineteenth century, and that it gives way, though gradually, to an opposite assumption and a contrary practice. Part of my purpose will be to demonstrate that the structural change was a deliberate and intentional interference with the older dominant pattern. By establishing the change as an observable trend in fiction, by establishing it as a distinct and deliberate tradition in its own right, I hope to be able to meet, and perhaps to challenge, the very basis of those complaints which have been widespread for decades against the endings of modern novels. No one can gainsay a fellow reader's or critic's sense that an ending is "unsatisfying." But it may be possible to suggest that the root of his dissatisfaction is an expectation that pertains to older forms, to assumptions which more recent forms have all along been bent upon undermining. By following the journey of experience through the work of Hardy, Conrad, Forster, and Lawrence, I hope to make evident the irregular but nevertheless cumulative and impressive turn to the form we have come to recognize as the modern novel.

3

Thomas Hardy: "Weddings Be Funerals"

We can begin conveniently with the best of Thomas Hardy's early books, *Far from the Madding Crowd*. The traditional form, the closed experience, is worth tracing in a single, rather conventional novel because once it has been established in some detail, it can serve as a clear and precise background. Against it we can measure Hardy's gradual and deliberate departure from the norm in those novels in which he did his greatest and most original work in fiction.

I

Far from the Madding Crowd (1874): "Repose . . . again"

1. BATHSHEBA'S INNOCENCE

In the peevish but precise words of Henry James, who did not find Hardy's heroine to his taste,

> the young lady is a flirt, and encourages them all [her shepherd, her neighbor, and her soldier]. . . . We cannot say that we either understand or like Bathsheba. She is a young lady of the inconsequential, wilful, mettlesome type.[1]

The lady, her shepherd, her neighbor, and her soldier: these are the four principal *dramatis personae*. But the expansion of inward expe-

rience in *Far from the Madding Crowd* centers on the life of Bathsheba Everdene, and her experience (as James suggests) is centered
on marriage. Not that the young lady *desires* marriage; on the contrary, throughout the earlier part of the story, she concentrates on
avoiding it. In her innocence, when she cries out against matrimony,
she does so in tones and language which strongly suggest Hardy's
own Sue Bridehead of twenty years later; but strikingly, Bathsheba
sounds even more strongly the personal tone of D. H. Lawrence's
Ursula Brangwen in *Women in Love,* forty-five years later: "I *hate*
to be thought men's property in that way, though possibly I shall be
had some day." [2] The voice just quoted is, oddly, Bathsheba's, not
Ursula's.[3]

Bathsheba's independence seems to have offended James. But the
permutations, climax, and denouement of her experience are built
directly on that independence: on a very highhanded flirtatiousness,
on her masculine energy, on her willfulness. In point of fact, as the
following discussion intends to show, the form of the story Hardy
tells deliberately takes shape as a "taming" of the heroine. The action
is therefore planned to allow the broadest possible scope at first for
what James finds objectionable: the young lady's high-spirited, man-
nish tendencies; gradually to chasten, torment, and weaken her; and
finally to make her manageable—in fact, to make her beg to be managed.

From the very first chapter, what Hardy intends to convey about
Bathsheba—tediously, clumsily, but at any rate clearly—is her temperamental disposition to exercise control over men. In chapter one
(Gabriel Oak conveniently spying for us), we learn, as she regards
her features in a mirror, that she imagines "dramas in which men
would play a part—vistas of probable triumphs" (5). She will soon
triumph—the right word—without yielding herself in love. In chapter two (Oak helpfully eavesdropping), we learn that Bathsheba,
hard at work, wishes she were "rich enough to pay a man to do these
things" (15). She will soon be rich enough. And in chapter three
(Oak still unobserved), we learn that she rides a horse first like a

boy, leaning over backwards, "her head over its tail, her feet against
its shoulders"; and then like a man, with her legs spread "in the
manner demanded by the saddle, though hardly expected of the
woman" (18).

Almost at once Bathsheba rescues Oak from probable death by
suffocation (23). She is rapidly becoming the novel's central actor—
its center of masculine energy and movement. Then, as he lets go her
hand, she teases him:

> "You may have it again if you like; there it is."
>
> .   .   .
>
> "There—that's long enough," said she, though without pull-
> ing it away. "But I suppose you are thinking you would like
> to kiss it? You may if you want to."
> "I wasn't thinking of any such thing," said Gabriel simply;
> "but I will—"
> "That you won't!" She snatched back her hand.
>
> .   .   .
>
> "Now find out my name," she said teasingly; and withdrew.
> (25)

Pages later, "waving a white handkerchief" and "panting like a
robin" (30), she races after Oak to explain, "I ran after you to say—
that my aunt made a mistake in sending you away from courting
me" (31). Now as Bathsheba herself is at pains to make clear, her
eagerness does not constitute a proposal of marriage, not even an
explicit "wanting" of Oak. "Why, if I'd wanted you I shouldn't have
run after you like this" (32). Nevertheless, that highly qualified
"proposal" is the seed from which the novel will flower. It is the first
of a series of increasingly audacious initiatives in love and of increasingly direct "proposals" to her menfolk, audacities which will recur
right down to the final chapters. As for any actual marriage, she
explains, "I should feel triumphant, and all that. But a husband—"
(33).

Every event, then, has until this early point in the novel developed
Bathsheba's moral disposition as that of a flirtatious "young lady of
the . . . wilful, mettlesome type." (I omit James's "inconsequen-

tial." Without benefit of the hindsight which shows us Lawrence, and with Hardy's own Sue Bridehead still twenty years in the offing, James can be forgiven for dismissing Bathsheba as of little consequence.) Then, in an abrupt and surprisingly cool reversal of herself, Bathsheba "predicts" her own quite opposite need and outlines the shape of her experience to come: "I want somebody to tame me; I am too independent; and you would never be able to, I know" (34). It will take in fact three men to tame Bathsheba: principally and most violently of course Sergeant Troy; but more gradually, Farmer Boldwood and Gabriel Oak will also contribute in essential ways.

Less than two pages further on, Bathsheba's independence of spirit becomes an economic independence as well. With fairytale speed, charm, and luck, the girl is suddenly elevated to power and prosperity by an unexpected legacy; Oak is reduced to poverty and dependence by a disaster to his flock of sheep; and the next great movement, the vast opening outward of the novel, is set to begin.

2. THE EXPANSION

For the next one hundred pages, roughly, Bathsheba is presented to the reader as "Farmer Everdene's niece; took on Weatherbury Upper Farm; turned away the baily, and swears she'll do everything herself" (103)—presented as farmer, employer, overseer, paymaster, and grain salesman. But though Bathsheba shatters conventions right and left, the center of the explosion is made clear enough: "there was potentiality enough in that lithe slip of humanity for alarming exploits of sex, and daring enough to carry them out" (102). We can safely concentrate our critical attention there.

When she discovers that there is only one farmer in the neighborhood who has failed to notice her charms, she sends him a valentine: "Carnation's sweet/And so are you." And—worse—"Marry Me" (109, 111). The man thus boldly wooed is Farmer Boldwood. (The play on words in his name extends in several directions, most notably to the opposition of "-wood—Oak"; Gabriel Oak, who continues to love Bathsheba and turns out to be—as his first name suggests—her guardian angel, yields his last name to a barrage of sub-puns in the text, e.g., "What a way Oak had, she thought, of enduring things"— p. 338.) Enthralled by the heroine's careless valentine, Boldwood becomes her second victim in love: she remains heart-whole.

But in the wars of courtship, Bathsheba's genius for dominating the field without yielding (either her person or her feelings) suffers a first setback. A soldier inflicts the opening wound. The metaphor of battle is implicit in Hardy's vocabulary: "brass and scarlet," "sound of a trumpet" (p. 184); "I am not of steel," "the gathers of her dress began to give way like lilliputian musketry" (p. 186).

The taming of Bathsheba now begins in earnest; and "taming" is here to be understood in an almost literal sense, as if Hardy has at the back of his mind the metaphor of the breaking of an untamed horse. (We recall the heroine's expertness with horses in the opening chapters.) Bathsheba receives an "instantaneous check" (184) which throws her "off her balance." She has been caught on, of all things, a spur. In the very first instant of their very first meeting, Sergeant Troy's spur (with Hardy's excellent aim) goes directly for the weakest spot in her defense, her skirt: " . . . something tugged at her skirt and pinned it forcibly to the ground" (184). For the full force of the event, it may be worth recalling Hardy's comment on a woman's dress in his earliest published novel, *Desperate Remedies*:

> . . . to a woman her dress is part of her body . . . her dress has sensation. Crease but the very Ultima Thule of fringe or flounce, and it hurts her as much as pinching her. . . . Go to the uppermost: she is there; tread on the lowest: the fair creature is there almost before you. (151)

Troy, in his frank manner, treads on the lowest: Bathsheba is there before him. Together they recite a magical spell, almost their catechism:

> "Are you a woman?"
> "Yes."

*   *   *

"I am a man."
"Oh!" (184)

The darkness in which Hardy allows them to meet provides him with the excuse his realism requires for that incantatory dialogue. And amply guarded with similar excuses, the expansion of Bathsheba's experience now proceeds both symbolically and by a series of *double-entendre*. Bathsheba tries to free her dress from Troy's spur. For the first time in a relationship with a man, she finds herself in "a position of captivity" (186)—"You are a prisoner, miss" (185)— where she must absolutely forfeit something. The wordplay on marriage to her soldier is driven home with a bludgeon as she struggles to free herself ("hitched," "hooked," "the knot of knots which there's no untying"—pp. 184, 187); but sexual captivity and forfeit are adumbrated much more cautiously: "she could free herself at the risk of leaving her skirt bodily behind her" (186). "Bodily" is suggestive, almost superfluously so. The sentence that originally followed four lines further on was apparently so suggestive[4] that it was withdrawn from the text after it had come out in the serialized version. "And then, her appearance with half a skirt gone!" [5]

Troy's spur gives place to his sword, and the stylized attack on Bathsheba's body and freedom of movement proceeds in the chapter which describes the ritualistic swordplay in the Hollow amid the Ferns: "stand as still as a statue" (211) . . . and "you have been within half an inch of being pared alive two hundred and ninety-five times" (213).

Significantly, Hardy now goes out of his way to mislead the reader by suggestion and implication, into thinking that he is witnessing the swift development of an illicit liaison between the two lovers. For several chapters the narrative point of view is carefully restricted for the most part to other characters, who surmise the worst. In chapter thirty-two Bathsheba, like a gypsy or a thief (see p. 239), disappears from her house and is tracked down on the highroad in the middle of the night: she has stolen away from her retainers to run after her Sergeant lover. "Ladies don't drive at these hours, miss,

as a jineral rule of society" (244). In chapter thirty-three she who has
always "concealed from the world under a manner of carelessness
the warm depths of her strong emotions" (237), is espied alone in
Bath with her Sergeant, "talking moving things, and once she was
crying a'most to death" (252). And in chapter thirty-four Farmer
Boldwood, who not far back has already concluded that she is a
"sweet, lost coquette" (236), now concludes that she has become
Troy's mistress. Unseen, Boldwood hears her invite Troy to her bed
in this style:

> "There's not a soul in the house but me tonight. I've packed
> them all off, so nobody on earth will know of your visit to your
> lady's bower." (263)

On the basis of the information so far presented, the conscientious
reader, too, must arrive at the same (unjust) conclusion. But we are
of course, all of us,[6] wrong. Troy produces a marriage license. Having carefully misled us, Hardy melodramatically corrects us. Bathsheba's history has apparently not been leading her into an illicit
sexual experience (as do the histories of Eustacia, Lucetta, Tess, and
Sue) but directly into marriage. Apparently: for, as we shall see,
Hardy has not really misled us at all, and Bathsheba's perfectly legal
marriage will turn out to be exactly the "illicit" sexual relationship
he has so far been at pains to suggest.

"Of love subjectively she knew nothing" (111) when, lightly, she
sent Boldwood the valentine which affected him so cruelly. In the re-
alignment and expansion of emotions that follow her marriage, she
experiences the utter abjectness of her dependence upon Troy's light
feeling for her—which, as he rapidly becomes indifferent to her,
takes on more and more overtly the form of cruelty. The taming
proceeds apace, again almost literally. When Bathsheba inquires,
with intuitive suspicion, the name of a woman whom she "thinks"
Troy knows (and who is in fact his former mistress, Fanny Robin),
Troy tells her to

> "Think if you will, and be—" The sentence was completed by
> a smart cut of the whip around Poppet's flank. . . . (301)

And not long after, she finds herself begging, "Now, anything short
of cruelty will content me. Yes! the independent and spirited Bathsheba is come to this!" (315). The subjugation has been rapid: the
cut of Troy's whip now becomes the pain of "dry-eyed sobs, which
cut as they came." And—

> She was conquered. . . . [*Once*] it had been a glory to her
> to know that her lips had been touched by no man's on earth.
> . . . She hated herself now.

The sound we hear distantly coming is the moan of Tess Durbeyfield and the cry of Sue Bridehead. Like them, but without their
passion, Bathsheba recalls how right she was when as a girl she had
once imagined there would be "a certain degradation in renouncing
the simplicity of a maiden existence." [7]

Soon Fanny Robin dies, and Bathsheba sinks to the morbidity of
opening her rival's coffin and to the humiliation of begging her husband for love. When Troy, in an outburst of necrophilic tenderness,
kisses the golden-haired corpse of Fanny Robin, Bathsheba pleads
with him to "kiss me too, Frank—kiss me!" (344). And at this point
the earlier "misleading" hints of illicitness and immorality are un-
covered again. Troy tells Bathsheba that, before God at least, Fanny
Robin is his "very, very wife!" (345).

"If she's—that,—what—am I?" Deliberately phrased that way,
Bathsheba's question virtually suggests an unpleasant answer for
which a variety of words must have been available to Troy. He uses
none of them; Hardy spares his readers that.[8] But Troy's answer
returns to the earlier, elaborate suggestion of an illicit passion barely
palliated by a marriage certificate, and his words are perhaps ultimately more degrading.

> "You are nothing to me—nothing," said Troy heartlessly. "A
> ceremony before a priest doesn't make a marriage. I am not
> morally yours."

Their marriage dies that instant—so Hardy tells us (see p. 345). But Bathsheba's reaction next morning, in her advice to a maidservant, is worth noticing: "If ever you marry . . . don't you flinch. Stand your ground, and be cut to pieces" (351). We remember the cut of the spur, the sword, the whip. She *will* stand her ground and be cut to pieces: the explosive process of narrative experience has not yet reached its most terrible pitch. We are, as it were, watching that explosion (or expansion) in mid-career, and it will behoove us in our exploration of her experience as a form, to observe *when* Bathsheba's experience attains its greatest intensity, and to ascertain *whether*— and *in what sense*—the explosion of her experience is finally contained. We can put all of this in Hardy's terms.

"Emotional convulsions seemed to have become the commonplaces of her history," Bathsheba reflects when Fanny is at last in her grave and Troy has left her. And yet emotional convulsions keep coming, deepening, and intensifying: Troy ostensibly "drowns"; then Bathsheba is gradually hectored and manipulated into accepting Farmer Boldwood's renewed proposal of marriage. Hardy's biggest gun, the emotional and moral climax of the plot, has now been mounted. When, at the very instant she actually accepts Boldwood's dubious proposal, Troy appears in the doorway, wrapped up to his eyes in a cloak, like a devil come from hell [9] to avenge her sin, her emotional convulsions—the combined intensification and degradation of her experience—reach the point of absolute moral extremity.

In fiction, those moments—or those many pages—which render a central character's realization that life has become morally impossible are often accompanied (is it only in fiction?) by the onset of illness and fever: the very intensity of the moral explosion brings on a physical deterioration. And not infrequently, those fully expanded and intensified moments in the structure are also accompanied by the suggestion of mental derangement—hallucination or insanity. Perhaps we are justified in regarding these processes as literary "rituals" or conventions—drawn of course from cultural conventions and psychological observation—which not only render but also mark the fullness of the formal expansion of experience.

"Ritual" events of this kind now occur in *Far from the Madding Crowd* over a sequence of about ten pages. At Troy's incredible reappearance in the midst of the celebration, Bathsheba wonders "whether it were not all a terrible illusion" (433). And "her mind was totally deprived of light" (434). When Troy seizes her to carry her off, "she writhed and gave a quick, low scream." Immediately, Boldwood shoots Troy. Bathsheba then performs "deeds of endurance" (437) which require "superhuman strain" (400). She undresses Troy's corpse and lays it out in graveclothes; when it is over, the "simple consciousness that superhuman strain was no longer required . . . put a period to her power to continue it." She cries, "—how can I live! O Heaven, how can I live!" She remains prostrate in bed for months while a last blow, the possibility that Boldwood will be executed for the shooting, hangs over her. " 'I do so hope his life will be spared,' said Liddy. 'If it is not, she'll go out her mind too' " (445).

3. THE CONTAINMENT OF THE EXPANSION

The rapid resolution of Bathsheba's intense distress now begins. Boldwood's life is spared by the Home Secretary, and

> Bathsheba revived with the spring. The utter prostration that had followed the low fever from which she had suffered diminished perceptibly. . . . (447)

A slow return toward (not to) the more narrowly limited moral situation that obtained at the opening of the book begins to take place. Hardy reminds us that "two years ago [Bathsheba] was a romping girl, and now she's this!" (445). Two years: four hundred and forty-five pages. The road back (though of course not all the way back) takes about eight months: but barely fifteen pages of the text.

Before giving us the events which will narrow the now widespread moral "desolation" (452) of Bathsheba's life, Hardy explicitly
adds up the extent of the damage. Her lovers are all gone. Her masculine energy has been laid waste: "it seemed to herself that she
never could again acquire energy sufficient to go to market, barter,
and sell." Oak, who has been managing her farm, plans to leave for
California. She believes he despises her and, worse, she believes that
his love has been "withdrawn just at his own pleasure." The taming,
the cutting down of Bathsheba to size, has been completed.

The restorative process of the ending, most notably the renewed
"proposal" of marriage which Bathsheba makes to Oak, is accompanied by frequent suggestions of a return to Bathsheba's girlhood. We
are told, when she calls upon Oak in the evening, "doubtful if it
were right for a single woman to call upon a bachelor who lived
alone, although he was her manager" (453), that "their lives seemed
to be moved back again to the days when they were strangers" (454).
She reminds the reader and Gabriel that "I was the first sweetheart
that you ever had, and you were the first I ever had; and I shall not
forget it!" And at last she admits "with a slight laugh, as they went
to the door, 'it seems exactly as if I had come courting you— . . .'"
(456). Gabriel's reply—" 'And quite right, too,' said Oak"—is a mild
vengeance.

The containment of her intense experience can, of course, be only
partial at best. "Bathsheba smiled (for she never laughed readily
now) . . ." (463) is Hardy's final comment. But not much more
than a page before the book ends, and immediately before she is
married, Bathsheba's horrific experience is squeezed down into (of
all things) a modified girlishness:

> Repose had again incarnadined her cheeks; and having, at
> Gabriel's request, arranged her hair this morning as she had
> worn it years ago on Norcombe Hill, she seemed in his eyes
> remarkably like the girl of that fascinating dream. . . . (462)

Now for the larger purposes of this book, I propose to step back slightly from a direct examination of *Far from the Madding Crowd* in order to consider the significance of its closed ending in more general terms. What I wish to suggest is simply that, although the events in this conclusion vary from those in other conclusions as novels vary from one to the next, the process (which the marriage here represents and in part helps to bring about) is familiar to all who read. It is a kind of coda *da capo,* or rather a movement *al capo,* toward the beginning. It is a process which not only resolves tensions and not only reduces them, but does all this by suggesting a movement *backward* away from their fullest expansion in the climax. A re-versal, a turning back: it is what happens, for example, to Tom Jones and Sophia Western (not their marriage, but the reversing effect of their marriage on their distressing experience). It is the process that Dickens was obliged to predict in the revised ending of *Great Expectations* by (at the very least) allowing Pip and Estella to walk out over the rubble of the book hand in hand. What we may, however, overlook is that Dickens did indeed write another structural version of the same *al capo* process into the original ending as well although it was not strong enough, apparently, without the ritual reinforcement of a promised marriage. There in the first ending Pip walks hand in hand with *little* Pip, and simultaneously shakes hands with Estella, whose "suffering" (the last sentence tells us) "had given her a heart to understand what my heart used to be."

The attempt to limit the expanding energy of the novel, to delineate a close that will contain the previously expanded moral and emotional disturbance, is a formal maneuver: the traditional assumption about how to end. The movement *al capo* is clearly only a variant of that more general form. Before I go on to compare the influence of either the general form or its variant on later works by Hardy, it may be useful to make two points. First, in the novel we have been considering, the final containment of the heroine's explosive experience is no mere last-minute shift or patching-up. The taming of Bathsheba has

been the story of her wounding—over and over, until she can stand
no more. But the ultimate process of reversal and healing is implicit
—it is ongoing—in the text all along. In the conclusion, it is true,
Oak abruptly rescues a humbled Bathsheba from the destructive desolation of her physical and spiritual weakness. But against and beneath the strong destructive tide of the book runs a clear and reverse
undertow: although in the opening events it is Bathsheba who rescues Oak from death and Oak whose farm is crushed by disaster, in
the four-hundred page expansion of that moral situation, it is Oak
who constantly rescues Bathsheba from the disasters of her love and
her farm. More precisely, he *succeeds* in rescuing her from farming
disasters—fire, sheep-poisoning, and storm; and having repetitively
attempted to rescue her from the disasters of love, he succeeds in
doing *that,* both at once now, in the ending.[10] The concluding and
conclusive process has been happening in other processes, in other
events, throughout.

Second, although a movement back toward the beginning is only
one way to suggest a delimitation of the climactic fullness of experience, it is surprising how often Hardy himself resorts to that sort of
episode in his efforts to achieve a closed construction. The departure of Michael Henchard from Casterbridge in "the working
clothes of his young manhood" (360), in the guise

> he had presented when entering Casterbridge for the first time
> nearly a quarter of a century before; except, to be sure, that the
> serious addition to his years. . . (361)

and so on, is perhaps the most explicit. Taken together with the
return of the sailor Newson; with Henchard's own return to poverty, alcohol, and hay-trussing; with his deliberate evocation of his
entry into the novel "reading a ballet-sheet" (367); and with his long
rehearsal of the details of his wife-selling: all in all, the *al capo* preoccupation in *The Mayor of Casterbridge* is perhaps also the most
elaborate. But there are other similar motifs of a closing "return" in
Hardy: Marty South's appearance, slipping from the shadows of the

fiction into the light of the last page of *The Woodlanders,* just as she illuminated its opening pages; Cytherea's abrupt decision on the last page of *Desperate Remedies*—

> "O Edward . . . you must do something that has just come into my head! . . . give me one half-minute's row on the lake here now, just as you did on Budmouth Bay three years ago"—

and of course the more somber "return" which we have just seen in *Far from the Madding Crowd.*

II

Tess of the d'Urbervilles' Sister

Tess Durbeyfield, at the beginning of her fiction, is hardly more than a child and yet partly a woman. She has "a luxuriance of aspect, a fulness of growth, which made her appear more of a woman than she really was" (48), and in effect seems "a woman when she was not much more than a child" (57). In the last chapter of *Tess of the d'Urbervilles,* as Tess is being executed, Angel Clare walks hand in hand with her sister, "a tall budding creature—half girl, half woman —a spiritualized image of Tess" (506), and so into the morning and out of the book. The final pages constitute a patent and deliberate attempt at an *al capo* maneuver. But to say *that* is to say little about the aesthetic validity of the final scenes, their actual effect on the reader. Like Tess, the reader has come a long journey from her "large innocent eyes" and "white shape . . . so soft in her thin white gown" (12; 16 f.) to her "spiritualized image" and those "same beautiful eyes" (506) in her sister. To appreciate the closing maneuver, or to deprecate it, it may be necessary to retrace the journey from innocence to experience.

I. TESS'S INNOCENCE

An overture in innocence is a common structural and moral requisite in Hardy's fiction. Susan Henchard's utter credulousness in the validity of wife-selling is the necessary seed of the fiction of her husband's tragedy. Hardy stresses her extreme simplicity, perhaps unduly, to gain our consent to its improbability; just as he stresses the innocence of Bathsheba Everdene, whom Gabriel Oak twice sees in the beginning "in a bird's eye view, as Milton's Satan first saw Paradise" (*Far from the Madding Crowd,* pp. 14, 3 ff.); just as he stresses Elfride Swancourt's "Miranda-like tremulousness" and inexperienced awkwardness in kissing ("You ride well, but you don't kiss nicely at all"—*A Pair of Blue Eyes,* pp. 2, 65 ff.). But in none of these does the inception and conception of innocence receive so much attention as it does in *Tess of the d'Urbervilles.* The emphasis in *Tess* is more pervasive; it is almost obsessive.

Tess's innocence of experience in both related senses—innocence of knowledge and innocence of guilt—begins, of course, with the subtitle: *A Pure Woman.* "It was disputed more than anything else in the book," Hardy sighed in the preface to the 1912 edition. *"Melius fuerat non scribere.* But there it stands." The subtitle, he explains, was added almost as an afterthought, "at the last moment, after reading the final proofs." But that *Tess* had been written with a pure woman aforethought is equally clear. Her purity is begotten by simplicity out of childishness: the weak simplicity of her father, "Sir John" Durbeyfield, (see his reactions in chapter one, especially page 8); and the appealing childishness of Joan, his "witless wife," (53), whose "intelligence was that of a happy child" (41). As the narrative turns from her father to Tess—at the corner of the Pure Drop Inn (12)—" 'Bless thy simplicity, Tess,' said her companions" (13).

Everywhere in the book, Hardy's notion that innocence involves chronology—innocence lying *before* experience on a linear movement through history and time—carries his imagination forever backwards: to "the wondering days of her infancy" (40); to Tess "in a pink print pinafore . . . marching on upon long stalky legs, in tight stockings which had little ladder-like holes at the knees, torn by kneeling" (41); much, much later to "the house where we were born . . . . We ought to think of it, oughtn't we?" (454); often to the question of who murdered whom in the d'Urberville coach "centuries ago . . . he killed her—or she killed him—I forget which" (451, but there are numerous references to the coach). And occasionally farther still, to Norman times: "some of Tess d'Urberville's mailed ancestors rollicking home from a fray had dealt the same measure even more ruthlessly toward peasant girls of their time" (91; see also pp. 422 and 491).

Still, Tess—we must believe—is innocent; and the novel rapidly and transparently assumes the dramatic shape and interest of the *psychomachia*. In the battle for her soul, as Tess, though not necessarily as Hardy, too, conceives it, Alec is the infernal tempter and Angel (like Gabriel) the minister to her salvation. A certain amount of direct and indirect emblematic usage of names is sprinkled through the text. When Angel comes to rescue Tess from his demonic rival Alec at the end of the book, the dialogue runs:

> "What name shall I give, sir?"
> "Angel."
> "Mr. Angel?"
> "No; Angel."

And Alec—whose reversion from Evangelism to Satanism is detailed in the last hundred pages—first appears on the scene of the novel smoking (44). His name—his real name—is Stoke; from "behind the blue narcotic haze" (47) of his characteristic cigar, having conducted her on a tour of the garden and offered her fruit ("she parted her lips and took it in"), he "watched her pretty and unconscious munching through the skeins of smoke . . . as she innocently looked down at the roses in her bosom." [11]

Tess Durbeyfield's own name certainly contains (like the subtitle) Hardy's argument for her innocence, the particular innocence on

which the formal expansion of the novel is based. But her name, as
the first chapter tells us plainly and the rest of the novel insists ex-
haustively, is no clear or simple matter. In a sense, *Tess of the d'Urbervilles* is indeed the story of a name—of the deception in a name.
That the name *d'Urberville* obviously suggests "city" in both Latin
and French [12] may possibly reflect Hardy's concern with the opposition between Alec's city wiles and Tess Durbeyfield's country innocence: the -ville and -field are plain enough. The only trouble with
this view is the perhaps trifling one that Hardy everywhere insists
that d'Urberville is Tess's name and not Alec's name. Moreover,
whenever the name crops up the one thing that Hardy's vision is
impelled to evoke for us is antiquity.

We know of Hardy's life-long interest in reading the German
metaphysicians (he was reading Hegel in 1886, shortly before the
composition of *Tess*),[13] and we can wonder, on the basis of evidence
in the text, whether it was not of all things the German prefix UR to
which he lent his imaginative attention—a possibility which is not
unrelated to his notion of Tess's Ur-innocence. Hints of the primeval, of atavism and of archaism, abound everywhere the name appears. Tess imagines "the d'Urberville lineaments, furrowed with in-
carnate memories representing in *hieroglyphic* the centuries of her
family's and England's history" (45, italics added). Her family, not
his: Norman warriors, family vaults, skeletons, and the rest. Alec's
house, to which Tess first goes—the house of d'Urberville—is "of
recent erection—indeed, almost new" (46). Alec himself, for no very
good realistic reason, actually makes his appearance from inside a
tent (see p. 44). And behind his house lies a primeval forest which
we are told quite explicitly is outside his boundaries. Hardy's description of the forest catalogues these details:

> venerable tract . . . primaeval date . . . Druidical mistletoe
> . . . aged oaks . . . enormous yew-trees, not planted by the
> hand of man. . . . All this sylvan antiquity, however, . . .
> was outside the immediate boundaries of the estate. (42 f.)

Ur is actually isolated for us as such in the text, and we are told in effect that it is the most characteristic syllable on Tess's tongue:

> The dialect was on her tongue . . . the characteristic intonation of that dialect for this district being the voicing approximately rendered by the syllable UR. . . . (13)

Much more, virtually everything connected with Tess or her name, tends to move Hardy's imagination backward through time. Twelve, nine, five:

> Phases of her childhood lurked in her aspect still. As she walked along today, for all her bouncing handsome womanliness, you could sometimes see her twelfth year in her cheeks, or her ninth sparkling from her eyes, and even her fifth would flit over the curves of her mouth now and then. (13)

And at the moment of her seduction Tess is asleep like an exhausted child:

> D'Urberville stooped and heard a gentle regular breathing. He knelt and bent lower, till her breath warmed his face, and in a moment his cheek was in contact with hers. She was sleeping soundly, and upon her eyelashes there lingered tears. (90)

After her seduction the movement is still further backward:

> It was only then that her still face showed the least emotion, a tear or two beginning to trickle down.
> "What are you crying for?" he coldly asked.
> "I was only thinking that I was born over there," murmured Tess. (97)

And when at the last moment in which we see her, not Alec now but Angel bends over her as she lies on the sacrificial slab at Stonehenge—like the expiation of another Holy Sinner on another rock who in Thomas Mann's story shrinks into small animal life—she is reduced still further:

> her breathing now was quick and small, like that of a lesser creature than a woman. (505)

The movement for most of the book until the climax is from Tess's family cottage at Marlott to the family vault at Kingsbere-sub-Greenhill (surely significant names). Angel—sleepwalking—lays her in a coffin (318); and Tess herself—like Chaucer's archetypal old man in the Pardoner's Tale who goes tapping the ground and asking it to open up for him—

> . . . bent down upon the entrance to the vaults, and said— "Why am I on the wrong side of this door!" (464)

At the climax of the action, the murder of Alec, Angel wonders whether some throwback in Tess may account for the strange quality in her which had

> extinguished her moral sense altogether. . . . [He] wondered what obscure strain in the d'Urberville blood had led to this aberration. There momentarily flashed through his mind that the family tradition of the coach and murder might have arisen because the d'Urbervilles had been known to do these things. . . . [He] supposed that in the moment of mad grief . . . her mind had lost its balance and plunged her into this abyss. (492)

And after the climax Angel carries her still farther back through time; the movement is from a Christian burial (463) through the crucifixion (470) to Druidical sacrifice to the sun (503 ff.). Angel asks for Tess at the hotel by her Christian name, Teresa (p. 482: despite the improbability of the play on words, one is tempted to wonder whether Crashaw's "She's for the moors and martyrdom" may have been on Hardy's mind),[14] and he then leads her through "half-woodland, half-moorland" (494) to her martyrdom at the Stone of Sacrifice (504). The movement then from the end of the penultimate section to the end of the last section of the novel is from the family vault to Stonehenge: "Older than the centuries; older than the d'Urbervilles" (502).

> "I don't want to go any further, Angel," she said. . . .

2. THE EXPANDING FORM

Tess's experience expands in a single direction: disintegration. And in keeping with that paradox, the disintegration begins from somewhere near "zero," close to the bottom, and continues downhill from there. This is not the pattern of *The Mayor of Casterbridge,* where Michael Henchard is almost immediately pushed upstairs from the bottom: we watch his descent from a second-story bow-window of the King's Arms Hotel, to a rotting clay hut with boarded-up windows in a ravine. In the traditional tragic design, as in *The Mayor of Casterbridge,* awfulness is (in part) the product of the height of the slip multiplied by the length of the drop. The fall of Tess, however, is in the pattern of Verga and Zola, writing within the same decade as Hardy, the fall of the repairman from the low roof, the fall from poverty to penury.

Tess of the d'Urbervilles has fallen before her story begins. Hardy's book opens with a heroine and a family whose finances and social status are marginal. Her moral innocence, as we have seen, is in large measure the *absence* of knowledge and experience. ("O mother, mother!" she cries when it is too late. "Why didn't you tell me there was danger in men-folk?"—p. 104) The elements of her disintegration are unspectacular—she loses the horse, her virginity, her husband, her boots, her job, the family cottage. And her progress along those external values which the world supplies for measurement is downward—economically, socially, morally—until she is finally incarcerated and executed: from near-zero to zero.[15]

The specific forms of her disintegration are those of exhaustion, attrition, dissolution, and death; and the line of that motion is relentless. This is not to say that there are no movements in the opposite direction—toward solution, resolution, a way out. Of these *Tess* has perhaps more than its fair share. But it is to say that those movements are, as we shall see, crippled by Hardy's deliberate reversal of

the narrative order he has used in his early works; and by his juxta-
position of hints of decay in the midst of growth.

A few comparisons with his early fiction may help to reveal the
shifting narrative order of recurrent episodes.[16] Angel's tracking-
down of Tess to a lodging house at Sandbourne bears an obvious
similarity to the search of Southampton hotels for the heroine of
Hardy's first published novel. But in *Desperate Remedies* the finding
of Cytherea (293 ff.) is a rescue, that is, a temporary resolution and
relaxation of the tension; the finding of Tess is designedly too late:
with the resulting murder of Alec, the moral tension is immediately
pushed a notch higher.

More significantly, the connection between love and death, while it
is prominent in Hardy's fiction from the beginning, is handled
differently in *Tess*. In *A Pair of Blue Eyes* Elfride is kissed by her
second lover while sitting on the tomb of her first and confesses the
fact to her third in the same graveyard. The dialogue runs:

> ". . . how, in the name of Heaven, can a man sit upon his
> own tomb?"
> "That was another man. Forgive me, Harry, won't you?"
> "What, a lover in the tomb and a lover on it?"
> "O—O—yes!"
> "Then there were two before me?" (362)

When ultimately she confesses the full details, Harry abandons Elfride as Angel abandons Tess. But though Elfride dies, she lives on
long enough to marry a fourth lover "so as to turn my useless life to
some practical account" (431). The difference is salient.

When Bathsheba opens the coffin of her rival in love, watches her
husband kiss the corpse, and hears him deny that she herself is morally his wife (*Far from the Madding Crowd*, pp. 340 ff.), she wants
to "escape his words at any price, not stopping short of death itself" (345). But in the next chapter she awakens under a tree "with
a freshened existence" to the "Chee-weeze-weeze-weeze" and "Tink-
tink-tink-tink-a-chink" of the birds, and recuperates by reading *The
Spectator* papers. This is another of those alternations which occur

in all novels and which we have already observed in *Far from the Madding Crowd:* events of rescue and repair knit up a thread here and there even as the main sleeve of the narrative comes apart in shreds as we read. But in *Tess* Hardy tampers with that design, tampers with our expectations. He stretches his hand consolingly toward the reader—toward Tess—and we see the relief we are explicitly invited by the author to see while in fact the event is blighted as it arrives in his palm.

Now Hardy is, of course, usually understood to produce this effect by prearranging the "ironies" of fate. In *Tess,* however, his technique is far subtler and proceeds not only by prearranged events but largely by a process of evocation and suggestion within events.[17] When, after Alec has literally stooped low to seduce Tess in the black foggy forest, Tess comes out into the sunlighted field for the dancing movements of the harvest, we cannot avoid a feeling of relief. The description of the harvest is vaguely tranquilizing and, though it is also, we perceive, vaguely mocking, we cannot avoid sensing that some warmth has been offered after coldness, purposeful activity after deathlike stillness, earthly love after soiling lust:

> stooping low, she moves forward, gathering the corn with both hands against her knees, and pushing her left gloved hand under the bundle to meet the right on the other side, holding the corn in an embrace like that of a lover. (111 f.)

But one sentence later, the passage is followed by:

> A bit of her naked arm is visible between the buff leather of the gauntlet and the sleeve of her gown; and as the day wears on its feminine smoothness becomes scarified by the stubble, and bleeds. (112)

This is the pattern of events which Hardy sets up and maintains.

The ritual of love embodied in the movements of the harvest comes to an end—love's harvest, surely—and Tess "unfastened her frock and began suckling the child" (113). The magic of the phrase is clear—the evocation of the nourishment of life. But the groundwork of evocation drops under the reader in the very next sentence: we watch one of the men "with absent-minded fondness, regretfully stroking the jar [of ale] that would no longer yield a stream." The parallel is certainly intended, but is it intended to hint at the drying up of life's nourishment in Tess, of nurture and love? The narrative continues, one sentence further on—

> When the infant had taken its fill the young mother sat it upright in her lap, and looking into the far distance dandled it with a gloomy indifference that was almost dislike; . . .

As bad as that, then? Perhaps not; the sentence goes on:

> then all of a sudden she fell to violently kissing it some dozens of times, as if she could never leave off, . . .

Surely this is some relief . . . or is it? The sentence reads on:

> the child crying at the vehemence of [Tess's] onset which strangely combined passionateness with contempt.

The see-saw continues down the page, and page by page.

Now we do not, after the calamity of Tess's seduction, either require or *necessarily* expect a healing or restoring bend in the stream of events. But when it is held out to us—with that satisfying turning movement so natural to and regular in the storyteller's art—we can hardly refuse our assent and belief. "Yet even now Tess felt the pulse of hopeful life still warm within her . . ." (125).

But everything in the novel till now—even if we are not familiar with the rest of Hardy—has already warned us against *believing* that. What I am suggesting is not merely that Hardy deals with the frustration of hope, the perversity of fate, or the irony of events. I am suggesting that he is playing with a narrative pattern; toying with and within an already established form; building his irony by the frustration of the reader's narrative expectations. ". . . [S]ome spirit within her rose automatically as the sap in the twigs. It was unexpected youth, surging up anew after its temporary check, and bringing with it hope, and the invincible instinct towards self-delight" (127). We *must* believe.

And so "The Rally" begins—Tess's rallying, the third "phase" of the novel. We read: "On a thyme-scented, bird-hatching morning in May. . . ." (131) Nor are we disappointed, not at all; only (as we shall see) cunningly deceived. The milk of life's nourishment having come to an end with the death of her child Sorrow, Tess leaves home again for the lush dairy where "as each animal lingered for her turn to arrive the milk oozed forth and fell in drops to the ground" (137). Tess sets to work at once. ". . . To my way of thinking, the cows don't gie down their milk to-day as usual," the dairyman notes (141).

Events at Talbothays are withered before they are out of the bud, and hang rotten on the branches of the narrative. The pastoral idyll is stained "with tall blooming weeds emitting offensive smells" (158). And Tess as she walks has been

> gathering cuckoo-spittle on her skirts, cracking snails that were underfoot, staining her hands with thistlemilk and slugslime, and rubbing off upon her naked arms sticky blights which, though snow-white on the apple-tree trunks, made madder stains upon her skin.

And all this "as she drew quite near to Clare." For the love idyll is stained at the same time and in the same way. Of what exactly is she afraid, Clare wants to know:

> "The milk turning sour?"
> "No."
> "Life in general?"
> "Yes, sir." (159)

Tess's sense of her own inward staining of course makes every movement toward hope also a movement toward despair. A "terror of ecstasy" (228) is Hardy's oxymoron for Tess's predicament as Clare insistently proposes. In terms of the quasi-logic of the storyteller's art therefore, a lover's proposal—an impulse toward narrative

"integration"—becomes in effect an impulse toward "disintegration."
Tess's "Rally" is converted into its opposite; the expanding disintegration of the first two "phases" continues unchecked; and proposal
and pastoral converge, sometimes within a single sentence, produc-
ing firecracker bursts of the diction of exquisite torment: "Tess flung
herself down upon the rustling undergrowth of spear-grass, as upon
a bed, and remained crouching in palpitating misery broken by mo-
mentary shoots of joy."

What follows of course, in the expansion of her experience, is her
marriage to Angel, her confession of her past with Alec, and Angel's
abandonment of her.[18] From here to the end, the current sweeps
clearly to death. From the moment Angel places her in an empty
coffin "as if a greatly desired end were attained" (318); to her own
desire for entry into the d'Urberville sepulchre on which Alec has
been "recumbent" (463); to her murder of Alec in bed—"the point
of the blade had touched the heart of the victim, who lay on his
back, pale, fixed, dead" (489); to her sacrifice on the sun-stone at
Stonehenge . . . the tide of events is unmistakable and strong. And
Tess's conscience—not her purity or the lack of it, but her moral
experience—drifts with the destroying tide:

> [the] original Tess had spiritually ceased to recognize [her]
> body . . . as hers—allowing it to drift, like a corpse upon the
> current, in a direction dissociated from its living will. (484)

The direction of the current, the expansion of Tess's innocence into
experience, has been toward disintegration and death.

3. THE THREE "CONTAINMENTS" OF TESS'S EXPERIENCE

Angel returns to rescue her—"too late" (483). In effect, he has come
back to repair her disintegration by "remarrying" her. And Tess's
"elopement" (499) with Angel in the last fifteen pages of the book—
the ironic "Fulfilment" (Hardy's title for the last "phase") of their
earlier unfulfilled honeymoon—is a ghastly parody of the classic ending of a novel, its traditional solution and consummation in mar-

riage. Theirs is consummated in an empty mansion, behind "shut-
tered windows, like sightless eyeballs," "in total darkness" while they
listen to the housekeeper "close the windows, fasten them, lock the
door, and go away" (496). They are in a tomb. (In the next paragraph Tess tells Angel for the very first time about the sleepwalking
episode in which he had placed her in a coffin on their *first* honeymoon.) The mockery of the usual formal conclusion is grim and, in
the circumstances, heart-rending. "Why should we put an end to all
that's sweet and lovely!" Tess asks (498). But Hardy is hurrying the
marriage-ending along toward a burial, in more senses than one; the
tradition we hear in Tess's voice goes back to Richardson's Pamela:
"I begged . . . he would by slower degrees, bring on my happiness,
lest I should not know how to bear it." In their now consummated
marriage, inside Angel's and Tess's honeymoon tomb lies the normal
moral and emotional resolution of fiction, "within was affection,
union, error forgiven: outside was the inexorable" (*Tess,* p. 498). But
the pressure of the events Hardy has structured is irresistible. And
the imitation of the older form, the containment of a novel's moral
and emotional climax by marriage, collapses.

But there is always the other familiar ending, the containment by
death. We move swiftly, within two pages, from Tess's "Ah, happy
house—good-bye!" (500) to Angel's "I think you are lying on an
altar" (502). But Tess's death cannot and does not "contain" or syn-
thesize her disintegrated experience. Nor does it bring, as novelistic
deaths used to do, relative relief, satisfaction, or ebbing after the flood-
tide of experience. To observe that more clearly by a similar exercise
in perspective, it may be useful to compare her death with its more
classical form in *Clarissa Harlowe.* The redemptive martyrdom of
Clarissa serves to contain the monstrous expansion of *her* innocence:
"in God's good time we shall meet in a blessed eternity," she writes
to Miss Howe, "never more to part." Hardy deprives the sacrifice of
Tess of even that comfort. "Tell me now, Angel, do you think we
shall meet again after we are dead?" Angel avoids replying. "What—
not even you and I, Angel, who love each other so well?" (503). The

expansion continues: resolution, containment, moral synthesis are possible neither in this life nor in the next . . . or rather, not for Tess. For there *is* 'Liza-Lu, "a tall budding creature—half girl, half woman." And on the (by now) mutilated and exploded form for experience in the novel, Hardy performs a perfunctory operation.

Until this point, as the present discussion has attempted to demonstrate in some detail, *Tess* has been written as a resistlessly expanding form of personal experience which has only pretended to alternate tension and relief in the usual narrative manner. Nevertheless, the events of the last chapter do suddenly create a "check": a narrow-ended structure. The shift is abrupt and unquestionably deliberate. Hardy had already been obliged to re-conclude *The Return of the Native* to suit the public taste; and it may have been with much the same consciousness of the same demand—for a moral synthesis after the climax, for a limiting "lesson"—that he deliberately chose to write the final chapter of *Tess* as he did, having learned his own lesson. But surely his entire approach in writing *Tess* until that point had been just as deliberately intended to contradict even the possibility of a lesson learned.[19] His own comment on the viability of providing a final resolution or solution for Tess's fictional experience was made much earlier in the novel.

> "By experience," says Roger Ascham, "we find out a short way by a long wandering." Not seldom that long wandering unfits us for further travel, and of what use is our experience to us then? Tess Durbeyfield's experience was of this incapacitating kind. (124)

To what extent then is it even *possible* for the reader to accept the fact that 'Liza-Lu explicitly and symbolically becomes Tess—her substitute or double—"a spiritualized image of Tess, slighter than she" (506)? Tess herself spells out the projection and continuance of her own experience in 'Liza-Lu. "She has all the best of me without the bad of me; and if she were to become yours it would almost seem as if death had not divided us . . ." (503). The spatial diminution of Tess indicated in "slighter than she"; and the moral refinement in "spiritualized" and in "all the best without the bad" are not irrelevant. What the final chapter clearly suggests is the contraction of the stream of Tess's moral experience at last through 'Liza-Lu. When Angel and Tess's sister walk hand in hand out of the book, that final event, that new and symbolic moral synthesis of Tess's experience is apparently, if astonishingly, intended to suggest a containment of the experience: intended, that is, to reverse and control the expanding momentum of destruction and dissolution.

The final Christian mood, the suggestion of the resurrection, the references to "Giotto's 'Two Apostles'" (506 f.); to "cathedral," "aisle," "nave," "spires of St. Thomas's," "pilgrim," "St. Catherine's Hill," and so on; the replacement of Druid paganism by Christianity —suggest Christian assumptions about sequence in life and literature, the climax of death resolved and contained by the life after death. It is a compromise (with his audience, we can speculate),[20] a formal constriction of events which, after the uncompromisingly explosive narrative form upon which Hardy has insisted until now, cannot persuade. Despite the author's strenuous effort to suggest a ritual, the strained outcome inevitably fails to perform successfully the ritual function of containing the novel to which it is tagged.

Are we then to assume that this obligatory conclusion is only another, and perhaps the cruelest, of Hardy's deliberate ironies? Can it be that this elaborately contrived mood of tragic resolution, ethical synthesis, and Christian salvation is not a compromise with, but a savagely ironic assault on, the rigidity of his readers' expectations? If one takes the conclusion in this vein, as a moral incongruity already undermined by everything in the novel, then the still open, still unreversed disintegration of experience in *Tess* comes indeed close to the form of experience in *Jude the Obscure*.

III

Jude the Obscure (1895): "The Ultimate Horror . . .
Enslavement to Forms"

Jude's word for his and Sue's experience is "experiment"; they are
"pioneers."

> "Perhaps the world is not illuminated enough for such experi-
> ments as ours! Who were we, to think we could act as pio-
> neers!" (425)

Their "views" have been "fearless" (416 f.); their "experiment" culminates in that memorably horrific (if clumsily rendered) event, the
death by hanging and suicide of their three children.

> "Then bitter affliction came to us, and her intellect broke, and
> she veered round to darkness. Strange difference of sex, that
> time and circumstance, which enlarge the views of most men,
> narrow the views of women almost invariably." (484)

The metaphor for form advanced in the first chapter of this book
suggested that the events in a novel give rise to a flooding stream of
moral experience, either dammed or uncontrolled in the ending. The
excerpt from *Jude the Obscure* just quoted suggests, in Hardy's own
terms, that the expansion and narrowing of a character's moral apprehension ("enlarge the views," "narrow the views") is produced
gradually by a stream of events ("time and circumstance"). The passage may serve to indicate at the outset what the rest of Hardy's text
confirms in great detail. The author's manipulation of the stream of
conscience in *Jude the Obscure*—the enlarging and narrowing of
"views"—is a conscious attempt to give his fiction a double structure:
to set the open form of experience directly and explicitly against the
traditionally closed form, and thereby, as we shall show, to convey
his meaning through deliberate counterpoint.

> Sue and himself had mentally travelled in opposite directions
> since the tragedy: events which had enlarged his own views of
> life, laws, customs, and dogmas, had not operated in the same
> manner on Sue's. (415 f.)

At the deaths of the children Hardy explicitly divides the novel's expanding stream of experience into two distinct branches: Sue's is diverted, redirected, and constricted; Jude's is allowed to continue and to widen.

Sue cries out: "I wish my every fearless word and thought could be rooted out of my history" (417). And Jude confirms with some horror the new current he sees in her: "After converting me to your views on so many things, . . . you suddenly turn to the right about" (423); "you threw off old husks of prejudices, and taught me to do it; and now you go back upon yourself" (424).

The composition of the ending of the book is extraordinarily rigid in its counterpointing of scene after scene.[21] Events after the death of the children are constructed as a careful inversion or mirror-image of events that have led up to it. Each individual scene reverses an earlier one and the entire course of events—so far as Sue is concerned— moves in a reversed direction. Hardy deliberately writes Sue's part of the score backward (while, as we shall see, he write Jude's part very much "forward"). One evening after her bereavement Sue, whose developing maturity from the beginning of the book has been away from the Church and toward religious Skepticism, comes home smelling of incense (416 ff.) and explains, "I have been in the fumes." (This incident reverses a recent one: she and Jude have been expelled from another church, while working together, because of Sue's pregnancy and unmarried state—pp. 363 ff.) Next in order after her bereavement Sue refuses to have any further sexual relations with Jude.

> He went to the bed, removed one of the pair of pillows
> thereon, and flung it to the floor.

•   •   •

> "We'll be dear friends just the same, Jude, won't we?" . . .
> Jude did not permit himself to speak, but turned and de-
> scended the stairs. (427 f.)

(This episode and the celibate relationship that follows it reverse an incident earlier than their expulsion from church. The precise point of their first sexual union is guardedly but unmistakably given earlier—see p. 359 and the later reference to it on p. 435; it was preceded by a long period of celibate union: "we are to be friends, not lovers!" —p. 292.) Next in order, Sue leaves Jude and returns to Phillotson's house. (Much earlier she left Phillotson's house and went to Jude.) Then she remarries Phillotson but does not consummate her second union with him—see p. 447—(as earlier she married but did not consummate her union with him.) Finally she forces herself to bed with her husband. The final stages in the reversal are made specific: "back in the house was one thing—this another" (480), says Phillotson. Sue is just as specific, not merely about her own intentions but, in effect, about the author's elaborate effort to secure a "reversal": "I jumped out of the window rather than that you should come near me. I have never reversed that treatment till now" (478).

That the course of Sue's explosively unconventional experience "veers round" after the death of the children, "goes back on itself," and "narrows"; that her experience undergoes a reversal and a contraction, is abundantly clear.

Alternating with these episodes occur the episodes of the other remarriage, Jude's to Arabella, which follow but mock the developments in Sue's remarriage. The contrapuntal texture of the novel's coda, then, has three voices: the ground bass of Sue's past (heard in the background); Sue's present experience (inverted, as we have seen, above it); and a second inversion, apparently parallel, echoing above both. But the obsessively strict parallelism of Hardy's composition is maintained with a continuous dissonance in that third voice, Jude's: "All right. I've—married you. She said I ought to marry you again, and I have straightway. It is true religion! Ha—ha—ha!" (464).

Thus to Arabella; to Sue; "We've both remarried out of our senses. . . . I was gin-drunk; you were creed-drunk" (471). Both marriages bring about the "melancholy wreck of a promising human intellect" (470)—again Jude's voice to Sue—both are "degrading, immoral, unnatural." Both, moreover, are undertaken as willful physical and moral humiliations—Jude into gin and bodily debility and Sue into sexual self-humiliation with Phillotson (see pp. 476 ff.).

Nevertheless, despite the parallelism, even despite his remarriage, Jude's experience after the children's death undergoes no reversal (of his own moral experience) but on the contrary undergoes an inexorable "enlarging." And this, too, is made abundantly clear. From the outset Jude's experience has been developing in a direction different from that of Sue. The unmoving finger pointing onward, with the legend THITHER, which he chiselled into a milestone on the road to Christminster (Oxford) in the ambitious opening section (85) and which he glances at again in the fevered final section (472), provides us with accurate directional signals, if any are needed. Jude's career has been the history of a disappointment. As Arabella was one of the first to aid in his eventually total frustration, so Sue seconded her:

> "I fear I am doing you a lot of harm. Ruining your prospects of the Church; ruining your progress in your trade; everything! . . . O I seem so bad—upsetting men's courses like this!" (285)

His final separation from Sue and his remarriage to Arabella do not reverse but only continue the long, halting, but undeflectable progress toward moral dissipation and disintegration which his history so studiously relates. He expires, quoting from the Book of Job, to the cheers of undergraduates becoming graduates. Both *before and after* the death of his children, every episode moves to create

> the larger picture of Jude's final total disillusionment with Christminster and with all of life. The loss of Sue and the death of his children in the "City of light," under the very walls of the "castle manned by scholarship and religion," destroyed the

> structure of his dream world and banished the phantoms which
> he had spent his life in creating and pursuing. . . . His will
> to live disintegrated.[22]

The stream of Sue's conscience thus flows at the end into marriage; the stream of Jude's conscience flows beyond marriage into
death. Following each branch separately after the fork in the current
which Hardy has explicitly provided, we arrive at both those familiar endings for a novel, a wedding and a funeral. But deliberately,
surgically, Hardy proceeds to clear away any possible misconceptions
about his use of the two traditional methods for concluding a novel.
His use is manifestly ironic. And it is therefore appropriate and by
no means accidental that here fiction's traditions become hyperbolic:
a double remarriage and a double funeral.

"Weddings be funerals 'a believe nowadays," the Widow Edlin
observes (481). The incident which inspires Mrs. Edlin's remark and
which in fact gives us our very last view of Sue Bridehead is this
one:

> Placing the candlestick on the chest of drawers, [Phillotson]
> led her through the doorway [of the bedroom], and lifting her
> bodily, kissed her. A quick look of aversion passed over her
> face, but clenching her teeth she uttered no cry. (480)

What Hardy is carefully up to is the attempt to deprive both the
book's wedding and the book's funeral of their customary effective-
ness for controlling the narrative expansion of experience. He will
provide no relief of emotional distress and no containing moral synthesis. Jude calls Sue's remarriage a "fanatic prostitution" (436) and
the "ultimate horror" (484). Lest his contemporary readers too easily
discount Jude's opinion as biased, Hardy insists grimly that Sue's
love for Jude continues with force (see the erotic outbursts on p.
471). By portraying the prolonged trembling and "aversion" with
which she gives herself finally to Phillotson, the author leaves no
doubt in the reader's mind that Jude's opinion is in fact Hardy's own
and the right one. The last say in the book is Arabella's. Her post-
mortem analysis of Jude's corpse deliberately rephrases the contra-

puntal relationship which Hardy has already established between Jude's death and Sue's living death: "She's never found peace since she left his arms, and never will again till she's as he is now!" Arabella's remark occurs as the last sentence of the novel not only because it is Hardy's opinion as well, but because it is his analysis of the final "shape" of Sue's experience.

At the end of *Tess* Hardy nowhere divorces himself from the final interpretation of the "shape" of Tess's experience which Tess herself provides; in the last chapter as we have seen, perhaps with an eye to the demands of his readers, he even encourages that interpretation.[23] The conclusion of *Tess,* though it is entirely inconsistent with everything that has gone before, is quite traditional, both in its form and in its implication. In *Jude* the author clearly separates himself from the interpretation Sue offers. Hardy's resort to a double marriage as the outcome of *Jude* is clearly of another order entirely from the usual resort to marriage in, say, *Tom Jones, Emma, Jane Eyre, Bleak House,* and *Middlemarch.* There the sound of the bells which summon readers to a wedding invariably signals a major resolution of the complexities of the protagonists' experience. And yet, Sue's own explicit intentions in remarrying and urging Jude to remarry are, of course, precisely the same—to establish a moral and emotional resolution for her career and Jude's. To that extent, the resemblance (in the structure that Sue, in her disordered state, *wills*) to earlier novels is a fair one. It is as if Hardy had arranged matters so that his own skepticism may undercut and shatter Sue Bridehead's fanatical, unreasonable dedication to the principles of Fielding, Austen, Brontë, Dickens, and Eliot.

The result is a formal irony: an irony, that is, of structure. The realities of Jude's experience reveal to us the illusions of Sue's experience. The double weddings which mock each other, and the mockery achieved finally by the symbolic double funeral, are parts in an uncompromising (if rigid) counterpoint. The parts, alternating and weaving against each other, produce an extraordinary coda that effectively attacks not only the conventions of life but also the conventions of fiction. For with that acidly ironic counterpoint Hardy manages to undercut the traditional structure of the novel and the novel's ending in two ways. Jude's formal remarriage and death provide no resolution but merely leave open his progress toward moral disintegration; Sue's attempt to restructure her "experiment" with experience as it *ought* to have been structured (in fiction only) provides her with a living death, a formal resolution but a moral dissolution. Hardy's attack on fictional conventions, brilliantly mounted in *Tess* but compromised in the final chapter of that novel, is now complete, and it is an attack on form:

> "And now the ultimate horror has come—her giving herself like this to what she loathes, in her enslavement to forms!" (484)

The "forms" of life are not unrelated to the form of fiction. The forms Jude refers to in the passage above are social and religious. But Hardy's care in arranging these very forms of social life as forms for the structure of experience in his fiction makes it clear that the line of his literary attack lies directly across that middle ground between imagination and life which the novel inevitably crisscrosses.

The result was not surprising. "I have been charged since 1895," Hardy grumbled seventeen years afterwards in a postscript, "with a large responsibility in this country for the present 'shop-soiled' condition of the marriage theme. I do not know" (p. x). Hardy says he does not know. But Jude says as he lies rotting in bed and contemplating Sue's marriage: "And I here. And Sue defiled!" (488).

All three of the novels we have examined in this chapter come to rest in both weddings and funerals. But Hardy's use of these fictional conventions is conventional only in *Far from the Madding Crowd*. In *Tess* and still more vehemently in *Jude,* he undermines the conventionally closed form of the flux of conscience by so weakening its most traditional fictional techniques for securing a "close" —marriage and death—that they cannot possibly resolve the dilemmas, reduce the tensions, or contain the expanding moral and emotional force of the story.

We have come a remarkable distance from Hardy's first novel, *Desperate Remedies* (1871), in which Cytherea ends her history, well reversed at last by the conveniences of death and marriage, by asking her husband Springrove to row her round the lake again *al capo*. We have come a remarkable distance by 1895 from the gradual "remarriage" of Grace and Fitzpiers at the end of *The Woodlanders* in 1886:

> "Say 'husband.' "
> "No, no; I cannot." (419)

She cannot. But within twenty pages she resolves to "take him back to her bed" (439)—a false ending after the endless frustration of Grace's marriage, as Hardy knew. But he did not yet dare to write the ending:

> the ending of [The Woodlanders]—hinted rather than stated— is that the heroine is doomed to an unhappy life with an inconstant husband. I could not accentuate this strongly in the book, by reason of the conventions of the libraries, etc.[24]

We have come, in fact, a long journey from the book-reversing wedding of Pamela and Squire B—, the controlling moral synthesis established by the funeral of Clarissa, the soul-appeasing death of the Man of Feeling, the all-resolving marriage of Elizabeth and Darcy, and the public shotgun marriage of Pip and Estella.

For literary weddings and funerals have served as literary rituals— sensitive, symbolic processes to contain the flood of fictional experience. And Hardy, if crudely, still monumentally and consciously, by undermining those bulwarks helped to divert the fictional stream of conscience. The public reaction was clear and immediate. The earlier dispute about the morality of *Tess*, which had divided English society, was immediately dwarfed by the "shrill crescendo" of abuse against *Jude* on both sides of the Atlantic.[25] At the outcry of moral outrage which accompanied the moral shift in the shape of experience, Hardy left off writing novels; but having already turned the stream, he left it running in what became the direction and channel of the twentieth century.

For despite Hardy's own defense, the offense in *Jude* was *more* than a matter of "some twenty or thirty pages of sorry detail deemed necessary to complete the narrative, and show the antitheses in Jude's life" (p. ix); those pages were, significantly, the end. And the attack on marriage—Hardy's alleged "responsibility . . . for the present 'shop-soiled' condition of the marriage theme"—was more than an onslaught against the institution of matrimony; it was also a reductive strategy which denied a widely cherished form for life and for narrative: an attempt to tamper with an influential if invisible matrix of assumptions about possible ends and possible endings.

4

JOSEPH CONRAD: "THE END, SUCH AS IT IS"

The year that saw the publication of Thomas Hardy's last important novel, *Jude the Obscure,* was the year of Joseph Conrad's first, *Almayer's Folly,* 1895. The "Folly" of the title is, the book tells us, a popular nickname for Almayer's "new house for the use of the future engineers, agents, or settlers of the new Company" [1]—a Company that remains a hopelessly unrealizable dream. But in a wider sense Almayer's folly is hope itself: the universe in which Conrad locates him permits no hope. On the last page of *An Outcast of the Islands,* Conrad's second novel and one in which Almayer appears again (as a younger man), his last words are the drunken shout: "I hope!"

> "Hope," repeated in a whispering echo the startled forests, the river and the hills.

The setting and the rhetoric are Conrad's, but the universal law of frustration comes close to that which regulates Hardy's world. What Conrad mocks on that same last page is Almayer's "rebellious attitude towards the scheme of the universe": the phrase is suggestive of Hardy.

Still, it is with something of a wrench now that we shift our gaze from Wessex and Christminster to the Malayan Archipelago and

Costaguana. As reflections in a mirror, as reflections of men and manners, Hardy's vision and Conrad's vision seem poles apart.

> Although their lives cover very nearly the same period of time, in a century when the English novel is popularly supposed to have been at its greatest, their work in tone and artistry and feeling and setting belongs not only to different centuries but almost to different worlds.[2]

One can hardly argue the point. But as reflections in the stream of conscience, as reflections of morals in motion, their visions have a peculiar consistency. The uncontained form of experience makes its appearance, as we have seen, late in Hardy's work; it appears in Conrad's work from the beginning. In the analyses of individual novels that follow, two things will become apparent: Conrad's impulse toward a finally open narrative experience and his awareness of a division in his impulse. By concentrating special attention on *Nostromo,* where the open pattern appears most fully developed in a central novel of full length, and on *Almayer's Folly,* where the same pattern can be shown to dominate the very inception of the novelist's created world, we will be able to trace the fluctuating importance of the form in Conrad's work generally. For an open form is not the shape of all of Conrad's novels. He was attracted to it—to what he recognized clearly as an unconventional moral and narrative vision —and suspicious of it. His appreciative comment on Henry James leaves no doubt that he was a good deal exercised over the relative moral validity of closed and open forms.

> . . . it is obvious that a solution by rejection must always present *a certain lack of finality,* especially startling when *contrasted with the usual methods of solution* by rewards and punishments, by crowned love, by fortune, by a broken leg or a sudden death. Why the reading public which, as a body, has never laid upon a story-teller the command to be an artist, should demand from him this sham of Divine Omnipotence, is utterly incomprehensible. But so it is; and *these solutions are legitimate inasmuch as they satisfy the desire for finality, for which our hearts yearn,* with a longing greater than the longing

for the loaves and fishes of this earth. Perhaps the only true desire of mankind, coming thus to light in its hours of leisure, is to be set at rest. *One is never set at rest by Mr. Henry James's novels. His books end as an episode in life ends. You remain with the sense of the life still going on;* and even the subtle presence of the dead is felt in that silence that comes upon the artist-creation when the last word has been read. *It is eminently satisfying, but it is not final.*[3]

The phrases I have italicized above reveal the simultaneous presence, in a single conscious criticism by Conrad, of two conflicting impulses: just as we will see them in the construction of his novels. To decide whether Henry James's novels are indeed formally closed or formally unclosed, whether "the life still going on" goes on with a containment of the work's own climactic moral movement or goes on without a containment of that moral movement, would require an additional chapter of analysis. But the passage on James should serve to suggest, as we embark on a consideration of Joseph Conrad, that it may be not only James who attempts "solutions" outside the "usual methods," not only James who struggles to find endings that are "eminently satisfying" without being "final."

I

Almayer's Folly (1895): "A Detailed Programme"

Conrad's first book is a slight affair; yet in a study of the transition from closed to open form at about the turn of the century, *Almayer's Folly* has a significance beyond itself. For Conrad did not simply conceive his earliest book in the open form; he did so in a detailed way which not only turned to the newer pattern but explicitly rejected the older one.

"Almayer's young hopes, his foolish dream of splendid future, his awakening, and his despair" (203): as Conrad phrases it, the course of Almayer's folly sounds roughly like the course of Jude's. But exactly like the author of that grand final work, Conrad in this slender, beginning work is by no means content merely to give us a narrative experience which is finally not closed. Like Hardy, he is preoccupied with the *necessity* of closing off the expanding moral agony of his central character; and like Hardy he is preoccupied with the necessity of making clear to the reader that no such closing off is *possible*. Almayer tries (as hard as any central character ever has) to reverse the disaster of the climax, he wrestles to achieve a moral reorganization which will contain the damage, and he fails. It is all very explicit. The closing of his stream of conscience is not simply ignored or discarded or unachieved; it is undermined by the author's intention. As in *Jude,* the specific tension between the necessity for a narrowing experience in fiction and the realities of a widening one becomes the recurrent tension through which the book is organized and which gives it form.

> The well-known shrill voice startled Almayer from his dream of splendid future into the unpleasant realities of the present hour.

That is how Conrad's first novel begins. And the rest of the page immediately identifies for us the two sources of Almayer's frustration: the "gold he had failed to secure" and the nonwhiteness of his half-caste daughter Nina (her mother is Malayan). The same page virtually outlines the course of the story to come—outlines it, that is, negatively, if the reader understands that every desire it mentions will be thwarted:

> He absorbed himself in his dream of wealth and power away from this coast where he had dwelt for so many years, forgetting the bitterness of toil and strife in the vision of a great and splendid reward. They would live in Europe, he and his daughter. They would be rich and respected. Nobody would think of her mixed blood in the presence of her great beauty and of his immense wealth.

In short, his daughter and his ducats. For the achievement of his ambitions, the merchant of Sambir has pinned his last remaining hopes on a young Malay prince named Dain Maroola, who will find for Almayer the gold he cannot find for himself. "Let only Dain return!"

These are the conditions of Almayer's innocence, and the central movement from innocence to experience in the book is his, not his daughter's or Dain's. The simple sequence of frustration built upon these conditions, which gives the story its fundamental structure, is exceedingly direct. In a few pages Dain, the instrument of Almayer's salvation, appears; moments later, he disappears; when he reappears the following morning he is—so far as Almayer knows—dead. Then

> Almayer raised his hands to his head and let them fall listlessly by his side in the utter abandonment of despair. . . . It seemed to him that for many years he had been falling into a deep precipice . . . and now, with an awful shock, he had reached the bottom. . . . (p. 99)

He is in fact only halfway through his short book; he has not yet reached bottom. But his own view of the affair is unimaginably desperate. Almayer thinks of himself in the third person:

> Why doesn't he cut his throat? . . . Why does he not die and end this suffering? He groaned aloud unconsciously and started with affright at the sound of his own voice. Was he going mad? Terrified by the thought he turned away and ran towards his house repeating to himself, "I am not going mad; of course not, no, no, no!" He tried to keep a firm hold of the idea. Not mad, not mad. (100)

Incredibly, the crises that follow this one are still more intense and even more desperately phrased.

With Dain supposedly dead, Almayer has lost his ducats. With Dain in reality alive (as Almayer soon discovers him to be), his situation is not better, but worse: not only his ducats but his daughter, now. Dain and Nina are in love; the lovers are scheming to flee together from the island forever; the total collapse of Almayer's universe is imminent. And the action arrives at its obvious climax in Almayer's unsuccessful attempt to shoot Dain. But the most intense point in Almayer's own expanding moral and emotional experience is in fact reached on the next page when he orders his daughter to leave Dain and come with him.

> As it dawned upon him that she did not mean to obey he felt a deadly cold creep into his heart, and pressing the palms of his hands to his temples, he looked down on the ground in mute despair. (177)

He "groaned in his extremity of rage and shame" (178). To himself he cries aloud: ". . . white men finding my daughter with this Malay. My daughter!" (184). He has reached the "completeness of his misfortune" (179).

> His features had lost all expression, and life in his eyes seemed to have gone out. The face was a blank, without a sign of emotion, feeling, reason, or even knowledge of itself. All passion, regret, grief, hope, or anger—all were gone, erased by the hand of fate, as if after this last stroke everything was over and there was no need for any record. Those few who saw Almayer during the short period of his remaining days were always impressed by the sight of that face. . . . (190)

All passion spent (outwardly; "inwardly he felt himself torn to pieces"—p. 194), Almayer even helps his daughter to escape with Dain.

What he then does is very interesting indeed, both in itself and in its bearing on the argument of this study. As we continue reading, we seem to be following a clear contraction of the expanded flux of conscience, a rendering of events which will contain the preceding moral and emotional movement into the climax. Almayer erases his daughter's tracks, literally.

> He fell on his hands and knees, and, creeping along the sand, erased carefully with his hand all traces of Nina's footsteps. He piled up small heaps of sand, leaving behind him a line of miniature graves right down to the water. (195)

Not only that; he burns every trace of his ambition for ducats: his "account books . . . in [which] he had intended to keep day by day a record of his rising fortunes . . . the desk, the paper, the torn books, and the broken shelves" (199). His trading post and office burned to the ground, he moves into his empty "Folly," the symbolic fool's cap of his life (see p. 201). Now all of these steps have been performed quite deliberately as part of a program:

> "Forget!" muttered Almayer, and that word started before him a sequence of events, a detailed programme of things to do. . . . Certain things had to be taken out of his life, stamped out of sight, destroyed, forgotten. (198 f.)

He discovers of course that even with every trace of his trading enterprise obliterated, even with "every vestige of Nina's existence . . . destroyed" (201), even with opium, he cannot forget (see p. 206). He dies. The book ends.

Almayer himself considers another possible ending. He actually considers leaving the island with the young Rajah Dain and his daughter Nina, changing "his heart if not his skin" (192), and living in the Rajah's princedom. This is the kind of conclusion (if one may regard it for the moment as a formal variety) to which Nostromo turns later on. The central self of the moral experience envisions an "opening"—a necessary but shaming conclusion in which, at the moment of crucial moral choice, he gives up the attitudes, ideals, dignity, and effort of a lifetime. But Almayer's self is unlike Nostromo's: Almayer's "idea of his duty to himself—to his race—to his respectable connections; to the whole universe" (192) prevails finally. The book's method of conclusion then—the struggle to forget —is a rigid decision, personal, social, and moral. And all the final events—from Almayer's erasure of his daughter's footprints to his last resort, opium—represent his attempts to close off, morally and emotionally, the intense disaster of the book's climax; to close off, in fact, the previous movement of twenty-five years of frustration culminating in the departure of his daughter and the utter loss of hope.

So, deliberately, the book's last pages are there for the conventional reason: to suggest finality by suggesting a containment of the climactic movement, a closing down and a tapering off of moral experience. Every reader must sense Conrad's intent to convey the gradual contraction of Almayer's inner life ("no news from this world had any interest for him"—p. 203); the contraction of his outer life ("an immense man-doll broken and flung there out of the way"—p. 204); and even the contraction of the tone and pace of the writing as, after all, Almayer slips into his unforgetful opium dream. In one sense then (for the moment ignoring the novelist's mockery in all this), we respond to the flux of experience in Conrad's first novel as if it were closed. Its arc is almost precisely that given in our definition: Almayer *attempts* to attain a new relation of the inward self to the outward world which will serve to contain—here to obliterate—the most distressing events in the momentum of his experience. Or to put it another way, his final situation—erasure, burning, and opium —corresponds in form to the usual attempt to conclude in marriage; marriage regularly serves to reverse the previous motion, comic or somber, into distress. The narrative then obliges us to assume that the attempt in marriage will work, unless we are given reason to think otherwise.

But the careful, the over-careful, the single point of Conrad's mockery is that Almayer's programmatic attempt cannot and does not work, not at all, not in the slightest. Despite the formal "sequence of events, a detailed programme of things to do . . . and then forgetfulness would come easy" (198), no moral or emotional containment of the overwhelming climax will ever be possible for his protagonist. In its form, in terms of the novelist's strategy, Almayer's resort to opium at the end of his stream of conscience closely resembles Sue Bridehead's resort to remarriage with Phillotson and Jude's resort to remarriage with Arabella. Each conclusion presents explicitly and studiously the failure of a necessary ethical and structural "form," the failure of the closed ending. The necessary ending *is* rendered—not abandoned—and it is rendered as a failure. That is, Conrad's first novel (appearing as we have noted in the same year as *Jude the Obscure*) insists by an arrangement of experience on the same elaborate *formal* contraction, while it insists ironically on the impossibility *in fact* of a contracted ending to experience, and insists secondly on the degradation involved even in the attempt. We are now close to the central moral organization not only of this small volume, but of much of Conrad's work: the very blatant irony of this story is that Almayer's folly, frustration, and degradation continue to expand after the climax despite his program for their containment. In thus mocking (too easily, too grossly in this tale) his central character's final effort to bring his life into accord with his own ideas and ideals, Conrad is both asserting and denying the familiar narrative and ethical myth.

The coincidence of a resemblance of form here, as one major novelist puts down and the next takes up the pen, cannot be imagined to be a matter of literary influence from one man to the other. But the "un-influenced" resemblance need hardly be so neat and exact for it to suggest that a question about ends and a gradual shift in the fictional organization of experience was taking shape near the turn of the century. The less plausible it seems to imagine a direct line of imaginative persuasion from any one novelist to the next, the more necessary it becomes to assume a widespread and pervasive literary (and cultural) phenomenon whose development took on, in effect, the force of a new, obligatory moral structure for the novel—the force, that is, of a literary myth.

II

Nostromo (1904): "A Malignant Growth"

"*Nostromo* is central for Conrad's work," Robert Penn Warren contends, and he goes on to write later in the same essay:

> If the central process that engaged Conrad is the process of the earned redemption, that process can only be rendered as "story,"

and any generalization about it would falsify the process. In-
stinctively or consciously Conrad was willing to give the terms
of the process, the poles of the situation as it were, but not an
abstract summary.[4]

The analysis of *Nostromo* that follows will focus attention on the
narrative process itself, on the expanding arc of responses between
"the poles of the situation." Its focus will therefore be on that moving point in the course of fiction at which structure and ethical interpretation intersect. In the arc from innocence to experience in any
novel, central characters invariably reach a point of maximum moral
and emotional intensity; or in Conrad's words, "a sense of an inconceivable intensity of existence" (*Victory,* p. 364). In the central convention of eighteenth- and nineteenth-century fiction, the emotional
intensity is reduced after the climax, and the moral imbalances par-
tially or wholly stabilized: the "eminently satisfying" ending is satisfying both structurally and morally. That pattern—the traditional
aesthetic and ethical pattern for the novel—is not the pattern of *Nostromo*.

I. THE CENTRALITY OF NOSTROMO

Can we begin with an analogy? Tom Jones in *Tom Jones,* Emma in
Emma, Tess in *Tess,* and Nostromo in *Nostromo*. The analogy—
which seems too obvious—is actually heavily weighted, the better to
reveal the weight of critical opinion, which leans ponderously the
other way. F. R. Leavis writes that in *Nostromo* it is, in fact, Martin
Decoud who "remains at the centre of the book, in the sense that his
consciousness seems to permeate it, even to dominate it." [5] Nostromo himself is the book's "lost subject," [6] according to Albert
Guerard. And Graham Hough suggests that the book has no center
in at least one important sense when he observes that until the very
end we do not "care"

> for what happens to the characters—the Goulds, the Avellanos,
> Decoud, Nostromo himself—with anything like the intensity

that we feel for some of Conrad's other personages—for Lord Jim, for Captain MacWhirr, for Heyst and Lena, or for Flora de Barral. And if anyone wishes to suggest that these are naïve criteria for the novel, I shall remain wholly unimpressed, for I believe they are of its essence.[7]

Lord Jim, MacWhirr, Heyst, and Flora de Barral are obviously central in their respective novels; is it at least partly because there are six or eight centers for our interest in *Nostromo* that we remain ultimately less interested in any one of them? We do not have to decide here upon the exact cause of our lack of intense concern for the characters,[8] but it remains important for an analysis of the structure of experience to determine whether we can conclusively choose the personal experience of any one character as dominant, central, or even indicative of the arc of responses—the total pattern of experience—shaped by the novel. As conclusively, for example, as we can say that the personal experience of Tess of the d'Urbervilles shapes the form of experience in *Tess of the d'Urbervilles*.

If not one single character's experience engages our intense concern in *Nostromo,* then that novel must be considered seriously flawed, and not by Graham Hough's standards alone. Conrad, in his essay on Henry James, observes that it is of the essence of fiction to record, not secondhand history, but the history of human experience. "Fiction," Conrad writes, is "human history, or it is nothing." [9] But a great deal depends upon where one places the accent, and how strongly, in "human history." As human *history,* as "public historical drama—the study, concretely rendered, of the play of moral and material forces, political and personal motives," *Nostromo* is, in F. R. Leavis's words, "one of the great novels of the language"; as *human* history, we are apt to feel (to recur to the same critic's admission), that "for all the rich variety of the interest and the tightness of the pattern, the reverberation of *Nostromo* has something hollow about it." [10]

Now it is not my intention to argue anyone into anxious sympathy with the titular hero; neither do I propose to discuss the excellence of

Nostromo. What I wish to do is to establish that there is plenty of evidence, both outside the book proper and in the text itself, to show that for better or worse, hollow or not, the *human* history of Nostromo himself is the novel's center, its center of attention and center of gravity. As for attention: Nostromo is the focus of Conrad's imagination and the focus of the novel's development and structure. As for gravity: he is the focus of its implications. I wish to show that if Nostromo is "lost" until the final third of the book, this phenomenon in itself is at least very deliberate and by design; that if until the end we do not "care" about what happens to Nostromo, this is by the same design. Nostromo is held in abeyance, "in solution" everywhere, until the ending crystallizes his experience by a very conscious stratagem—so that he is necessarily central to the book. This novel gets there in its own way, but the analogy with *Tom Jones* and *Emma* will hold: Nostromo in *Nostromo.*

Now I wish to show this clearly because, if we grant that Nostromo's experience dominates the book not in its title or in its conclusion only, but at its very core, then we can say that the stream of conscience which the whole novel creates, and which is vastly complex, is controlled by Nostromo's experience: and his experience expands disastrously and limitlessly. In his career, unlike that of some of Conrad's earlier heroes, no attempt—not even an attempt—at a reversal or containment of his moral and emotional experience is suggested. The expansion, once it occurs, is full-blown; it is virtually an explosion of conscience, irreversible. And that formal and meaningful change in the regular shape of the conventional novel, here very deliberately organized, comes close to being this novel's point—of departure, of order, of view.

2. THE FRAME OF THE TEXT

Fiction cannot always be held accountable for matters of fact. Nostromo takes Martin Decoud and the silver to sea. Decoud and the silver disappear; Nostromo returns. But the bare possibility of an enormous theft and a calculated murder—the theft of an entire cargo of silver ingots and the unexplained disappearance of an eminent citizen (the only witness)—all this provokes *no* investigation and *no* suppositions in the province of Sulaco: amazing! Conrad has arranged events—the collision at sea, Hirsch's hysterical story—so that Nostromo's lie must sound like the truth to all reasonable men. " 'I believe you, Capataz,' said the doctor, drily" (435). (Dr. Monygham is the only person in the novel who is allowed to suspect the truth, and he is obliged to keep his opinion to himself.) But in the last analysis it is Nostromo's reputation that places him above public investigation or private doubts. He is absolutely, Conrad insists with tedious irony, "incorruptible."

In the prefatory note to *Nostromo,* written years after the novel itself, Conrad speaks of an anecdote about an "unmitigated rascal" who had committed such a theft of silver in South America: he had heard the story in his youth and he was reminded of the incident by a chance copy of a book he came across.[11] The story of the theft, which I will call here the "germinal incident" for the novel, stirred him to write again after there had "seemed somehow . . . nothing . . . to write about" (pages vii-ix). If the "unmitigated rascal" of Conrad's memory, whom he conjures up for us in his preface, had been placed squarely in the events of the novel Conrad actually wrote, we can see at once the possibility or probability of a premeditated theft and murder. But such a character, Conrad explicitly tells us, and such a story did not appeal to his imagination. It was only when he could imagine the Nostromo we now have, a man who seems absolutely "incorruptible," that he "had the first vision of a twilight country which was to become the province of Sulaco" (p. ix). The unthinkableness of the present Nostromo's corruption, and the thought that he is indeed finally corrupted, with emphasis on that word *finally,* gives the book not only its meaning but its form.

The novel, that is, flows from the energy of a special conception of the process of experience. Nostromo's experience dominates the novel: not only from the safety of the preface, the vantage point of the title, and the hindsight of the conclusion, but all along and from within. For although, as we read along, his story at first seems impeded by a cityful of other personages and other stories,[12] and he seems as a character to crawl out only "finally" from under a vast bulk of economics, politics, and history,

> there was something in the genius of that Genoese seaman which dominated the destinies of great enterprises and of many people, the fortunes of Charles Gould, the fate of an admirable woman. (452)

Nostromo's experience becomes emblematic—a pattern for the corrupted experience of others, and a pattern for the corrupted experience of the country.

The experience of "Nostromo"—the man, the book—was clearly a disturbing one for Conrad. The narrative itself (as we will presently observe) is full of images and scenes of torture as well as of fraud and crime. And the manner in which Conrad speaks of the book in his letters and notes has a most peculiar consistency, as if the book itself has been both a torture and a fraudulent crime. Here are a few quotations, wrenched out of their contexts, in which of course they were not intended to have the suggestion I am here suggesting that they do indeed have.

> I hardly dare avow my audacity. (May 9, 1903)[13]

> I am dying over that cursed *Nostromo* thing.
>
> .   .   .
>
> When it's done I'll never dare look you in the face again. (July 8, 1903)[14]

> Finished! Finished! . . . And all the time horrible toothache . . . had to wire for dentist (couldn't leave the work) who came at 2 and dragged at the infernal thing which seemed rooted in my very soul. The horror came away at last, leaving however one root in the gum. Then he grubbed for *that* till I

leapt out of the chair. Thereupon old Walton said: "I don't think your nerves will stand any more of this."

.   .   .

Wasn't sure I would survive. [The book this time, not the toothache.] (September 1, 1904)[15]

The strain has been too great, has lasted too long. (September 3, 1904)[16]

I feel a great humbug. (October 7, 1904)[17]

For in regard to that book I feel a great fraud . . . my audacious effort. (October 31, 1904)[18]

And written thirteen years later, the "Author's Note" to *Nostromo* still has the special accent of the effects of a crime: "anxiously meditated," "impending change in my mentality," "I can not in any way be held responsible" (p. vii). He speaks of the germinal anecdote as "completely *destitute of valuable* details" (all italics in this passage are added), a story which he had heard in his youth but which he later *"came upon"* and *"picked up"* from someone else's book (viii).[19] The word "valuable," having been applied to the *story* of the theft, now appears in connection with the theft itself: "A rascal steals a large parcel of a *valuable* commodity [silver]—so people say" (ix). But the word is at once re-applied to the *story:* "It's either true or untrue; and in any case it has no *value* in itself." The defensive note is remarkable. But it changes as soon as Conrad—confounding anecdote and treasure, Nostromo and himself—realizes that *he* might indeed write such a novel: "It was only when it dawned upon me that the purloiner of the treasure need not necessarily be a confirmed rogue, that he could even be a man of character. . . ."

3. THE WEAVING OF THE TEXT

"Nostromo" is "our man" (*nostr'uomo,* "our man" in Italian); and Ourman is the hero of this secular morality in the same sense that Everyman is the hero of the more famous morality. Ourman's centrality, of course, is not so easily achieved. The tying together of multifarious careers in *Nostromo,* and in particular the tying-in of the hero's corrosion with the corrosion of the world, is a kaleidoscopic affair. "Nostromo's activities are picked up almost solely by fragmentary comments for nearly two hundred pages," [20] it is true, but as we might expect, these fragments are marshaled strategically. At the end of Part One, Nostromo, penniless, gives away silver. He "jingled in his palm the increasing hoard of [his] silver buttons" (130). He gives them to "a pretty Morenita" girl, and it is no accident that in the act of giving away silver he is seen as a lover. A gradual attempt to make more precise the vague connection of silver with love with corruption is where the book is heading; it ends with the corruption of love. Nor is it accidental that we are then reminded, by a chronological jump, of Nostromo's connection with the loss of an entire cargo of silver. As Part Two opens, immediately afterwards, we are just as deliberately reminded, by another disconcerting shift, that "the fate of national honesty trembles in the balance" (135)—as Nostromo's balance goes, so goes the nation's. Much later, the "magnificent Capataz" is "thrown off his balance" (523) by becoming, like the nation, "the slave of the treasure."

The tying together, the weaving of Nostromo's life into the bigger, thicker, more important texture of the novel—he is "indispensable," he "saves" every major character in one fashion or another, and then he "saves" the nation as a whole—thus becomes a method for the formal expansion of his experience. For example, he says of himself when he and Martin Decoud have embarked with the treasure that "it has been tied for safety round Nostromo's neck" (256). And Decoud's response is not "I see," but

> "I see it," murmured Decoud.

The interlocking chain of images of torture, already mentioned, which Conrad carefully weaves from character to character, and finally back to Nostromo, helps put the latter still more firmly at the book's center. A Jewish merchant named Hirsch is tortured by being

suspended in the position of the "estrapade" (see pp. 448 f.).[21]
Hirsch's physical position before he dies is precisely the spiritual position in which Decoud is tortured into suicide:

> The solitude appeared like a great void, and the silence of the
> gulf like a tense, thin cord to which he hung suspended by both
> hands. . . . He imagined it snapping with a report as of a
> pistol—a sharp, full crack. (498 f.)

(Hirsch, too, still suspended, dies by a pistol shot.) Decoud's "last
thought was: 'I wonder how that Capataz died'" (501). When the
Capataz Nostromo appears on Decoud's beach and sits in Decoud's
position ("in nearly the same pose, in the same place") we learn that
he is tormented "through a night of sleeplessness as tormenting as
any known to Decoud." We have here, in other words, a remarkably
rigid case of writing in parallels, namely, Hirsch, Decoud, Nostromo. (But we have not mentioned other tortures: Monygham's, p.
372 ff.; Sotillo's, p. 460—all linked together.) Perhaps the most rigid
moment in this particular series occurs when we see Nostromo, near
death, embrace his Giselle. When Decoud drowned, he went down
weighted with silver ingots. It is now years later, but:

> weighted with silver, the magnificent Capataz clasped her round
> her white neck in the darkness of the gulf as a drowning man
> clutches at a straw. (545)

And of course when Nostromo is finally shot and killed, it is beneath
the "tree under which Martin Decoud spent his last days" (553).

The formal parallel between Charles Gould and Nostromo, "the
two racially and socially contrasted men, both captured by the silver
of the San Tome Mine" (as Conrad later put it in his "Author's
Note," p. xi), is just as painstakingly drawn. The ironic adjective for
Gould (repeated for emphasis: see p. 521) is "incorrigible" as Nostromo is "incorruptible." Mrs. Gould meditates:

> He did not see it. He could not see it . . . but she saw clearly
> the San Tome Mine *possessing, consuming, burning up the life*
> of the last of the Costaguana Goulds. (521 f.)

The italics are added to emphasize *as a form* the point Mrs. Gould makes next, that Charles is

> the last of the Goulds. The last! She had hoped for a long time, that perhaps—But no! There were to be no more. (522)

For Charles Gould and Nostromo, "both captured by the silver" of the mine, also share parallel forms of experience—irreversible expansion into corruption—and share that pattern with the "expansion" of the mine:

> more soulless than any tyrant, more pitiless and autocratic than the worst Government: ready to crush innumerable lives in the expansion of its greatness. (521)

By all these means, in effect by knitting up the pattern of everything with that of everything else—by tying the silver round Nostromo's neck, Nostromo's development to that of the others, all of them back to the mine, and the whole caboodle to the political life of the nation—Conrad gives (or intends to give) the expansion of Nostromo's experience a greater amplitude and intensity than his individual experience possesses in itself (or indeed could possess, given the simple lines of his character). The seemingly kaleidoscopic structure of experience turns out in fact to have been all along concentered, although not concentrated, on Nostromo.

4. CLIMAX AND CONTINUING EXPANSION

As Conrad and his characters never tire of remembering, the "most agitated period of their lives" was the Sulaco Revolution and in particular those few most anxious days when, it turns out, Nostromo "saved" the silver and returned from the sea to "save" the country (in the same dark sense) by summoning General Barrios. This is the fulcrum on which the events of the novel finally turn. The theft at sea—the "germinal incident"—becomes the extraordinary climax of individual and national experience. We can therefore speak with just as much confidence about a moral and emotional climax in the pattern of experience for the book "about" Nostromo, as we can of such a climax in, say, the book about Tess—that confrontation of Tess and Angel in the parlor when, as Alec's mistress, she has just come down from Alec's bedroom. From that moment on, Tess tries hopelessly to reverse and contain the preceding direction of her experience by destroying Alec and by clinging to her second honeymoon with Angel. What we wish to decide about *Nostromo* is this: whether the book's movement as a whole experience—as a kaleidoscopic whole—from its opening in a panoramic explosion of disruption and corruption to its climax (the theft, Decoud's suicide, the seizure of the city by revolutionists) is or is not completed by a change in the direction of that expanding process. Is there a final impulse toward a closing off of the flux of conscience of the whole book, toward a containment of the mounting disruption and corruption?

Disillusioned with the public reception of his efforts to save the silver and tempted by Dr. Monygham ("the king of the devils has sent you . . . to meet me"),[22] Nostromo decides to "grow rich slowly" (p. 503; cf. p. viii). But this choice—to "grow rich slowly"—is exactly what happens to the country as a whole. Indeed, everything that happens to Nostromo after the theft continues to become the pattern of experience for everyone else. After the successful War of Separation in Sulaco, the mine, miraculously preserved (like the treasure, and both by Nostromo), enslaves its owners, the Goulds, and enslaves everyone it benefits: the country collectively. Nostromo "become[s] the slave of a treasure with full self-knowledge" (523). What happens in the national process—

> "Will there never be any peace? Will there be no rest?" Mrs. Gould whispered. "I thought that we—"
> "No!" interrupted the doctor. "There is no peace and no rest in the development of material interests."

and in the social and economic process—

> ". . . the men have grown different. Do you think that now the mine would march upon the town to save their Señor Administrador? Do you think that?" (511)

happens to Nostromo—

> Nostromo had lost his peace; the genuineness of all his qualities
> was destroyed. . . . His courage, his magnificence, his leisure,
> his work, everything was as before, only everything was sham.
> (523)

And the connection between Nostromo and the political process is
made as actual as possible:

> "They are conspiring for the invasion of Costaguana. And do
> you know where they go for strength, for the necessary force?
> To the secret societies amongst immigrants and natives, where
> Nostromo—I should say Captain Fidanza—is the great man.
> What gives him that position? Who can say? Genius? He has
> genius. He is greater with the populace than ever before. It is
> as if he had some secret power; some mysterious means to keep
> up his influence. (511)

In the last two chapters, the novel comes to rest squarely on the
character of Nostromo. Until now the events in which he has figured
have been webbed in suggestive patterns. His experience is now dis-
covered to be at the exact center of the web, and the book closes—as
it has all along suggested it would—with Nostromo.[23] We therefore
can and must expect to see either some reversal or the further malig-
nant growth of corruption in Nostromo himself. What we are given
is at first sight disappointing.[24] Nostromo's inner rottenness now becomes a rottennness in love: he enters into a secret liaison with Giselle, the sister of his fiancée Linda. (Conrad, of course, *writes* that
his hero is now corrupt to the core, totally; but the only corruption
he really treats is erotic.)

Love in the novel "comes late, not as the most splendid of illusions,
but like an enlightening and priceless misfortune" (513). But that is
Dr. Monygham's love. Nostromo's love is a tedious business, so
much so that it becomes difficult to agree with F. R. Leavis:

> His return to find the new lighthouse standing on the lonely
> rock hard by his secret, and his consequent betrayal into devious

paths in love, are magnificent and characteristic triumphs of symbolism.[25]

It seems easier to agree with Albert Guerard:

> Yet all this, really (and given the inevitably embarrassed treatment of sexual passion) is unworthy of the novel that has gone before.[26]

But unworthy as it may be (so far as treatment goes), Nostromo's new and additional immoralism, years after the moral and emotional climax, is clearly a continuing expansion of his stream of conscience and in the same direction. (This disintegrating movement, too—the rotting of love—is given its due parallel within the Gould family, and on the national level in the corruption of political loyalties and patriotic love: see pp. 511 f.) Pretending to court one girl, Nostromo clandestinely courts the other because she is by nature more corrupt. And his love for her is itself corrupt, as Mrs. Gould reminds us: "Very soon he would have forgotten [her] for his treasure" (561). Appropriately, he is shot on account of his deception as he crawls for more silver. It is an explosive finale, a "fine grand-opera effect." [27]

When Mrs. Gould then goes to him as his confessor, "monastically hooded" (558), he confesses to her while he lies dying that he is "Nostromo the thief. . . . I have said the word. The spell is broken!" Broken, but not altered or reversed; there is no containment for Nostromo. He confesses still further: the silver "holds me yet" (559).

He dies, but the event of his dying serves to bring about no moral or emotional containment in the novel.[28] It is an end without being a reversal of the climactic momentum. More: once Nostromo is dead, Conrad bends every effort to keep the end of the novel from "closing" the experience: Nostromo's domination continues. This is how the novel "closes":

> "Is he dead?" she cried, bending over.
> "Yes, my poor girl. I am coming round," the doctor answered from below.

.   .   .

"... But I shall never forget thee. Never!"

.   .   .

"Never! Gian' Battista!"

Dr. Monygham, pulling round in the police-galley, heard the
name pass over his head. It was another of Nostromo's triumphs,
the greatest, the most enviable, the most sinister of all. In that
true cry of undying passion that seemed to ring aloud from
Punta Mala to Azuera and away to the bright line of the hori-
zon, overhung by a big white cloud shining like a mass of solid
silver, the genius of the magnificent Capataz de Cargadores
dominated the dark gulf containing his conquests of treasure
and love.

"You remain with the sense of the life still going on; and even the
subtle presence of the dead is felt in that silence that comes upon the
artist-creation when the last word has been read. It is eminently
satisfying, but it is not final," as Conrad said of James. Nostromo's
"triumphs" are still going on. They must. For surely it is Conrad's
point that the process which the novel depicts from its very begin-
nings in the nation and in Ourman—the corruption of the spirit by
"material interest"—is not only still going on, but still expanding.[29]

Of another hero in an earlier book, Conrad wrote:

> When he stepped off the straight and narrow path of his pecul-
> iar honesty, it was with an inward assertion of unflinching
> resolve to fall back again into the monotonous but safe stride
> of virtue. . . . (*An Outcast of the Islands*, p. 3)

No such resolve enters Nostromo's mind, and no such impulsion
enters Conrad's book now. In *Nostromo* he writes:

> A transgression, a crime, entering a man's existence, eats it up
> like a malignant growth, consumes it like a fever. (523)

This is a pronouncement about form as well as about psychology
and morality; the form of *Nostromo* is that of a malignancy. Once
the cancerous growth begins, it consumes Nostromo's life and the
novel in a single forward-moving development.

III

"Appendages"

Kenneth Burke once defined literary form as "an arousing and fulfilment of desires." [30] But in Hardy's later novels, as I tried to show
in the chapter on Hardy, form might well be defined as the emotional and aesthetic opposite of that, as a deliberate arousing and
frustration of desires. And in much of Conrad's fiction (to stretch
Burke's definition a bit), form might be defined as the arousing and
confusing of desires. Some such effect, at least, seems to be the result
if not the intent of the labyrinthine narration in *Chance,* for example, and even more particularly of the fragmented or kaleidoscopic patterns in *Nostromo.* As Conrad himself saw fit to put it,

> the thought for effects . . . (often at the cost of mere directness
> of narrative) . . . can be detected in my unconventional group-
> ing and perspective, which are purely temperamental and
> wherein almost all my "art" consists. . . . It is fluid, depend-
> ing on grouping (sequence) which shifts, and on the changing
> lights giving varied effects of perspective.[31]

That these "effects of perspective," as Conrad calls them, are consciously chosen is evident; that they are "purely" temperamental is
questionable. They are certainly temperamental, but they are pat-
ently related to a trend in literature which transcends, or subsumes,
temperament in its bias for those interior effects "often at the cost of
mere directness . . . wherein almost all [their] 'art' consists"—the
fragmented and kaleidoscopic art of Joyce, Pound, Eliot, Virginia
Woolf, Faulkner, and others whose "temperaments" were apparently
kin.[32]

Conrad, according to Ford Madox Ford, had an immense grasp of
the "architectonics of the novel, over the way a story should be built
up so that its interest progresses and grows up to the last word." [33]
Ford goes on to tell us of his and Conrad's agreed preference for

startling, disjunct, impressionistic techniques; and of their speculations about the *progression d'effet* in fiction.

> There is just one other point. In writing a novel we agreed that
> every word set on paper—*every* word set on paper—must carry
> the story forward and that, as the story progressed, the story
> must be carried forward faster and faster and with more and
> more intensity. That is called *progression d'effet,* words for
> which there is no English equivalent.[34]

"Varied effects" are one matter, *progression d'effet* another, related,
and more dubious matter. Nothing could be more evident than that
such a theory of effects, without temperamental safeguards or intelli-
gent compensations, will lead directly to sensationalism. But in his
best work Conrad manages to avoid the impression of a merely
mounting sensationalism by at least two distinct safeguards. The
first is precisely that formal arousing and yet *confusing* of the
reader—those "unconventional . . . fluid . . . shift[ing] . . . changing . . . varied effects of perspective" which (as in *Nostromo*) successfully interrupt and redirect the increasing flow of tensions: Conrad's sense of page-by-page form. The other safeguard (wherever it
controls the narrative) is his peculiar sense of the central experience,
an over-all architecture which keeps the *progression d'effet* from
finally becoming or resembling a mere skyrocketing of intensity.

The central experience in a Conrad story—the sequence of inward
and outward responses—traces almost invariably the hero's dogged
refusal to embrace whatever moral and emotional expansion events
still more doggedly force upon him; and formally, that pattern of
experience operates as a brake against any mere mounting of
"effects" into sensationalism. Conrad's novels are continually *about*
to open outward. One is aware of an imminent explosion as the
"progression" intensifies; but the inward refusal holds the cumulative force in check under increasing pressure; and the story "opens"
only at the end. There is a sudden crumbling of resistance, an erup-
tion at maximum moral intensity. The point I wish to make is that
these last throes of emotional response only *seem* to be crucial con-

tainments of disturbing moral experience. They seem that way because Conrad is divided against himself, and consciously so.

In *Almayer's Folly* (1895), the protagonist's rapid dissolution into
an opium dream in the last pages; in *Nostromo* (1904), the titular
hero's abrupt immoralism, commencing on page 503 out of 566 pages
in all, followed by his unavailing confession; in *Under Western Eyes*
(1911), Razumov's last-minute self-punishing confession; in *Victory*
(1915), Heyst's suicidal renunciation of his mistrust; in *Chance*
(1914), Flora de Barral's final realization of trust: these are all preceded by book-long resistance against the violent expansion of a
clenched conscience, of a restricted moral experience. And the moral
experience opens that the book may close.

Lord Jim (unfortunately for the neatness of any time-scheme,
1900) is an obvious exception: Conrad does *not* imagine always, as
he does in *Nostromo,* an expanding current of conscience which is
finally not reduced, controlled, or contained by his ending. Nevertheless, the recurrence of the conflict of intentions in Conrad deserves
observation. It is the struggle between his effort to "close" his form
morally and his refusal to do so; and I refer to a conflict both in his
critical mind and in his imaginative work. The two impulses can be
discerned in both clearly. They are not only opposed but contradictory; as a result, the imagined "ends" to which they give rise are
morally ambiguous conclusions; and that specific tension in Conrad
helps to indicate the slow turn of the novel, the progressive emer-
gence of a finally open experience as normative for fiction.

Now there is ample evidence that *The Nigger of the "Narcissus"*
(1897) is written in a closed form. We can turn to the evidence in a
moment. But the matter is not so simple. First, there is Conrad's
intention—his insistence on writing an incomplete fiction because
life itself is incomplete:

> Dear Garnett,
> Of course nothing can alter the course of the *Nigger*. Let it
> be unpopularity; it *must* be. . . . As to lack of incident well—
> it's life. *The incomplete joy, the incomplete sorrow, the incom-*

plete rascality or heroism—the incomplete suffering. Events
crowd and push and nothing happens. You know what I mean.
The opportunities do not last long enough. Unless in a boy's
book of adventures. Mine were *never finished.* They *fizzled out*
before I had a chance to do more than another man would. Tell
me what you think of what you see. I am going on. Another 20
pages of type—or even less—will see *the end, such as it is.*[35]
[Italics added]

". . . the end, such as it is." What *is* the end, and what has led up
to it? The slow process of moral corruption among the crew of the
"Narcissus" increases gradually to a crisis; *after* the crisis, corruption
is checked: closed. The dead body of James Wait, whose living
presence on board ship has caused mounting havoc, slides off the
plank finally (his corpse catches on a nail first!) and "the ship rolled
as if relieved . . ." (441): closed. The traditional form is here not
only perfectly rendered and achieved, but aptly symbolized: it is the
voyage of experience; and the ship makes port. And the men? Well,
they disembark of course. And yet Conrad works for pages thereafter to give us that astonishing, continuing picture of the men: still
"the dark knot of men drifted in sunshine." On and on—after all,
they still have to be paid, to quarrel, to drink . . . why?

He has told us why, or told Edward Garnett: "incomplete . . .
never finished . . . fizzled out. . . ." He is attempting to make real
the pattern of fiction by making it resemble the pattern of "life"
(rather, *his* vision of *his* life). The struggle to produce something
"incomplete" is a positive need, and for more than one good reason.
True, his own adventures "were never finished," but that reference
to "a boy's book of adventures" is touchingly suggestive. For writing
elsewhere, Conrad complained precisely of the misfortune that in
other novels of the sea, in Marryat, and in James Fenimore Cooper,
"the stress of adventure must end fatally in inheritance and marriage." [36] For Conrad the reverse must be true: not a boy's book. He
is struggling toward the vision of fiction in which "events crowd and
push and nothing happens."

And this is just what happens as events crowd and push their way to the end of *Victory:* nothing. Considering the nerve-reaching intensity by which events mount to the final holocaust, "nothing" may sound absurd. But I would suggest that something of the sort—the ending in which "nothing happens"—was the effect Conrad intended to create by cutting the story off short with the extraordinary chop he gives it. Those few pages in which Heyst reaches "an inconceivable intensity of existence" occur after we have followed a long and obvious climax to a clear crisis in Heyst's experience: he watches Lena apparently betray him with Ricardo. And, as usual in fiction, the moment is hallucinatory. Hideous doubt "seemed to spread itself all over him, enter his limbs, and lodge in his entrails. He stopped suddenly, with a thought that he who experienced such a feeling had no business to live—or perhaps was no longer living (p. 391 f.)." Moments later, he realizes that Lena has been shot sacrificially, in protecting him. At this point, conventionally and conveniently, Heyst's immediate revulsion of feeling might have led to a reversal, that is, a moral and emotional containment of his central, mounting experience: of his "infernal mistrust of all life." But does it? Davidson troubles to intone:

> "Practically the last words [Heyst] said to me, as we came out on the verandah, were:
> 'Ah, Davidson, woe to the man whose heart has not learned while young to hope, to love—and to put its trust in life!' "

So: trust in life? Containment? The closed form? Davidson says so. But incredibly, that is all; it is two pages from the end; and it is not much. We are then actually given not a containment but a conflagration. Heyst burns himself, Lena's corpse, the bungalow, and the novel. All of this is accomplished by means of Davidson's brief report. It is very much as if Conrad's need to close morally without actually *giving* us that closing, his need for an "incomplete" experience in fiction (as well as a complete experience) does not permit him to do the obvious. The obvious is there, it is obligatory for the

moralist, but for the artist, it is old hat; *he will not render,* in terms
of further events and relationships, the process of reversal, reduction,
or containment. No wonder Ford Madox Ford was moved to observe that "the ends of [Conrad's] books have sometimes the air of
being rather slight compared with the immense fabrics to which
they are the appendages." [37]

In fact the "slight" ending provides no closing of the form at all.
Leavis calls that final victory "ironic," [38] but while the statement is
transparently true, it suggests that the moralist in the critic has here
inclined him to understatement. Certainly the overstated and un-
qualifiedly moral view of the conclusion that follows, another critic's,
will not do:

> So the Samburan mystery closes, dark passions spent. From
> immersion in the evil come to him there, Heyst has fashioned
> a triumphant victory, a victory over his own cold heart—a noble
> prince at the last, in tragic death with his beloved.[39]

There is a good deal to be said for Kingsley Widmer's forthright
assault against

> the moral-sentimentalist view of *Victory* which sees Heyst as
> undergoing a progressive redemption from skepticism to love.
> But the actual pattern runs from skepticism to demonism to
> despair. And that fits the pattern of the romantic skeptic else-
> where in Conrad, as with Decoud in *Nostromo.* . . . There
> is no rebirth. The very opposite of it, Heyst's flaming suicide, is
> not "trust in life."[40]

The disagreement and the ambiguity and the irony can be phrased
succinctly in terms of the flux of conscience: after the expansion of
experience, Conrad *only seems* to provide his reader with the closed
form. The old pattern has been carefully grafted by a few suggestions onto the trunk of the newer form. The victory, if it is one, is
therefore Conrad's, a technical victory achieved by pyrotechnical
means. And the means do not justify the end.

In another sense, the conflict in Conrad's impulses interferes with.

Chance. Published the year before *Victory, Chance,* too, despite many and obvious formal differences, traces the long process by which someone achieves "trust in life." That is the story it tells, and the central self in that experience is Flora de Barral. But in *Chance* Conrad almost incredibly attempts his two species of conclusion separately; there are two separate endings, neatly packaged in the layered wrap of the narration. There is the ending of Flora de Barral's story of trust; and then, abruptly, there is the surprise ending of the narrator's own story (narrated by another narrator). And if *Chance* must be considered an ultimately less effective work than its successor, it is fair to indict as cause, not only the burdensome complexity of the narrative method, but the two endings. For it is in order to achieve both of them, one after the other, that the complex narration was conceived, that it is allowed to wind the actual story of Flora creakily around, and is finally encouraged to uncoil like a rusty spring: a delayed-action trap. The story is open, but the narrative frame is closed.

With Captain Anthony, Flora de Barral finally after four hundred pages—like Heyst more quickly with Lena—discovers trust. And immediately—*exactly* as the bungalow burns a hole in *Victory*—down go the ship and Captain Anthony in a wreck, on the next page, though the narrator tells us that time has elapsed between Flora's discovery of trust and the wreck (p. 438). Flora's "complicated bad dream of existence" (442) is over, and the story opens outward. But as we move out through the wrappings of narrator after narrator, we discover that we are in for still another ending—an entirely traditional marriage ending. Many years after the shipwreck, Powell, one of the narrators super-added to Marlow, will marry Flora: and alas, "the stress of adventure and endeavour must end fatally in inheritance and marriage."

Powell has been a "false trail" because he represents a false direction for Conrad, a distortion of that special sense of narrative architecture which strengthens Conrad's work generally and which strengthens *Chance* until close to the second ending. As we approach the second ending we read the following unbelievably banal paragraph:

> The afternoon was well advanced before I approached the cottage. The amenity of a fine day in its decline surrounded me with a beneficent, a calming influence; I felt it in the silence of the shady lane, in the pure air, in the blue sky. It is difficult to retain the memory of conflicts, miseries, temptations and crimes of men's self-seeking existence when one is alone with the charming serenity of the unconscious nature [sic]. Breathing the dreamless peace around the picturesque cottage I was approaching. . . . (442)

And so on. Here is a closing of his form with a vengeance, and the vengeance is inflicted on style, ethics, and structure all at once.

If one looks at the process of inner response to outer pressure, one observes in Conrad—in the best of Conrad—a series of central characters whose inward posture is an intensely strained resistance against an outward threat. "The genius of Conrad was directed to intensifying the life of a man or a woman . . . ," V. S. Pritchett remarks. "His characters live on the edge of a great anxiety." [41] And just there at the nervous edge of the fiction, in Conrad as in Hardy, one observes the hesitation—the impulses both toward and against the conventional closing of the narrative's expanding complication and intensification of conscience. For "the usual methods of solution" are, in Conrad's skeptical view, "legitimate inasmuch as they satisfy the desire for finality for which our hearts yearn with a longing greater than the longing for the loaves and fishes of this earth." The words are so pointed as to suggest not only the moral form of fiction with which this study had been concerned, the closed experience, but Conrad's awareness of it as, specifically, mythic *and* questionable. It is an ironic awareness; it is a skepticism about the end of experience not everywhere embodied in his work. Yet Conrad's attraction to an open narrative form which will be "eminently satisfy-

ing, but . . . not final" brings us to the threshold of the radical vision of conscience that shapes the flux of experience in the twentieth-
century novel. Hardy's sour refusal to make ends meet in his novels,
and Conrad's "appendages" ("the end, such as it is"), are moments
in a gradual change in the temper of fiction which is clearly more
than temperamental. In the twentieth century, fiction will create a
new fable. It will soon be telling its readers that experience is unreduced and irreducible. The novel will soon not only refuse to be
"final," but insist on its right to be not even "satisfying."

5

E. M. Forster: "Expansion. Not Completion"

> Expansion. That is the idea the novelist must cling to.
> Not completion. Not rounding off but opening out.

This description of the form of the novel—or perhaps we ought to call it a wish—is E. M. Forster's. (It comes from the chapter on pattern and rhythm in his *Aspects of the Novel*.[1]) It may at first glance seem to describe succinctly the open form whose influence and rise in English fiction have been under investigation here in this study. In fact, however, the context from which the passage has been excerpted makes it clear that Forster is not speaking of an open structure at all but of the total final effect on the reader, the after-effects of his reading.[2] The analogy Forster makes is with music.

> When the symphony is over we feel that the notes and tunes composing it have been liberated, they have found in the rhythm of the whole their individual freedom. Cannot the novel be like that? [3]

A wish, certainly. But the writer who, when he speaks as a critic, makes that particular wish, will bear watching. Books by a novelist who claims that "the idea the novelist must cling to" is "not completion" deserve our attention. And not only at first glance but on second thought as well, the passage—description, wish, perhaps gentle manifesto—may have more than passing significance for a study of the structural development of the novel. Its wishful phrasing, its almost haunting resonance, suggests the possibility of a literary commitment that may conceivably overflow the boundaries and definitions of its immediate context. Taken in a wider sense, the passage can tell us a good deal not only about rhythmic and musical expansion, but about the organization of conscience in Forster's novels.

The excerpt dates from the twenties; the evolving practice which it (perhaps accidentally) reflects came earlier. Except for *A Passage to India,* all of Forster's novels appeared between 1905 and 1910: to place them in the framework of this study, it may be helpful to point out that all the early novels appeared between Conrad's *Nostromo* and his *Victory.* In Conrad's work, concluding episodes which elsewhere in fiction, after a final crisis, delineate a containing reorganization of experience, have eroded. Episodes of "the struggling regenerative process" (George Eliot's phrase) [4] appear almost vestigial or are absent. In Forster, the changing treatment of the underlying form of experience in the novel is carried a step further. The traditional shape (expansion followed by tapering) is reversed entirely; we are given its mirror image.

In reading Forster's novels we may at first seem to be wading knee-deep in the usual flooding stream of experience, following its bends as it swells through events to a formal climax (a climax to be succeeded presumably by a final containment—a "rounding off.") But we find as we read along that the novelist has begun instead to render a long, intensifying, and quite successful attempt by his central characters to *restrict* their emotional and moral experience. The contraction of conscience at last reaches its extremity; and the crisis and conclusion create a sudden "opening out."

That formal antinomy—an expanding narrowing followed by a widening closing—that paradox is Forster's, not mine, and that form is his characteristic conception of experience. The variations he plays on the paradox and pattern will be explored in the following pages.

I

A Room with a View: "The Whole of Everything at Once"

To trace the Forsterian form of experience in *A Room with a View,*
it is convenient to begin with the title. The scenes and chapters into
which the events of conscience in the novel naturally fall are rooms
and views. In rooms, order reigns and proprieties are observed: the
deadening Cockney pension in Florence, Mrs. Honeychurch's dimly
lighted living room, Mrs. Vyse's "well-appointed flat," the Misses
Alan's "clean, airless establishment." But the contrived pressures of
the story push the cast of characters forward and out—to the window, the lawn, the trees, the hills—where the view is grander.
Whenever they are out of doors, disorder reigns and proprieties are
ignored: adults tumble childishly on the lawn (174),[5] nakedness is
exhibited among the trees (202-4), a violent knifing occurs in the
piazza (70), and Lucy Honeychurch is kissed amidst violets (110).
The scenic and emotional textures of the novel are woven by a constant opposition between the warp of convention and the woof of
desire, between English viewpoints and Italian vistas: rooms, that is,
and views. But the opposition is more than a tension; it is an expansion, a direction of movement.

> Life, so far as [Lucy Honeychurch] troubled to conceive it,
> was a circle of rich, pleasant people, with identical interests and
> identical foes. In this circle, one thought, married, and died.
> (171)

The tensions of the story compel Lucy beyond this "circle," out
through ever-widening circles of experience.

> Italy worked some marvel in her. It gave her light, and—
> . . . more precious—it gave her shadow. . . . She did develop
> most wonderfully day by day. (138 f.)

"Her senses expanded;" and "this conception of life vanished" (171).
The passage from England to Italy is of course a parallel direction

of movement. The book begins and ends in Italy; but it opens with an English view ("two rows of English people . . . portraits of the late Queen and the late Poet Laureate . . . the notice of the English church") and it closes with an Italian view ("they heard the river, bearing the snows of winter into the Mediterranean"). Corresponding with both these movements is Lucy's emotional passage from the unconventional but narrow grasp of her fiancé, "mediaeval" Cecil Vyse, to the more modern and embracing views of George Emerson.

> "I had got an idea—I dare say wrongly—that you feel more at home with me in a room." [Cecil is speaking.]
>
> "A room?" she echoed, hopelessly bewildered.
>
> "Yes. Or, at the most, in a garden, or on a road. Never in the real country like this."
>
> "Oh, Cecil, whatever do you mean? I have never felt anything of the sort. You talk as if I was a kind of poetess sort of person."
>
> "I don't know that you aren't. I connect you with a view—a certain type of view. Why shouldn't you connect me with a room?"
>
> She reflected a moment, and then said, laughing:
>
> "Do you know that you are right? I do. I must be a poetess after all. When I think of you it's always in a room. How funny!"
>
> To her surprise, he seemed annoyed.
>
> "A drawing-room, pray? With no view?"
>
> "Yes, with no view, I fancy. Why not?"
>
> "I'd rather," he said reproachfully, "that you connected me with the open air."
>
> She said again, "Oh Cecil, whatever do you mean?" (165-6)

The novel's "view" gathers meaning as the story tumbles on. In the elder Mr. Emerson's opinion (clearly Forster's as well) the proper view is the truth of feeling and of bodily love. His attitude, and the impassioned viewpoint of Italians, and the seductive panoramas of the natural world join in an unholy alliance to threaten Lucy's respectability.

> Lucy did not look at the view either. She would not enjoy any-
> thing till she was safe [away from George Emerson] at Rome.
> (106)

It is precisely at this point in the novel, after she has been exposed
to the mountains over Florence and the view, that Lucy's deliberate
narrowing of emotional and moral apprehension sets in. She flees;
she returns home, becomes engaged to Cecil Vyse (certainly his
name fits the structure). And her constriction progresses to an extreme. She becomes not less, but more like her chaperone, the frozen
and withered Miss Bartlett.

> "Oh, goodness!" her mother flushed. "How you do remind
> me of Charlotte Bartlett!"
> *"Charlotte?"* flashed Lucy, pierced at last by a vivid pain.
> "More every moment." (294)

Commenting on another heroine's narrowing "views," Thomas
Hardy wrote:

> Strange difference of sex, that time and circumstance, which
> enlarge the views of most men, narrow the views of women
> almost invariably. (*Jude the Obscure,* p. 484)

Allowing for the difference between Forster and Hardy, and between the comic and the tragic vein, what happens to Lucy Honeychurch is not unlike what happens to Sue Bridehead.

> She gave up trying to understand herself, and joined the vast
> armies of the benighted, who follow neither the heart nor the
> brain, and march to their destiny by catch-words. (265 f.)

Forster says it of Lucy; it might, with a few changes to the language
of Hardy, have been said of Sue. The content of events—"time and
circumstance"—varies; the narrowing of views in response to events
is similar in form. Threatened by the expanding pressure of events,
Lucy

> pretended to George that she did not love him, and pretended
> to Cecil that she loved no one. The night received her, as it had
> received Miss Bartlett thirty years before. (266)

Between the early expansion and the final pages, then, the shape of Lucy's experience despite, or rather on account of, the pressure of events is a narrowing shape, like that of a funnel. Since the last chapter presents us with a grand reversal of the funnel, a panoramic widening of Lucy's views and our view of Lucy, we may perhaps imagine the full shape of her experience (resorting to Forster's term) as something like that of an hourglass. By the next-to-last chapter, we have arrived at the waist of the hourglass. (Forster's own use of the term "hour-glass shape" in *Aspects of the Novel*, Chapter Eight, is a different one, but even that usage may find some justification in *A Room with a View*. Until the penultimate chapter there is a strong trace, in Forster's conception of Lucy and Miss Bartlett, of a convergence and crossing of their characters.) Then in the last pages *before* the last chapter, old Mr. Emerson, whose views are the widest in the book, utterly reverses Lucy's funneling experience by bidding her "remember the mountains over Florence and the view." With a great effort, he succeeds.

> He gave her a sense of deities reconciled, a feeling that, in gaining the man she loved, she would gain something for the whole world. . . . It was as if he had made her see the whole of everything at once. (310 f.)

The last chapter portrays Lucy's expansion. The "water-tight compartments in her" (144) do finally break down. She marries George —acknowledging that, as Mr. Emerson has said, "love is of the body; not the body, but of the body" (307)—and she and George return to Florence.

> He carried her to the window, so that she, too, saw all the view. They sank upon their knees, invisible from the road, they hoped, and began to whisper one another's names. Ah! it was worth while; it was the great joy that they had expected, and countless little joys of which they had never dreamt. They were silent. (315)

A Room with a View concludes expansively. But with the neatness of a mirror image, it also concludes traditionally and conveniently with love and marriage. Tradition here is deceptive and convenience has been converted. In *Aspects of the Novel* Forster writes:

> Love, like death, is congenial to a novelist because it ends a book conveniently. He can make it a permanency, and his readers easily acquiesce, because one of the illusions attached to love is that it will be permanent. . . . [Novelists] usually end their books with marriage, and we do not object because we lend them our dreams. (55)

While this is certainly true, it is also true that the usual marriage ending does more than close a book conveniently with the illusion of permanence. Traditionally, the marriage of convenience (to the novelist) serves to turn and reverse the direction of the experience he has put into motion; to control and reduce the expansion that has led into the climax. Tom Jones's chaotic imprudence and his mounting "character of a libertine" (XVIII, x) obviously do not *merely* end in the permanency or stability of his marriage with Sophia; they are controlled and reduced by his new relationship to her. As Jones says:

> "The delicacy of your sex cannot conceive the grossness of ours, nor how little one sort of amour has to do with the heart."—"I will never marry a man," replied Sophia, very gravely, "who shall not learn refinement enough to be as incapable as I am myself of making such a distinction."—"I will learn it," said Jones. "I have learnt it already." (XVIII, xii)

Containment of the expanding stream of conscience rounds off the novel: the pattern is familiar—it is as true (formally, while the content always varies) for *The Vicar of Wakefield, Jane Eyre,* and *Far from the Madding Crowd* as it is for *Tom Jones.*

But it is not true for *A Room with a View.* On the contrary, quite the reverse is true. The novel gives us the slow but inexorable dwindling of Lucy's experience and conscience under the mounting pressure of events until the climax (her talk with Mr. Emerson); and the climax is succeeded by a marriage which creates in an episode the very broadest emotional and moral possibilities that the story has attempted to achieve:

> [Mr. Emerson] had robbed the body of its taint, the world's taunts of their sting; he had shown her the holiness of direct desire. (311)

> •   •   •

> They sank on their knees, invisible from the road, they hoped. . . . (315)

In *A Room with a View* the marriage resolution serves as a magnification, not a containment; it unleashes, rather than contains.[6]

II

Where Angels Fear to Tread: "Unimaginable Tracts Beyond"

The shape of experience in *Where Angels Fear to Tread*[7] is in the same mold, an inversion of the traditional shape, but with a difference that suggests the more persuasive and less tidy pattern of expansion which Forster delineates in his last, most satisfying work, *A Passage to India.* In *Where Angels Fear to Tread* we learn that Miss Caroline Abbott is "appallingly narrow" (113).[8] When Italy and an Italian threaten to widen her consciousness of the beauty of physical love, Miss Abbott, like Lucy Honeychurch, tightens her awareness.

> "Help me!" she cried, and shut the window as if there was magic in the encircling air. (124 f.)

Philip Herriton too is narrow.

> "I seem fated to pass through the world without colliding with it or moving it. . . . I don't die—I don't fall in love. And if other people die or fall in love they always do it when I'm just not there." (151)

Under the pressures of events and before the climax, Caroline resorts to prayers to God (see pp. 147 and 183) to keep herself heartwhole, free from Gino Carella's diabolic grip on her passions. And

Philip irresponsibly continues to be uninvolved, and to look on dispassionately at what finally turns out to be a kidnapping. But their narrowness and their resistance are about to crack. When at the climax of the novel Philip is tortured by the fiendish Gino, and Caroline holds her beloved Gino in her arms, their mutual "consciousness of wider things" (113) undergoes an extraordinary degree of amplification.

> Her eyes were open, full of infinite pity and full of majesty, as if they discerned the boundaries of sorrow, and saw unimaginable tracts beyond. (172)

She discovers that she has indeed fallen in love with "the son of an Italian dentist" (181).

> "I love him, and I'm not ashamed of it. I love him, and I'm going to Sawston, and if I mayn't speak about him to you sometimes, I shall die." (181)

And Philip "was assured that there was greatness in the world" (173). He discovers that he has "reached love" (176) for Miss Caroline on one side, and that on the other he has reached a "vision of perfect friendship" and "alarming intimacy" (174) with Gino.

There are no narrowing episodes after this final expansion: for Caroline, the "close" for her flux of conscience would indeed have been the traditional fictional conclusion in marriage. Unlike marriage with George Emerson, marriage with Gino, as Lilia's story has made abundantly clear earlier in the novel, would inevitably lead Caroline to a destructive constriction of experience.[9] In fact, there have already been two closed forms of experience in the same novel, with which we may contrast Philip's and Caroline's: Lilia's—whose liberating slam of the door to the doll's house in which Mrs. Herriton had kept her leads her to a gate straiter than any known in Sawston—and Harriet's.

> Harriet, after a short paroxysm of illness and remorse, was quickly returning to her normal state. She had been "thoroughly upset" as she phrased it, but she soon ceased to realize that any-

thing was wrong beyond the death of a poor little child. Already she spoke of "this unlucky accident," and "the mysterious frustration of one's attempts to make things better." (177 f.)

For Caroline Abbott there is no such "returning to her normal state," but only a returning to England. "This woman was a goddess to the end" (184). And as for Philip:

> Out of this wreck there was revealed to him something indestructible—something which she, who had given it, could never take away. (183)

"To such a height was he lifted" (184).

The specific expansion which the novel has treated has not been at all the kind of relationship that a marriage to Gino, or Philip's marriage to Caroline, might ratify and enhance. The novel has treated the expansion of consciousness: of moral apprehension and emotional grasp. The experience shaped by the fiction expands to its climax in the episode of the torture of Philip—to his near martyrdom and to Caroline's beatification (see p. 172 f.)—and it leaves them "transfigured" (183). Their expanded consciousness remains open, indeed, barely endurable; there is no closing down, except as they minister to Harriet in the last sentence, "to close the windows lest the smuts should get into Harriet's eyes."

Where Angels Fear to Tread, perhaps on account of the absence of marriage, seems to end somehow less completely than *A Room with a View,* and no doubt this is deliberate. "The novel ends with an almost intentional weakness, petering out in sad discourse," Lionel Trilling puts it. "Yet its effect is invigorating."[10] The moment of climax ("This episode, which she thought so sordid, and which was so tragic for him, remained supremely beautiful" [184]) is neither resolved as a dramatic action by a denouement in marriage, nor reduced as a progress of the conscience by the fading of intensity or awareness. The lack of an episode which might provide a sense of finality; instead, the sense of incompleteness,[11] separation, and a life ahead made more difficult by expanded awareness: all this brings us closer than *A Room with a View* to the form of *A Passage to India.*

III

A Passage to India: "A Frustration of Reason and Form"

The structure of E. M. Forster's last novel has not always seemed a questionable shape. In the earliest book-length study of Forster, Rose Macaulay wrote that

> *A Passage to India* is, in fact, a remarkably well-built tale, with significant approach, tense suspense, highly dramatic crisis, brilliantly narrated denouement, and fine close.[12]

In one of the latest book-length studies of Forster, J. B. Beer, without alluding to Rose Macaulay, writes that

> there is no spectacular denouement, no final revelation concerning the events in the cave, only Adela's denial that Dr. Aziz followed her. And if this negation is all that is to be offered, the key events of the trial ought to come at the end of the novel. Why is there a long sequence dealing with irrelevancies such as the festival? [13]

Between these two books lie twenty-five years of criticism. Between them lies, for example, Lionel Trilling's frank uneasiness:

> It is not easy to know what to make of the dominant Hinduism of the third section of the novel. The last part of the story is frankly a coda to the plot, a series of resolutions and separations which comment on what has gone before. . . .[14]

It is not easy.

In his notes to the Everyman edition, Forster once explained that the three divisions of his book represent the "three seasons of the Cold Weather, the Hot Weather, and the Rains, which divide the Indian year." This is certainly disarming, and offers little help to those critics who propose to analyze Forster's thought in the novel by examining its three-part structure. More recently, interviewers tried to clear up the clouded issue of the "dominant Hinduism of the third section of the novel" by putting to Forster the exact question,

"What was the exact function of the long description of the Hindu festival in *A Passage to India?*" He answered,

> It was *architecturally* necessary. I needed a lump, or a Hindu temple *if you like*—a mountain standing up. It is well placed; and it gathers up some strings.[15] [Italics added]

Nevertheless, J. B. Beer, who cites Forster's explanation, cites it only to reject it because "it answers one question only to raise another." [16] Beer's own answer is that

> the Hindu festival . . . is a final image of all-inclusive reality, through which some of the chief characters must pass before his novel can be concluded.[17]

An all-inclusive reality. Or a lump. (Or *if you like,* a Hindu temple.)

> It is acknowledged on all sides that thought is the most important element in Forster's novels. . . . This point has been made by virtually every critic who has written on Forster.[18]

Thought in Forster has given rise to thought in his critics with alarming results. "The threefold division of the book"—

> "Mosque," "Caves," and "Temple," . . . represent also a kind of Hegelian Thesis-Antithesis-Synthesis; or, more properly perhaps, the statement of the problem, and two opposite resolutions.[19]

This thought is awesome. But no: a later critic feels that that "interpretation does violence . . . to the meaning of the novel," and he asserts that, as the three-part structure unfolds,

> as Forster moves from mosque to cave and from cave to temple, from the Way of Works [Part I] to the Way of Knowledge [Part II] and the Way of Love [Part III], his acquiescence is always tentative.[20]

Not Synthesis, then, but something more "tentative" than that, preservation from any "repugnant extreme" and from "consummate union." [21] But no, not at all: for another voice on the thought-behind-the-structure claims that

> in the structure of the novel, "Caves" *separates* "Mosque" from "Temple." Thus Forster reveals the division inherent in India in the two attitudes toward life. There is *nothing* between them. [22] [First italics added]

And another voice issues a still grimmer warning:

> In my outlook, then, there is an equation between the first and third sections of the novel: the two leading creeds of India are both presented and, for one reason or another, both are found wanting. . . . The middle section links the two and gives the clue as to their ultimate meanings. . . . They ultimately come to a curious resounding echo which the finite and limited human ear has not been able to interpret however much it has tried. . . . [23]

Like the critics,

> the strands of the novel are unified by the thematic principle that unity is not to be obtained. [24]

I have raised these puzzling voices because I wish to show here as clearly as I can that Forster's last novel gives rise to a stream of experience whose pattern is analogous to that of the earlier novels. That is, Forster's careful arrangement of the three-part structure produces an inversion of the traditional form of fiction. But to show that parallel is to suggest, as I see it, that the structure has a less specific philosophic or speculative import than is usually attributed to it. The structure expresses Forster's vision, certainly: his constant narrative vision of experience. As for his other vision—of Hinduism, Synthesis, and ultimate metaphysical realities—it is his vision of the novel, his insistence on a finally open flow of conscience, that organizes the former as its material. His vision of experience uses that material, dominates it, and produces the structure of *A Passage to India*.

There are four central characters in *A Passage to India* whose initiation into a fullness of experience we must consider, and three separate *rites du passage*. Mrs. Moore's "vision," the first of these, takes place in the pitch blackness of a cave. "Vision" is, of course, the wrong word for her experience since she sees little and is overwhelmed by what she hears. Serpentine echoes murmur, "Pathos, piety, courage —they exist, but are identical, and so is filth. Everything exists, nothing has value" (149).[25] Thereafter, the fright of what she has heard and understood never leaves her. "The more she thought over it, the more disagreeable and frightening it seemed. . . . The echo began in some indescribable way to undermine her hold on life." Her experience in the novel moves in a single direction, with no reversal or containment. Obsessed, separated internally from further events, she attempts to return to England, but her echoes stay with her, and she dies with them.

Mrs. Moore is in fact "the most successful among those characters of Forster's who expand to embrace the universal." [26] Whether one regards her story as finally one of disturbing spiritual enlightenment or one of destructive "spiritual muddledom" (208), the expansive— the finally expansive—quality of her experience is unmistakable. Its inexorable effect on her has received ample comment from every critic. Although I have no wish to minimize the importance to the novel of Mrs. Moore's part in it, or of Adela Quested's part, the question with which I am concerned here—the final shape of experience in the novel—depends ultimately on what one makes of the relation between Aziz and Fielding. Since this is so, our attention to Mrs. Moore and Adela must be relatively brief.

For Adela Quested, the moment of initiation into a fullness of experience is not her scare, moments after Mrs. Moore's, in another cave. Rather, Adela's cave provides only the first fright, the first part of a *rite du passage* which is not completed until her trial: *her* trial as well as Dr. Aziz's. With respect to the expanding form of her experience, the vexed question of what happened to Adela in the cave matters not at all.[27] Whether she imagined that she was assaulted, or was in fact assaulted by an anonymous native guide, that moment is a halfway point—the same point in either case—in the climb to the summit of her experience. Either way her passage is coherent. As she climbs to the cave with Aziz, the tale leads her unsuspecting thoughts along the path of her coming loveless marriage, of physical attraction, of plural wives—along the line of her own greatest resistance and into her own terrifying cave. If Mrs. Moore's "vision" is a fury of sound, Adela's is a fury of touch.

She is nearly destroyed. In an attempt to narrow and seal off the effects of the fury, she accepts in her extremity the interpretation (attempted rape) offered by the local English community. That interpretation is quite correct. Adela's experience in the courtroom leads her again along the same path: the first person she sees is almost naked and splendidly formed.

> The Court was crowded and of course very hot, and the first person Adela noticed in it was . . . the man who pulled the punkah. Almost naked, and splendidly formed, . . . he seemed to control the proceedings. (217)

Adela sees a good deal in that courtroom.

> Her vision was of several caves. She saw herself in one, and *she* was also outside it, watching its entrance. . . . (229: italics added)

She withdraws her charges against *Aziz*. This is her moment of widest moral vision, and after it there is no contraction.

> Though the vision was over, and she had returned to the insipidity of the world, she remembered what she had learnt.

Hers is the second expanding and unclosed experience in the novel. In form it corresponds in many respects to Lucy Honeychurch's. An Italian carriage driver leads Lucy to an unexpected assault made upon her by George Emerson. The native driver does *not* attack her, of course, nor in this case does Lucy hallucinate her kiss—

even though her vision is made to seem hallucinatory. But the carefully arranged assault serves as the early major explosion of experience; Lucy's attempts thereafter to narrow its effects give way finally to a greater climax and a greater expansion. And Lucy's marriage with George corresponds formally to the very different relationship Adela achieves with Fielding.

In the case of Fielding and Aziz, the movement from relative innocence to relative experience is in essence a movement from separation to mutual friendship—to a friendship that is nearly impossible. Although it is not by any means adequate to say that *A Passage to India* is *essentially* the story of Fielding and Aziz, it is finally their story. As we suggested earlier by way of example, the marriage of Tom Jones and Sophia connects and organizes wider issues of prudence, virtue, and civilization. Similarly, the union between Aziz and Fielding is more than a personal friendship. It is everywhere conceived and rendered as the friendship between an Indian and an Englishman, as the union of the civilizations of India and England, as the meeting of East and West.

A marriage of true minds is held out like a promise, always a little out of reach. The obstacles of circumstance, the trials of good faith, the emotional separations which threaten to destroy a final consummation, the growing crucial-ness to the novel's moral resolution of whether they will or will not be united at the end: all this and much more makes of their friendship the structural and ritual equivalent to the marriage of hero and heroine in the traditional novel. At first the marriage of Adela Quested and Ronny Heaslop, which Mrs. Moore has come to India to aid and abet, seems to play the usual structural role which the issue of marriage regularly plays (will they or won't they?) in organizing events and meanings. But the considerable moral issues it raises gradually subside into the background as the wider moral issues surrounding the marriage of true minds come to the foreground.

The story of Aziz and Fielding is tossed about in the wake of the other two stories, Adela's and Mrs. Moore's. It is they who bring

Aziz and Fielding together at an afternoon tea—or rather, it is their *story* that brings the friends together. It is on the ladies' account that Aziz arranges the ill-fated Marabar expedition. It is the ensuing trial of Aziz—and Adela—that provides a trial of friendship on Fielding's part. It is the conflict over the latter's connection with Adela that eventually draws the two men apart. And it is Mrs. Moore whose spirit blows the ashes of friendship to flame again in the final pages.

How high the flames reach there, what light they finally cast on the novel's total form, are questions that remain to be discussed. But let us briefly examine first the earlier progress to a closeness and warmth of intimacy. When Aziz is arrested for attempted rape after the Marabar trip, Fielding is forcibly separated from him; but Aziz believes that Fielding has deserted him. Thereafter, however, Fielding so dedicates himself to his friend's cause that the trial not only restores Aziz's good name but also, and more importantly perhaps for the book's central concerns, brings their friendship to its fullest bloom.

Yet at this point the countercurrent which will eventually undermine their friendship sets in. The reversing current—in our terms, the concluding motion—has its tiny source in an episode that appears to be only an accident. In the wild scramble out of the courthouse, Adela and Fielding are thrown against each other. Attempting to protect her, Fielding fails to join the victory procession for Aziz. It is a failure which the latter never forgets (see p. 292). Even Fielding acknowledges the distressing implications of the event.

> The English always stick together! That was the criticism. Nor was it unjust. Fielding shared it himself, and knew that if some misunderstanding occurred, and an attack was made on the girl by his allies, he would be obliged to die in her defence. He didn't want to die for her, he wanted to be rejoicing with Aziz. (233)

Despite admitted impediments, the marriage of true minds is consummated that same evening when Aziz and Fielding lie in bed, having endured their *rite du passage,* motionless now under the stars on the roof of a mansion (Ch. XXVII). This is the moment toward which their expanding and deepening stream of conscience has all along been wending its impeded way. If in Forster's novels as we observed earlier, marriage tends to resolve conflicting issues of conscience in an expanding direction rather than a limiting one, this union of friends—the trust, restfulness, and peace which they have achieved, the great intimacy and nearly perfect relationship—seems an analogous moment of expansion: an analogous chapter, for example, to the last chapters of both *A Room with a View* and *Howards End*. Here it is not a last chapter, but *A Passage to India* permits no further deepening of their intimacy.

The reversing and narrowing current sets in rapidly. Aziz suspects Fielding of devious designs—hidden motives in protecting Adela, designs on her person and her money—and now on every hand impediments multiply.

> "Aziz, you have forgiven me the stupid remark I made this morning?"
> "When you called me a little rotter?"
> "Yes, to my eternal confusion. You know how fond I am of you."
> "That is nothing, of course; we all of us make mistakes. In a friendship such as ours a few slips are of no consequence."
> But as he drove off, something depressed him. . . . (278 f.)

Passing through Venice on his return to England, Fielding realizes the existence of "a serious barrier" between himself and his Indian friends. The postcards he sends strike Aziz as "so cold, so unfriendly . . . something was wrong" (293). Finally Aziz concludes unjustly that Fielding has married his enemy Adela and cheated him of the money he might have received in a suit for damages. Their friendship is ruptured totally. "It was the end of a foolish experiment."

But the book of course does not end here. If we recognize that Forster is working with an opening form, a mirror image of the expected classical arrangement of experience, we may suspect that we are ready for the final expansion, the climactic opening outward. In *A Passage to India* that impulsion begins abruptly with the magnificent Hindu celebration. We can see now the aptness of Forster's own explanation, which J. B. Beer, the reader will recall, rejects as begging the question.

> Interviewers: What was the exact function of the long description of the Hindu festival in *A Passage to India*?
>
> Forster: It was architecturally necessary. I needed a lump, or a Hindu temple if you like—a mountain standing up.[28]

He needed some way of counteracting the dying wave of friendship and of bringing about the final expansion of conscience. Beer's objections make sense only if one assumes that Forster is working in the traditional mold, the expanded but finally contained form:

> Why, when the climax of the book has been passed, should such a lump be "architecturally necessary"? The answer can only be that it is there for some purpose other than the dramatic demands of the plot. In other words, we have to cope with the possibility that the structure of the novel does not consist simply of an arrangement of events. Behind that structure there is another, an arrangement of the novel's meaning.[29]

The arrangement of the novel's meaning lies precisely in the arrangement of events, not hidden behind it. And "the" climax of the book has not been passed, because the shape and resolution of experience—a more fundamental form in the novel than the shape and resolution of the action, or its form as drama—have not been fully molded yet.

We have arrived at the narrowest point in the stream: an expansion is to come. Borrowing our terms from Forster again and imagining the novel's shape as that of an hour-glass, we may conceive that we have arrived at its waist. A bare thirty pages from the book's end: it is an odd place for a waist. But the sudden sweep of experience ahead, though slight in number of pages, is as vast—almost, but not quite—as the preceding one.

Part III, then, the brief last section, opens in the midst of a Hindu religious festival. Nothing, we are warned, is

> dramatically correct; this approaching triumph of India was a muddle (as we call it), a frustration of reason and form. (284 f.)

That, surely, is explicit. Fielding has returned to India; in the course of the celebration, he and Aziz meet again, two years after their separation. There have, in the interim, been a couple of marriages. Aziz "had married again—not exactly a marriage but he like to regard it as one" (293). And Fielding, we learn later, is "not quite happy about his marriage" (318). It is the marriage of true minds that is about to be re-consummated.

For a while their mutal coldness and enmity continue. But finally, as Aziz opens impulsively toward Ralph Moore, the movement of expansion begins all over again.

> "Then you are an Oriental." [Aziz] unclasped as he spoke, with a little shudder. Those words—he had said them to Mrs. Moore in the mosque in the beginning of the cycle, from which, after so much suffering, he had got free. Never be friends with the English! Mosque, caves, mosque, caves. And here he was starting again. (311)

A bit later:

> "Perhaps I will just take you out on the water now, for one short half-hour."
> Was the cycle beginning again? His heart was too full to draw back. (312)

The climax of experience is imminent.

Aziz and Mrs. Moore's son Ralph, Fielding and Mrs. Moore's daughter Stella, take to the water now in separate boats, the better to watch the Hindu festival. The novel has been about passages over water from as well as to India, about voyages of return through the Indian Ocean, the Red Sea, the Mediterranean. We have already been taken through rituals of passage by which Mrs. Moore, Adela, and Fielding turn homeward: through a sea-burial, through Egypt,

and through Venice. And these rituals have not been rendered without a certain fitful humor. (Lady Mellanby's remark about the
frying-pan—page 210—may be typically Forsterian, but the mission-
ary's comment on the Lesseps statue in Egypt must surely have been
written by Ionesco: "He turns to the East, he *re*turns to the West.
You can see it from the cute position of his hands, one of which
holds a string of sausages"—p. 266.) Whatever one may think of
these, the final ritual is a good deal more fanciful. The two boats
collide, whirl round, are struck by the symbol of God that the
Hindu worshippers have cast upon the water, and then capsize,
flinging the four passengers overboard.

> They plunged into the warm, shallow water, and rose strug-
> gling into a tornado of noise. The oars, the sacred tray, the
> letters of Ronny and Adela, broke loose and floated confusedly.
> Artillery was fired, drums beat, the elephants trumpeted, and
> drowning all an immense peal of thunder, unaccompanied by
> lightning, cracked like a mallet on the dome. (315)

And the next sentence disposes of our lingering doubt that this
bizarre bit of stage business can possibly be the book's climax:

> That was the climax, as far as India admits of one.

One may of course be inclined to object that as a climax for experience, as a culminating episode for the flow of inner events and
outer events in the novel, the dunking—no matter how noisy—is
unsatisfactory and undramatic, a mere tangle of oars, letters, and
thunder, hardly a proper *event* at all. And Forster himself suggests
precisely that on the next page:

> ragged edges of religion . . . unsatisfactory and undramatic
> tangles . . .

But for better or worse, there cannot be much doubt that this is the
climax, even if we did not have Forster's word for it. For what takes
place is a reunion and a benediction: the Hindu celebration of the
birth of God provides the same catalytic service in bringing the

friends together as Mrs. Moore, Adela Quested, and the aftermath of their twin furies of sound and touch provided earlier.

Appropriately then, the next and last chapter begins: "Friends again. . . ." And the "remarriage" it celebrates is not merely a resolution after a separation; it is an expansion after a moral and emotional contraction. To see the point of this distinction a bit more clearly, the reader is asked to recall that very different remarriage of Sue Bridehead and Phillotson at the end of *Jude the Obscure. That* remarriage is a final contraction of experience after an expansion. Forster's reunion is a formal inversion of that shape; we have come past the waist of the hour-glass to a point in its shape which is almost full width.

> This reconciliation was a success, anyhow. After the funny shipwreck there had been no more nonsense or bitterness, and they went back laughingly to their old relationship as if nothing had happened. Now they rode between jolly bushes and rocks. (317)

The overturning in the water finds its counterpart on the land:

> the whole semi-mystic, semi-sensuous overturn, so characteristic of his spiritual life, came to end like a landslip and rested in its due place, and he found himself riding in the jungle with his dear Cyril [Fielding]. (320)

(We do not need to trace here, since they are peripheral to the central shape of experience in the novel, the various expansive resolutions brought about rather hurriedly in the last chapter, which extend to all the minor characters.)

Then suddenly the expanding impulse comes to an end. Fielding and Aziz, "aware that they could meet no more" (316), aware that "they must inevitably part" (319), begin to quarrel. What we must now decide is whether the very last pages render events which serve to taper, contain, reduce, or reverse the expansion of their reunion. They agree to disagree on politics, theoretically: "with abstract hate" (320). And disagree they do, violently.

> "We shall get rid of you, yes, we shall drive every blasted
> Englishman into the sea, and then"—he rode against him
> furiously—"and then," he concluded, half kissing him, "you
> and I shall be friends." (322)

In a novel whose expansion has been the difficult relationship of
friendship, this can hardly be viewed as a narrowing movement. "He
rode against him furiously . . . he concluded, half kissing him."
This is not still another reversal of the book's direction. But it *is* an
expansion of conscience blocked, a direction left uncertain, a new
and final opening outward left incomplete. Like his earlier novels
but more perfectly and more precisely than those, *A Passage to India*
embodies Forster's wish for a novel of "Expansion. . . . Not completion."

> "Why can't we be friends now?" said the other, [Fielding],
> holding him affectionately. "It's what I want. It's what you
> want."
> But the horses didn't want it—they swerved apart; the earth
> didn't want it. . . . "No, not yet," . . . "No, not there."

It is enlightening to set, directly against that ending, the ending of
D. H. Lawrence's *Women in Love*.

> "But to make it complete, really happy, I wanted eternal
> union with a man too: another kind of love," he said.
>
> .   .   .
>
> "You can't have it, because it's false, impossible," she said.

The parallel is sufficiently obvious, but what makes it significant is
that both novels are written in a form that deliberately departs from
—and in Lawrence's case emphatically denies—the dominant and
traditional form of the novel.

> The contrast between [Forster's] ironic-fictional design and
> Jane Austen's is now clear. Her balancing of possible interpre-
> tations, since it depended on well-defined beliefs, led inevitably
> to a choice and a resolution. Hers was the irony that moves to-
> ward the cancellation of irony. Forster's pattern leads to no such
> resolution.[30]

Indeed, Forster's pattern, as we have seen, is an inversion of the established design. Conrad, one supposes, might have approved of the design of Forster's novel. Still, Conrad's sentiment—

> It is eminently satisfying, but it is not final

—finds itself perhaps overzealously echoed in Forster's agreement—

> Not completion. Not rounding off but opening out.

And Forster's wish finds itself perhaps overfulfilled by Lawrence's novels.

6

D. H. Lawrence: "The Wave Which Cannot Halt"

I

"An Absence of Any Conclusion in View": A Study in Assumptions

The *locus classicus* in the criticism of D. H. Lawrence's fiction remains his own warning to Edward Garnett:

> But somehow—that which is physic—non-human, in humanity, is more interesting to me than the old-fashioned human element —which causes one to conceive a character in a certain moral scheme and make him consistent. . . . You mustn't look in my novel for the old stable *ego* of the character. There is another ego according to whose action the individual is unrecognizable. . . .[1]

It is illuminating to set against Lawrence's impression of what he was doing, another impression. Virginia Woolf, sympathetic but nevertheless worried, noticed that in the world of Lawrence's fiction the reader

> must hurry on. But to what?
> Probably to some scene which has very little to do with character, with story, with any of the usual resting places, eminences,

and consummations of the usual novel. The only thing that we are given to rest upon, to feel to the limits of our powers is some rapture of the physical being. . . .

But, perhaps, because such a state cannot satisfy for long, perhaps because Lawrence lacks the final power which makes things entire in themselves, the effect of the book is that stability is never reached.[2]

Surprisingly, Virginia Woolf's essay is concerned exclusively with *Sons and Lovers* whereas the first passage, in Lawrence's letter to Garnett, refers to *The Rainbow*.[3] Even in their embryonic form apparently, Lawrence's intentions, interests, and direction were already clear to that uncommon reader, Virginia Woolf. "That which is physic" is what interests Lawrence; "some rapture of the physical being" is his resting place, Virginia Woolf observes. "The old-fashioned human element" of consistent character holds only limited interest for Lawrence; his "eminences" have "little to do with character," Virginia Woolf feels. There are other parallels; but most striking of all is their agreement to disagree. "You mustn't look in my novel for the old stable ego," Lawrence insists. "The effect of the book," Virginia Woolf notes critically, "is that stability is never reached." Can we draw at once the apparent connection between a new conception of character—the unstable ego—and a new conception of form—the unstable novel? Whatever one makes of Paul Morel's return to the glowing town on the last page of his novel, or of Ursula Brangwen's vision of the rainbow on the last page of her novel, neither *Sons and Lovers* nor *The Rainbow* ever reaches formal stability. And though it will be fruitless to question which came first, character or form (both of which I wish to investigate here), it is clear that by the time of *The Rainbow* at least, a new unstable ego arrives in the shell of a new unstable structure.

Lawrence's novels do lack the "consummations of the usual novel." It is even a first principle of form in his fiction that the novel and the novelist should seek to reject, deliberately, disconcertingly, that particular "final power which makes things entire in themselves." Another final power, which continues to distress his readers, is his. The "consummations" of his novels may be (and have been) found wanting; but to find them so, readers and critics have had to weigh them in an inaccurate balance. They have had to measure his fiction by aesthetic intentions and critical assumptions not merely upset by Lawrence's conclusions (in which case their expectations *would* be a valid standard for judgment), but upset by the entire construction which has led to those conclusions. That imaginative construction is a highly organized form, a fictional structure which not only is left, but indeed must in the end be left, still open and expanding: never stabilized.

Lawrence's most dedicated champion,[4] F. R. Leavis, has puzzled over an "imperfection" found at the far end of *The Rainbow*: "the absence of an inevitable close." But he reassures us that it really does not matter.

> As for the imperfection of *The Rainbow*, the absence of an inevitable close matters, when one sees what the book does, not at all. A more serious criticism, perhaps, bears on the signs of too great a tentativeness in the development and organization of the later part; signs of a growing sense in the writer of an absence of any conclusion in view.[5]

Astonishingly, Leavis levels his "more serious" indictment at the entire "later part" of the novel. Yet surely we may suppose that there exists some connection between the "tentativeness" of the entire later section and the "imperfection" of the ending. Seeing that connection, the critic sees it not as formal or imaginative coherence, but as the inadvertent product (forgivable) of some difficulty in the novelist: "No real conclusion of the book, only a breaking-off, is possible—if only because the Lawrence who started it has changed too much." [6] Accepting with gratitude the perfectly accurate perceptions that prompted these remarks, one is tempted nevertheless to amend them in this way: There is no absence of an inevitable close, only an absence of *the* inevitable close. There is no "tentativeness" whatever in the later part of *The Rainbow*, but (as I hope to show) an organization which differs from the kind that leads to *the* inevitable close. "The development and organization of the later part" do produce "an inevitable close," precisely one in which "only a breaking-off is possible." And indeed there are "signs" in great profusion and for hundreds of pages, that by every means at his command, the writer is attempting to produce "a growing sense" in the *reader* of "an absence of any conclusion in view."

What Lawrence does with such painstaking preparation in *The Rainbow* he had already done, but with virtually no advance preparation, in the earlier *Sons and Lovers*.

> But no, he would not give in. Turning sharply, he walked towards the city's gold phosphorescence. His fists were shut, his mouth set fast. He would not take that direction, to follow her. He walked towards the faintly humming, glowing town, quickly.

The End. But "nothing in [Paul Morel's] previous history persuades us that he could unfalteringly do"[7] what Lawrence here makes Paul do, as Mark Schorer was the first and not the last to point out. It *is* unpersuasive, that ending. But it is not a capricious impulse on Lawrence's part. The failure of his technique here is related to the success of his technique and the progress of his discoveries in later novels.

In an earlier letter to Garnett, Lawrence protested (and protested too much):

> I tell you it has got form—*form:* haven't I made it patiently, out of sweat as well as blood. It follows this idea: . . .[8]

An analytic summary of the novel's form follows, and ends this way:

> [Paul] gets a woman who fights for his soul—fights his mother. The son loves the mother—all the sons hate and are jealous of the father. The battle goes on between the mother and the girl, with the son as object. The mother gradually proves stronger, because of the tie of blood. The son decides to leave his soul in his mother's hands, and, like his elder brother, go for passion. He gets passion. Then the split begins to tell again. But, almost unconsciously, the mother realizes what is the matter, and be-

gins to die. The son casts off his mistress, attends to his mother
dying. He is left in the end naked of everything, with the drift
towards death.

But as others have often observed, this is not the way the novel ends
at all. Lawrence's summary (which remarkably forgets or deliberately ignores the novel's last paragraph) is clearly a description of
what we have here been calling the closed form: that dominant tradition of the novel which expands to a "wide" climax of conscience
and then works its way back to a narrow-ended last chapter. But in
fact the ending asserts that Paul "would not take that direction."
What impulse, what impulsion (what compulsion perhaps?) led
Lawrence to alter in a last paragraph the direction he claims to have
"patiently and laboriously constructed"[9] throughout the novel that
leads up to it?

Lawrence's "artistic powers," Louis Fraiberg comments, "lapse
here long enough to let him write an incongruous conclusion to
Paul's story." [10] Incongruous and unpersuasive: but is it possible that
the last five sentences bear witness to something that is not quite or
not merely the failure of artistic powers? Can we regard them instead as a pre-vision of—or even a compulsion toward?—a new form
which will only be artistically grasped and successfully created in
The Rainbow? That last, deliberate bending of the form signifies at
the very least some inner necessity in the author,[11] his *refusal* to close
off a book already and necessarily closed.

> The last paragraph of the book, which has seemed to some
> an affirmation of victory for life and for Paul, can yield this
> meaning only if the plain tendency of all that has gone before
> is ignored or if the book is regarded as leading to a sequel in
> which all will be reversed.[12]

If we *can* regard the last paragraph of *Sons and Lovers* less as a
blunder and more as a recognition and an assertion—an insight unachieved but nevertheless asserted—we will be on surer grounds for
understanding what Lawrence painstakingly does achieve in *The*

Rainbow, where the same formal organization is in no way tentative, blundering, last-minute, or unpersuasive.

The direction that distorts the last page of *Sons and Lovers*—regarded not as an impulse of "affirmation" but as an impulse at all costs to open up an already closed form—carries over to *The Rainbow* and informs it from first to last page.

> One could speak of a sort of overflow principle in [Lawrence's] work ("overflow" was what Wordsworth called those passages which he could not accommodate in his poems) whereby the interests, attitudes, methods. and also the mannerisms of one novel flow not only into other novels, but also into the travel books, poems, letters, and essays.[13]

What Herbert Lindenberger here remarks in Lawrence is in a way true of all writers. Indeed, the overflow, not only among writers but within the work of individual writers, of interests, attitudes, methods, and mannerisms, is the groundwork of literary history. Yet, having admitted all that, one is still forced to acknowledge that what is true of all writers is still more true of Lawrence. Graham Hough is constantly obliged to go about his critical work on Lawrence in this way:

> "And whom shall I submit to?" Aaron said.
> "Your soul will tell you," replied the other.
>
> With these words the book ends. It is . . . a mere hint of a new philosophy, not yet an exposition of it. Lawrence is doing what he so often does, ending a book with the foretaste of what is to come. This emphasises the essential character of *Aaron's Rod,* which is that of an interim report. And because the question of power and its implications are only touched on here, we are absolved from discussing it further at the moment. Its fuller exposition is in the contemporaneous *Fantasia of the Unconscious.* . . . Our next task is to pursue the themes of power and leadership as they appear in the novels immediately succeeding *Aaron's Rod.*[14]

Ending as Lawrence "so often does . . . with the foretaste of what is to come"—this is open-ended form with a vengeance.

It is hardly possible to miss the idiosyncrasy of Lawrence's endings, but it has been easy to misjudge them by misjudging the structure of events which leads into them. David Daiches writes:

> But the novel [*The Rainbow*] has already said more than this,
> has already proved itself too complex to be concluded by a
> simple vision of hope such as the rainbow.[15]

We have already mentioned F. R. Leavis's charge that "no real conclusion of the book, only a breaking-off is possible"—a charge whose
judgment, though it is thumbs-down, seems more accurate. For the
rainbow is not too simple a vision to "conclude" a complex book; to
the extent that such criticism points to a flaw in the formal flux of
conscience, it misjudges the direction of that flux in *The Rainbow*.
The final rainbow is an attempt, managed with some artistry, not to
"conclude," an attempt to stop without concluding, an anti-conclusion, if you like. Manifestly impossible—so one is tempted to conclude
oneself, an attempt headed for failure; but then one is brought up
short by the realization that Lawrence has succeeded with at least
two readers by their own admission: F. R. Leavis and David Daiches.
Graham Hough, too, notices regretfully that

> the book can have no proper ending. . . . [When Ursula] has
> an intuition of regenerating power in her visionary encounter
> with the wild horses, when she sees the vision of the rainbow
> with which the book ends, . . . —we can only feel that this is
> quite insufficiently based, nothing in the book up to now has
> led up to it.[16]

Everything in the book (I will try to show) has led up to it; and
indeed it is *therefore* true that the book can have no "proper" ending.
Echoing F. R. Leavis, Roger Sale in "The Narrative Technique of
The Rainbow" writes that

> Lawrence becomes a victim of that tentativeness Leavis has
> described so well in connection with the novels of the early
> twenties. He writes on and on, looking for a place to stop,
> almost as though he were mindless of the methods used and
> terms established in the first half of the novel.[17]

If the view advanced here is correct, it is not Lawrence but Lawrence's critics who are "looking for a place to stop," and who in so doing have not been sufficiently mindful of the methods and terms established in the first half of the novel.

These terms and methods were not established in *Sons and Lovers;* but the parallel between the endings themselves has been observed by Mark Spilka in "The Shape of an Arch: A Study of Lawrence's *The Rainbow.*"

> Yet the ending holds true enough. . . . Ursula Brangwen becomes a woman in these final pages, in the same way, essentially, as Paul Morel is born a man at the end of *Sons and Lovers*. . . . Clearly the rainbow is a sign of her potential fulfillment.[18]

The words "born" and "potential" are suggestive: an ending which is barely a beginning. But whereas the impulsion toward that sort of an ending merely caps the earlier work, it dominates the internal imaginative organization of *The Rainbow* totally. For here it is not merely that the historical saga *à la* Bennett and Galsworthy gives way to the temper of the modern novel (*à la Jude the Obscure*); and not merely that in *The Rainbow* two earlier generations of Brangwens make way for a modern generation; but that here with the utmost propriety the dominant traditional form of experience in fiction—explicitly expected by those two earlier generations—is forced to give way within a single vast fiction to the form for experience which controls the novel for the first half of the twentieth century.

Women in Love is written even more explicitly in that open form. Graham Hough succinctly observes that its conclusion "brings into unexpected prominence another theme that has been subordinate but recurrent throughout the book—the relationship between man and man." [19] Observing the same point, David Daiches tries valiantly but hesitantly to ascribe to the book a few of the traditional virtues.

> Rupert Birkin . . . in the end does achieve a satisfactory relationship with Ursula, whom he marries, but only after many characteristically Lawrentian scenes of struggle and doubt and

alternating movements of repulsion and attraction in the course
of which much of Lawrence's mature view of men and women
is given concrete embodiment and symbolization. But the conclusion of the novel, with Gerald dead, Gudrun fascinated by
an attractively corrupt German sculptor, and Ursula and Rupert
facing each other, is far from embodying a final solution. Rupert demands more than a satisfactory relationship between man
and wife, and the novel ends on a question.[20]

One can catch here the implication that there is something wrong
with a novel which—no, not which does not embody a final solution,
but which is *far* from embodying a final solution, and one which
brings into "unexpected prominence" a subordinate but recurrent
theme.

All of these aesthetic, formal, and moral assumptions rise to the
surface vividly in F. R. Leavis' sympathetic evaluation of *Women in
Love,* forming a Procrustean bed in which Lawrence's achievement
must perforce lie down:

> Birkin and Ursula as a norm, contemplated in the situation
> they are left in at the close of the book, leave us wondering
> (and, it must in fairness be added, leave Lawrence wondering
> too). That is, if a certain symmetry of negative and positive
> was aimed at in *Women in Love,* Lawrence has been defeated
> by the difficulty of life: he hasn't solved the problems of civiliza-
> tion that he analyzes.[21]

By now this study's own point of view—and its peculiar complaint
—will have been sufficiently obvious. What Lawrence's work *does*
has been perceived, with accuracy and acumen, while at the same
time what it does has been evaluated according to expectations
which his work has all along been undermining. Whether his work
successfully creates any other norm by which it can reasonably be
judged, the remainder of this chapter will inquire. In an examination
of *The Rainbow,* Edward Engelberg has suggested convincingly that
Lawrence's fiction deliberately attempts to break loose from "enclo-
sures" and strike out toward climaxes that are not "coincident with
[the reader's] prophecies." [22] What I wish to do here is first to present

in greater detail the structure of events through which such a form is achieved;[23] and second, setting Lawrence's achievement in the context of the present study, to identify his characteristic form as the open-ended flux of experience.[24] For it is imperative to acknowledge with Edward Engelberg that

> those who accuse Lawrence of a sleight of hand at the end of his novels fail to see the intuition and later the consciousness of his purpose, for he was quite aware that his conclusions were not the neat, conventional climaxes that satisfy a reader's expectations. . . . Such endings he would have considered "immoral." [25]

And one ought to acknowledge the explicitness of Lawrence's own statement:

> "Nothing outside the definite line of the book," is a maxim. But can the human mind fix absolutely the definite line of a book, any more than it can fix absolutely the definite line of action for a living being? [26]

Those who criticize Lawrence for failure to organize his fiction toward an inevitable close, ought in fairness to recall his harsh judgment in *Women in Love* of Gerald Crich, whose strength, readers will recall, was "hollow":

> Only let him grip hold of a situation, and he would bring to pass an inevitable conclusion.[27]

II

The Rainbow: A "Developing Rejection of Old Forms"

From first page to last page the organization of *The Rainbow* is planned to provide, inevitably, for the absence of any conclusion. The interaction between the inner tensions of character and the outer pressures of plot, place, and pace give rise to waves or climactic movements of experience which are constantly prevented from falling and closing. The movement is always "outward" from a center, "beyond" a limit, and into the "unknown."

The novel begins with a five-page introductory passage. The first paragraph tells us that for generations each of the Brangwens had been

> aware of something standing above him and beyond him in the distance.
>
> There was a look in the eyes of the Brangwens as if they were expecting something unknown, about which they were eager. They had that air of readiness for what would come to them, a kind of surety, an expectancy, . . .

The suggested experience of a movement which will not finally cease, the organic rhythm whose very moment of falling back is the beginning of an impulsion forward, is just as deliberately evoked for us on the second page.

> But heaven and earth was teeming around them, and how should this cease? They felt the rush of the sap in spring, they knew the wave which cannot halt, but every year throws forward the seed to begetting, and, falling back, leaves the young-born on the earth.

The anonymous Brangwen women, out of whom come the novel's three generations, looked out to the "world beyond" (the third page insists) : "faced outwards" to the world of men, to "what was beyond, to enlarge their own scope and range and freedom." To a Brangwen woman, her own menfolk lacked "outwardness and range of motion," and were on this account less attractive than the vicar, who had "a range of being" (the fourth page continues to insist).

> She knew her husband. But in the vicar's nature was that which passed beyond her knowledge.

"The wonder of the beyond was before them," the fifth page tells us (over and over), holding out for us characters who "moved in the wonder of the beyond." As it turns out, the impulse beyond knowledge into the unknown, predicated by the introduction, is the energy which not only shapes the several arcs of experience of which *The Rainbow* consists, but determines and even makes imperative the absence of the "inevitable" conclusions of fiction. Instead of a limited conclusion, instead of a close that is knowable and hence delimiting, we are given ultimately Ursula's rejection of the known and knowable Anton Skrebensky. And the falling of that wave ("which cannot halt") is followed by the rainbow image: the pledge not only of a new world, but in effect of Ursula's union in *Women in Love* with the still unknown and unknowable Birkin.[28]

The contrary force, the energy of closure and constriction which produces the tension out of which the novel rises, begins exactly here as the five-page introductory section ends and the narrative proper opens: a canal is constructed within a high embankment that closes off the Marsh Farm of the Brangwens from the world beyond. "So the Marsh was shut off from Ilkeston, and enclosed in the small valley bed." The novel, the inexorable struggle outward and beyond any limiting terminus, begins.

The separate stories of the three generations in *The Rainbow* are all told not merely with careful regard for, but actually in explicit terms of, openings and closings, expansion and constriction. Lydia Lensky, the Polish lady whom Tom Brangwen marries in the first chapter, represents for Brangwen, we learn, that which is foreign, unknown, and, he soon discovers, unknowable.[29] She herself is entirely closed to life when he first meets her (see pp. 43-9); it is because he compels her to open herself to him that she takes him for her second husband. For Tom Brangwen, the movement is "beyond":

> he saw her hands, ungloved, folded in her lap, and he noticed the wedding-ring on her finger. It excluded him: it was a closed circle. It bound her life, the wedding-ring, it stood for her life in which he could have no part. Nevertheless, beyond all this, there was herself and himself which should meet. (32)

As the Brangwens begin to move outward from the Marsh, a series of foreigners provides a sense of direction: a "small, withered foreigner" (19) and his girl; Lydia Lensky; Anna Lensky; Anton Skrebensky; and ultimately (in *Women in Love*) the sculptor Loerke. (The direction of movement from the enclosed lowlands of the Marsh Farm at Ilkeston leads, as Ursula keeps remembering in the later book, to the open pinnacles of the Swiss Alps.) Even before he meets Lydia, very early in *The Rainbow,* young Tom Brangwen takes a trip by horse away from the Marsh Farm to a distant tavern.

> His mind was one big excitement. The girl and the foreigner: he knew neither of their names. Yet they had set fire to the homestead of his nature, and he would be burned out of cover. Of the two experiences, perhaps the meeting with the foreigner was the more significant. But the girl—he had not settled about the girl.
>
> He did not know. He had to leave it there, as it was. He could not sum up his experiences. (19)

No resolution, no settling, no summing up. Only the movement out:

> He balked the mean enclosure of reality, stood stubbornly like a bull at a gate, refusing to re-enter the well-known round of his own life.

That is why he marries Lydia Lensky. The marriage which "terminates" their courtship is in no sense the usual resolution of tensions, in no sense the usual containment of hitherto expanding impulses. On their wedding night, Tom Brangwen reflects:

> Behind her, there was so much unknown to him. When he approached her, he came to such a terrible painful unknown. How could he embrace it and fathom it? . . . If he stretched and strained for ever he would never be able to grasp it all, and to yield himself naked out of his own hands into the unknown power! . . . What was it then that she was, to which he must also deliver himself up, and which at the same time he must embrace, contain? (50 f.)

The very success of their union lies in its irresolution: "he seemed to live thus in contact with her, in contact with the unknown, the unaccountable and incalculable" (52).

The first chapter ends (as do each of the larger internal divisions of the novel) with a suggestion of the rainbow on which the last page of the book will rest.

> Then somewhere in the night a radiance again, like a vapour. And all the sky was teeming and tearing along, a vast disorder of flying shapes and darkness and ragged fumes of light and a great brown circling halo. . . . (42)

But the fact that the interlocking stories of the three generations simply balance, just as one story gives way to the next, on the image of the rainbow arching in the heavens, is in itself not really very impressive. It is the fact that in each case the rainbow arch is conceived as a circle half concluded, as an open circle leading out and beyond, in short as a doorway to the next generation and the next story, that gives firm evidence of Lawrence's intentions from the start to provide us finally with only tentativeness, with the absence of conclusion. (The original title, *The Wedding Ring*—the "closed circle" which Lawrence refers to on page 32—gave way to the final title *The Rainbow*.[30] It is no small matter that the original title might serve in a pinch as a title for the majority of novels ever written, and no accident that "a closed circle" might describe the traditional shape of the novel generally.) As the book turns to the story of Anna Lensky, we are told that Tom and Lydia

> had passed through the doorway into the further space, where movement was so big, that it contained bonds and constraints and labours, and still was complete liberty. She was the doorway to him, he to her. At last they had thrown open the doors, each to the other, and had stood in the doorways facing each other, whilst the light flooded out from behind on to each of their faces, it was the transfiguration, the glorification, the admission.
>
> .   .   .
>
> . . . she was the gateway and the way out, . . . she was beyond, and . . . he was travelling in her through the beyond. Whither?—What does it matter?
>
> .   .   .
>
> [Anna's] father and mother now met to the span of the heavens,

> and she, the child, was free to play in the space beneath, be-
> tween. (pp. 87 and 88)

In that way the story of the child Anna begins.

It "ends" a hundred pages further on, or rather it yields to the story of the child Ursula, in the same way:

> [Anna] had a slight expectant feeling, as of a door half opened.
> . . . A faint, gleaming horizon, a long way off, and a rainbow
> like an archway, a shadow-door with faintly coloured coping
> above it. Must she be moving thither? [Whither?—What does it
> matter? (p. 88)]
> Something she had not, something she did not grasp, could
> not arrive at. There was something beyond her. But why must
> she start on the journey? . . .
>
>   .   .   .
>
> [At dawn] she said, "it is here." And when, at evening, the
> sunset came in a red glare through the big opening in the
> clouds, she said again, "It is beyond."
> Dawn and sunset were the feet of the rainbow that spanned
> the day, and she saw the hope, the promise. Why should she
> travel any further?
>
>   .   .   .
>
> With satisfaction she relinquished the adventure to the un-
> known. She was bearing her children.
> There was another child coming, and Anna lapsed into vague
> content. If she were not the wayfarer to the unknown, if she
> were arrived now, settled in her builded house, a rich woman,
> still her doors opened under the arch of the rainbow, her thresh-
> old reflected the passing of the sun and moon, the great travel-
> lers, her house was full of the echo of journeying.
> She was a door and a threshold, she herself. Through her an-
> other soul was coming, to stand upon her as upon the threshold,
> looking out, shading its eyes for the direction to take. (pp. 183-
> 184)

The "direction" of the last section of the novel, the tentativeness of the last pages, the inevitable inconclusiveness toward which Ursula's story will drive her, can hardly be imagined to be a weakening of artistry in the novel. (To conceive of the story's final direction as a sort of failure or wavering is a failure in reading or a wavering of the critical imagination; it is the triumph, that is to say, of habit.)

At Anna's wedding, directly in the middle of her story, Lawrence takes care to warn us that her stepfather, Tom Brangwen, still remembering his own wedding, was still wondering even now

> if he ever should feel arrived and established. He was here at Anna's wedding. Well, what right had he to feel responsible, like a father? He was still as unsure and unfixed as when he had married himself. His wife and he! With a pang of anguish he realized what uncertainties they both were. (124)

And just in case the "direction" or the "end" which the novelist envisions for his novel should not as yet be entirely clear, he adds:

> When did one come to an end? In which direction was it finished? There was no end, no finish, only this roaring vast space. Did one never get old, never die? That was the clue. (125)

This "clue" is embedded in the midst of a wedding ceremony, traditionally "The End" of fictional careers; and the entire meditation on how one finishes is embedded in a longer passage (too long to quote) which for two pages burns intermittently with the prismatic colors of the rainbow "whilst the heavens shimmered and roared about them." And *that* entire passage concludes:

> Always it was so unfinished and unformed!

Much the same form ("always . . . unformed") molds the story of Will Brangwen, Anna's husband. As *his* story ends, or rather as it gives place to the story of his child Ursula, we read:

> He was aware of some limit to himself, of something unformed in his very being, of some buds which were not ripe in him, some folded centres of darkness which would never develop and unfold whilst he was alive in the body. He was unready for fulfilment. Something undeveloped in him limited him, there was a darkness in him which he *could* not unfold, which would never unfold in him. (197)

And much, much later in the novel, we learn that he was still

> in one of his states of flux. After all these years, he began to see
> a loophole of freedom. . . . The growing up of his daughters,
> their developing rejection of old forms set him also free.
>
> He was a man of ceaseless activity. Blindly, like a mole, he
> pushed his way out of the earth that covered him, working al-
> ways away from the physical element in which his life was cap-
> tured. Slowly, blindly, gropingly, with what initiative was left
> to him, he made his way towards individual expression and in-
> dividual form. (335)

Slowly, gropingly, but not blindly, Lawrence is creating a novel
whose individual form ought not to be missed.

"The growing up of [Will's] daughters" is, as we shall see, a "developing rejection of old forms" not only for them but for their novelist. (Gudrun's rejection of old forms waits for *Women in Love*.)
The never finished, "unformed" form in which Ursula's story is conceived and, it is only fair to say, fulfilled, is held before our eyes
dazzlingly in *The Rainbow*. Of her mother, Anna, we have already
read:

> With satisfaction she relinquished the adventure to the un-
> known. She was bearing her children. (184)

Of Ursula (at another crucial wedding, her brother Fred's) we read:

> Waves of delirious darkness ran through her soul. She wanted
> to let go. She wanted to reach and be among the flashing stars,
> she wanted to race with her feet and be beyond the confines of
> this earth. She was mad to be gone. (298 f.)

"Why should she travel any further?" (183) is the question her
mother, Anna, asks. Ursula, we are told much later, "was a traveller
on the face of the earth" and "like a bird tossed into mid-air" (394).

One has only to consider the way in which for hundreds of pages
Lawrence renders Ursula's relation to other people, and especially to
Skrebensky, to see the astonishing consistency with which he sets in
motion the finally unstable conclusion of her experience.

> And still [Skrebensky] had not got her, she was hard and bright
> as ever, intact. But he must weave himself round her, enclose

> her in a net of shadow, of darkness, so she would be like a
> bright creature gleaming in a net of shadows, caught. (301)

> She believed that love was a way, a means, not an end in itself,
> as Maggie seemed to think. And always the way of love would
> be found. *But whither did it lead?* (388) [Italics added.]

> Ursula suffered and enjoyed . . . Maggie's fundamental sadness
> of enclosedness. Maggie enjoyed and suffered Ursula's struggles
> against the confines of her life. And then the two girls began to
> drift apart, as Ursula broke from that form of life wherein Mag-
> gie must remain enclosed. (389)

> Nay, if [Skrebensky] had remained true to her, he would have
> been the doorway to her, into the boundless sky of happiness and
> plunging, inexhaustible freedom which was the paradise of her
> soul. Ah, the great range he would have opened to her, the il-
> limitable endless space for self-realization and delight for ever.
> (414)

Indeed, when she and Anton make love ("She would not love him
in a house any more. . . . She was free up among the stars"), Lawrence's vocabulary moves in a single sentence from "clasped,"
"clenched," and "close" to "open" and "unfathomable":

> She took him, she clasped him, clenched him close, but her eyes
> were open looking at the stars, it was as if the stars were lying
> with her and entering the unfathomable darkness of her womb,
> fathoming her at last. It was not him. (438)

And when she realizes that she will have to leave him, she thinks:

> He seemed completed now. . . . He seemed added up, fin-
> ished. She knew him all round, not on any side did he lead into
> the unknown. (447)

> "It isn't supposed to lead anywhere, is it?" said Dorothy, satir-
> ically. "I thought it was the one thing which is an end in itself."
> "Then what does it matter to me?" cried Ursula. "As an end
> in itself, I could love a hundred men, one after the other. Why
> should I end with a Skrebensky?" (448)

> The trouble began at evening. Then a yearning for something
> unknown came over her, a passion for something she knew not
> what. (450 f.)
> "Well, what have I done?" he asked, in a rather querulous
> voice.
> "I don't know," she said, in the same dull, feeling voice. "It is
> finished. It has been a failure." (454)

The word "finished" here means not only "over" but "complete,"
"perfected." The entire fiction which has gone before has made Ursula's point luminously clear. The narrative has taken the greatest
pains to establish in its own terms that whatever is perfected or per-
fectable, "has been a failure"; whatever is to be perfect, must lead
only into the unknown. To task Lawrence's novel with a failure to
provide a finished conclusion becomes, under these circumstances,
more than a trifle absurd.

The shape of "the wave which cannot halt" on page two, and the
energy of the incessant quest for the unknown on page 299 ("She
must leap from the known into the unknown . . . her breast
strained as if in bonds"), provide, then, the energetic shape not only
of Ursula's experience but of the entire fiction which her personal
history "concludes." The saga of the Brangwens which begins on
page one by telling us

> There was a look in the eyes of the Brangwens as if they were
> expecting something unknown, about which they were eager

ends when Ursula rejects Anton Skrebensky:

> He was that which is known. (465)

That ending ("It was the unknown, the unexplored, the undiscov-
ered upon whose shore she had landed, alone, after crossing the
void") capped by the rainbow image in the last paragraphs, is more
than a convenient example of an open form in fiction; it is almost a
manifesto for a form that is still expanding as the novel closes. Nor is
it possible to regard this energetic impulsion merely as a provision
for a "sequel" in *Women in Love*. For the latter's ending is, if any-

thing, still more of an anti-conclusion. (Both novels are "finished" works in one sense of that term; but both have expanding ends.) And in *The Rainbow* specifically, the opening end has been coming for a long time and from a long way back.

The contrary direction of energy, narrative impulses toward a desirable final restriction of experience and a "finished" conclusion, do also run through Ursula's story. Since these impulses provide a necessary tension, it is not surprising that they become more frequent and more insistent in the last chapter, *after* Ursula has rejected Skrebensky. Indeed the fossil remains of the customary novelistic "finish" in marriage and death are imprinted on the final section of the book like ghostly forms. Ursula writes to Anton, asking him to take her back and marry her; and in an extraordinary moment, just as if she herself were the novelist of her story, Ursula looks forward to "the time when she should join him again and her history would be concluded for ever" (458).

She repents her violation of the normal course of development. "I cannot tell you the remorse I feel for my wicked, perverse behaviour" (457). She will "live simply as a good wife to him. What did the self, the form of life, matter?" (456). Self? Form of life? All this is of course a direct inversion of what she has thought earlier:

> *Self* was a oneness with the infinite. To be oneself was a supreme, gleaming triumph of infinity. (416 f.)

And it is a direct reminder of the passage already cited, in which

> Ursula broke from that *form of life* wherein Maggie must remain enclosed. (389)

Indeed, the entire passage which stands almost at the opening of the last chapter can be read as a succinct definition of the closed form of experience in fiction, just as the present study has all along, and less succinctly, defined it. In that passage, in her penultimate decision, Ursula rejects the expanding form of the novel and bows her personal will to the force of cultural convention and literary tradition

which demands a closed form for experience. (The italics below are
of course mine.)

> What did the self, the form of life, matter? Only the living from
> day to day mattered, the beloved existence in the body, rich,
> *peaceful, complete, with no beyond, no further trouble, no fur-*
> *ther complication.* She had been wrong, she had been arrogant
> and wicked, wanting that other thing, that fantastic freedom,
> that illusory, conceited fulfilment which she had imagined she
> could not have with Skrebensky. Who was she to be wanting
> some fantastic fulfilment in her life? Was it not enough that she
> had her man, her children, her place of shelter under the sun?
> Was it not enough for her, as it had been enough for her
> mother? She would marry and love her husband and fill her
> place simply. That was the ideal. (456 f.)

That is certainly the ideal, the "inevitable" conclusion. And the ideal
is full of echoes: Ursula is with child, she will be "rich," she will live
"in the body," in a "place of shelter," and "under the sun," as her
mother, Anna, did. Quite plainly, Ursula's next-to-last choice echoes
Anna's last choice in that passage which stands at the end of Anna's
cycle of experience and stamps its form:

> Soon, she felt sure of her husband. She knew his dark face and
> the extent of its passion. She knew his slim, vigorous body, she
> said it was hers. Then there was no denying her. She was a rich
> woman enjoying her riches.
> And soon again she was with child. Which made her satisfied
> and took away her discontent. She forgot that she had watched
> the sun climb up and pass his way, a magnificent traveller
> surging forward. . . . [She was] settled in her builded house,
> a rich woman. . . . (184)

This choice then, Anna's, becomes precisely Ursula's next-to-last
decision, the choice of a closed form; the parallel should indicate
beyond the possibility of doubt Lawrence's coherent plan throughout the novel for the expanding form on which it closes. For Ursula,
who has everywhere been shown as a "magnificent traveller surging
forward," and whose travels will quite literally continue to the Alps

in a later novel, cannot finally tolerate the closed ending. Her almost-final decision to be bound by Skrebensky (whom she must finally reject) drives her to a state of physical fever and mental hallucination bordering on madness.

> Why must she be bound, aching and cramped with the bondage, to Skrebensky and Skrebensky's world? Anton's world: it became in her feverish brain a compression which enclosed her. If she could not get out of the compression she would go mad. (464)

This is that recurrent point in fiction, the point of fever, nightmare, despair, and disorder which we have observed in earlier chapters of this study, and which regularly signals the most intense and expanded point in the climactic form of experience in fiction. Here Ursula's moment of agonizing moral choice is accompanied by her nightmare vision of the thundering horses ("It was the crisis. . . . Then suddenly, in a flame of agony, she darted, seized the rugged knots of the oak-tree and began to climb"—p. 461); and it is accompanied by delirium ("She was very ill for a fortnight, delirious, shaken and racked. . . . In her delirium she beat and beat at the question"—p. 463). Regularly of course, in the form of fiction which Lawrence has all along been challenging, these moments are followed by episodes which reduce the intensity achieved and narrow the stream of conscience.

Lawrence, who has no such plans, is thus faced by a considerable problem of technique: what sort of episode can follow nightmare and delirium without reducing their intensity; what sort of episode can reduce the moral disorder while expanding the moral scope of Ursula's experience in the *same* direction as that in which it has been evolving? Given Lawrence's purposes, which are the obverse of the usual novelist's usual purposes, it is difficult to imagine a more successful solution[31]—a resolution in openness—than Ursula's vision of the rainbow as a "finish" for the flood of experience.

> As she grew better, she sat to watch a new creation. (466)

III

Women in Love: "More Urgent Proof," a Manifesto in Fiction

Ursula's travels—her transcendence of her own limited "self," of the limited "world" of her provincial childhood, and of the conventional "form of life"—are projected with complete and explicit consistency in *Women in Love*. Traveling to the Swiss Alps with her husband Rupert Birkin, who remains "unknown" to her and in a sense unknowable, she finds herself thinking

> of the Marsh, the old, intimate farm-life at Cossethay. My God, how far was she projected from her childhood, how far was she still to go! In one lifetime one travelled through aeons. The great chasm of memory from her childhood in the intimate country surroundings of Cossethay and the Marsh Farm—she remembered the servant Tilly, who used to give her bread and butter sprinkled with brown sugar, in the old living-room where the grandfather clock had two pink roses in a basket painted above the figures on the face—and now when she was traveling into the unknown with Birkin, an utter stranger—was so great, that it seemed she had no identity, that the child she had been, playing in Cossethay churchyard, was a little creature of history, not really herself.
>
> •   •   •
>
> So long as they were moving outwards, she was satisfied. They came to Zurich, then, before very long, ran under the mountains, that were deep in snow. At last she was drawing near. This was the other world now. (pp. 445 ff.)

The book-long evolution of the relationships among Ursula and Gudrun, Gerald and Birkin—an interweaving of experience which Mark Schorer has called a "fluid, dance-like movement"[32]—mounts toward its crisis in the "other world." We might glance briefly here at the final phases in the choreography. For Gudrun and Gerald, the gradual drift toward a duel to the death culminates at last, high in the snow, in Gerald's deathgrip on Gudrun's throat. After that, Gudrun packs off to Dresden to enter into a still more sinister dance offstage with the German sculptor Loerke. And Gerald keeps climbing until he is finally frozen to death. For Ursula and Birkin, the other two central dancers, the crisis in experience occurs after Gerald's death in a curtain-stopping *pas de deux:* but we will come to that shortly.

It is, in fact, not at all difficult to show that the dance of experience or the stream of conscience in *Women in Love* is left entirely inconclusive, or to show that its ending is left open and expanding. But what is perhaps more interesting to observe is that Lawrence has actually embedded an explicit essay on the theory of fiction within the very text of his novel, almost in the manner of Fielding and Gide. That is to say, Lawrence debates how to write a novel, and specifically how to end one, while he writes and ends his novel. Fielding's rather more wide-ranging literary discussion can be separated, more or less, from his narrative proper; whereas the notes and plans made in the course of Gide's novel by Gide's Edouard, for a novel to be entitled "The Counterfeiters," can hardly be pried loose from *The Counterfeiters* without damaging the narrative itself. But Lawrence's discussion is still less separable from the body of the novel than Gide's. What Lawrence's characters think and say about themselves and their fate remains (despite what I intend to do to those passages) the very stuff of narrative, not of exposition. Nevertheless, as an examination of the language in which their observations are phrased will at once reveal, their remarks are certainly, and at the same time, calculated theoretical and formal statements.

Consider the following remark by Ursula. In conversation with her sister Gudrun on the opening page of the book, she decides that marriage is "more likely to be the end of experience" than it is to be an experience of any sort. The significance of that remark, made in the first chapter by Ursula, who in the last chapter of her last novel explicitly rejected Skrebensky to prevent the possibility that "her history would be concluded for ever," is worth attention. It is in its own

way a consideration and a rejection of the conventional marriage
ending. When Ursula marries in this second novel, she will do so in
the middle of the story, and she will do so because marriage with
Birkin—he and she both say so explicitly (see pp. 360 f., 408, 410 f.,
414)—will not constitute an end or an ending in any sense of those
words. (Gudrun does not marry.)

Less than halfway through the novel and before marrying, Ursula
also considers the ending in death. "I am at the end of my line of
life" (217), is the way she begins.

> She had travelled all her life long along the line of fulfilment,
> and it was nearly concluded. She knew all she had to know, she
> had experienced all she had to experience, she was fulfilled in a
> kind of bitter ripeness, there remained only to fall from the tree
> into death. And one must fulfil one's development to the end,
> must carry the adventure to its conclusion. And the next step
> was over the border into death. So it was then! There was a cer-
> tain peace in the knowledge.
>   . . . One can never see beyond the consummation. It is a great
> and conclusive experience. (217)

From the terms in which Ursula couches her reflections, it is clear
that she analyzes and regards her life as if she were a novelist treating the fiction of her experience.[33]

Ursula does not die. She marries Birkin and travels to the Conti-
nent; and so it turns out to be neither death nor marriage but a
trip—traveling—which defines the last section of her history. As she
stands with Birkin on the prow of the ship, "the sense of the unreal-
ised world ahead triumphed over everything" (443).

But we are concerned here not so much with the specific ways in
which Lawrence achieves his open ending as with his discussion
within the novel of the theory of the open conclusion. Observations
like those of Ursula's above (Birkin's lengthy speculations in Chapter XIX, pp. 289-90, on Gerald's probable end, provide another example) occur in a scattered way here and there through the body of the
text.[34] But toward the end they occur (though still covertly) with

such concentration that it is not unreasonable to regard the final section of *Women in Love* as a remarkable essay on finality in fiction. The novel does not simply move toward "The End": it talks about itself as it moves there or thereabouts, all the while ringing a variety of changes on the terms "end" and "conclusion." Indeed, the final section becomes in its own way a deliberate *apologia* for what Virginia Woolf called Lawrence's abandonment of "the usual resting places, eminences, and consummations of the usual novel." Only quotation in detail can reveal the elaborateness and self-consciousness of what is in effect the novel's preoccupation with itself not merely as experience or meaning, but as a form for the achievement of both.

> [Gudrun] wanted to climb the wall of white finality, climb over, into the peaks that sprang up like sharp petals in the heart of the frozen, mysterious navel of the world. She felt that there, . . . among the final cluster of peaks, there, in the infolded navel of it all, was her consummation. (467)

> [Gerald] had the faculty of making order out of confusion. Only let him grip hold of a situation, and he would bring to pass an inevitable conclusion. (475)

> A certain violent sympathy, however, came up in [Gudrun] for this mud-child [Loerke]. There was no going beyond him. (486)

> "And what *is* the end?" [Gerald] asked.
> Birkin shook his head.
> "I've not got there yet, so I don't know. Ask Loerke, he's pretty near." (487)

> [Ursula] felt so doomed up here in the eternal snow, as if there were no beyond. (494)

> "Do you *feel*, Ursula," Gudrun began, rather sceptically, "that you are going-away-for-ever, never-to-return, sort of thing?" (498)

> "There's something final about this. And Gudrun seems like the end, to me," [Gerald said]. (501)

"Over, is it?" [Gerald said to himself.] "I believe it is over. But it isn't finished. Remember, it isn't finished. We must put some sort of a finish on it. There must be a conclusion, there must be finality." (526)

All possibility—that was the charm to [Gudrun], the lovely, ir- ridescent, indefinite charm,—pure illusion. All possibility—be- cause death was inevitable, and *nothing* was possible but death.
She did not want things to materialise, to take any definite shape. (533 f.)

"*Wohin?*"
That was the question—*wohin?* Whither? *Wohin?* What a lovely word! [Gudrun] *never* wanted it answered. Let it chime for ever. (536)

[Gerald] was weak, but he did not want to rest, he wanted to go on and on, to the end. Never again to stay, till he came to the end. . . . (539)

Birkin tapped and entered [after Gerald's death]. His face was white and expressionless. She knew he knew. He gave her his hand, saying:
"The end of *this* trip, at any rate." (542)

As readers of the book will recall, and as all of the passages ex- cerpted above clearly suggest, both Gerald and Gudrun do indeed reach a kind of dead end in the novel: Gudrun ends with Loerke, who is the "rock-bottom" of her continuing corruption and whom there is "no going beyond"; and Gerald ends alone among the ice peaks, become "cold, mute Matter" (546). The two characters who have perverted the living mysteries come appropriately to the inevi- table conclusion. For them, there is "no beyond": they are frozen solid (Gerald) at the very height and buried alive (Gudrun) in the lowest mud (see p. 486) when they have reached the damning extremities of their narrative motion. (Their ends correspond to two of the circles in Dante's *Inferno,* torments which are equally without end.) Their experience is now over, but it has been left unclosed.
And appropriately, Ursula and Birkin, who in the course of the

fiction have gained "faith in the mystery . . . new, deep life-trust" (547), find themselves in a state or, rather, a flight of transcendence in which they can arrive at no possible conclusion. Earlier in the book they do arrive at one of the usual eminences and consummations of fiction. It is rather unusually phrased as a "wonder, the wonder of existing not as oneself, but in a consummation of my being and of her being in a new one, a new paradisal unit regained from the duality" (423). And we duly learn in the next paragraph that "they were married by law on the next day." But, in fact, Birkin has already warned Ursula (and the reader-critic) that he will not rest content with the ending in marriage.

> "It's the problem I can't solve. I *know* I want a perfect and complete relationship with you: and we've nearly got it—we really have. But beyond that. *Do* I want a real, ultimate relationship with Gerald? Do I want a final, almost extra-human relationship with him—or don't I?"
>
> She looked at him for a long time, with strange bright eyes, but she did not answer. (415 f.)

The problem is given as insoluble; and it is phrased as a question which Ursula does not answer.

Given the form for experience toward which, as we have shown, Lawrence has been coherently working, it is therefore appropriate (and not, as has been suggested, a weakness in construction)[35] that the open question should recur in the ending and remain there, crucial and unsolved, after the climax of the book. That ending is even a satisfying one, provided of course that one does not unreasonably insist on deriving one's satisfactions only from the fulfillment of expectations and assumptions already perforated and pulverized everywhere in the novel. The entire book—even the very limited number of quotations from it presented above—has made its form evident. The lack of resolution which Lawrence achieves is imperative: the "saved" must end irresolute, only the damned can afford finality.

The climax in experience for Ursula and Birkin, the passage of widest moral and emotional apprehension, occurs in the watch over Gerald's corpse.

> . . . suddenly his heart contracted, his own candle all but fell from his hand, as, with a strange whimpering cry, the tears broke out. He sat down in a chair, shaken by a sudden access. Ursula who had followed him, recoiled aghast from him, as he sat with sunken head and body convulsively shaken, making a strange, horrible sound of tears.
>
> .   .   .
>
> "He should have loved me," he said. "I offered him."
> She, afraid, white, with mute lips answered:
> "What difference would it have made!"
> "It would!" he said. "It would!" (546)

There is no stabilizing of the flux, not even after Ursula and Birkin return to England.

> "Aren't I enough for you?" she asked.
> "No," he said. (548)

The narrative—and Birkin—have already made sufficiently clear that the marriage ending in eternal union is not enough: "to make it complete, really happy, I wanted eternal union with a man too."

> "You can't have [two kinds of love], because it's false, impossible," she said.
> "I don't believe that," he answered.

The End

Thus the book as a whole remains disquietingly—hence satisfyingly —and quite monumentally open after its crises: "the novel ends on a question." [36]

For us, however, another question remains: have we *really* been looking at a theory of endings in fiction or merely a theory of ends in life? The question can perhaps best be considered in this more general form: can we distinguish at all properly between a theory about life when it is expressed in fiction, and a theory about fiction? Lawrence himself would most probably have rejected the possibility of

the distinction, lock, stock, and barrel. But eschewing shabby compromise, we can, I think, find accord by agreeing that it is right and
proper that a novelist should conceive his theory of life in the shape
of novels, that he should think in novels when he thinks of life.

> . . . A more severe,
>
> More harassing master would extemporize
> Subtler, more urgent proof that the theory
> Of poetry is the theory of life.[37]

In the background of Lawrence's novel we hear Gerald Crich mut-
tering "in a trance" on page five hundred and one, "It's a complete
experience. . . . It's not finished—." And we ponder what it is that
Birkin has in mind when, after considering all the possible ways in
which Gerald might have saved himself from freezing and have
gone on to Italy, he admits:

> He might! And what then? . . . What then? Was it a way
> out? It was only a way in again. (545)

Theory of life or theory of the novel: one takes one's choice. But
the evidence in *Women in Love* makes it safe to say that Lawrence
—his critics to the contrary—regarded a conclusive ending as a corruption of the form of life *and* the form of fiction.

IV

The Stream of the Unconscious

Psyche and physics, self and world. The interlocking of the inner
dimension of character with the outer dimension of events gives rise
to the force and flow of fiction, to the long narrative flux of experience that will be finally narrowed or remain finally expanding. So
far we have traced Lawrence's anti-conclusive structure of events; we
have followed his calculated theory and practice of an unstable
novel. But we have not come to terms with his treatment of the

inner dimension, the self in fiction. That treatment is perhaps his most startling technical innovation, and it is crucial to the open form he creates. It leaves the structure of experience in his work finally uncontained in an extraordinary sense.

> Long ago we watched in frightened anticipation when Freud set out on his adventure into the hinterland of human consciousness. He was seeking for the unknown sources of the mysterious stream of consciousness. Immortal phrase of the immortal James! Oh stream of hell which undermined my adolescence! I felt it streaming through my brain, in at one ear and out at the other. And again I was sure it went round in my cranium, like Homer's Ocean, encircling my established mind. And sometimes I felt it must bubble up in the cerebellum and wind its way through all the convolutions of the true brain. Horrid stream! Whence did it come, and whither was it bound? The stream of consciousness! [38]

Lawrence's contribution to the technique of the novel—a rather widespread critical assessment now holds—is in some sense as original as James Joyce's.[39] But *which* sense is less easy to agree about. The originality of Joyce's technique centers in his treatment of consciousness; the center of Lawrence's originality has seemed harder to find. At one time and another, critics have variously suggested the spontaneity of the novelist's "daimon"; his personal involvement in the novel; his reliance on symbolic scenes; his recourse to a timeless and spaceless narration; his awareness of the crucial significance of full sexual realization.[40] Each of these explanations is on its own grounds valid, and in varying degrees all of them are helpful in seeing more clearly what Lawrence has accomplished. None of them explains, however, the peculiar—and highly characteristic—intensity of Lawrence's rendering of consciousness in a passage like this one:

> It hurt him as he watched as if he were at the stake. He felt he was being burned alive. The strangeness, the power of her in her dancing consumed him, he was burned, he could not grasp, he could not understand. He waited obliterated. (*The Rainbow,* p. 172)

Of course we can always fall back on the explanation that Lawrence focuses on "the felt quality of erotic passion and of religious emotion"; that while Proust, Joyce, and others were investigating consciousness, Lawrence "was exploring almost entirely its emotional properties." [41] But this method of approach does not tell us much about Lawrence's remarkable contribution to fiction beyond assuring us that he outdoes Samuel Richardson in conveying the motions of the heart. From that approach we are then obliged, in conscience, to go on to regard Lawrence's "flux of passion" as not merely a form of exploration but also a form of exaggeration, "a constant extremity of statement which becomes wearing." [42] And having accepted this sort of an explanation—which must surely be the most widely held one—as entirely valid, we still have not explained Lawrence's special power. Yes, a highly emotional style, or an exaggerated diction for exaggerated states of feeling, will serve as an explanation for

> It was black, mad, shameful torture, the frenzy of fear, the frenzy of desire, and the horrible, grasping back-wash of shame. (*R*, 175)

And it may serve to explain

> He felt he wanted to break her into acknowledgment of him, into awareness of him. (*R*, 56)

Perhaps. But it is less adequate as an explanation for "He felt he was being burned alive. The strangeness, the power of her in her dancing consumed him." It is inadequate because Lawrence here goes so far beyond any mere exaggeration of feeling, that "overstatement" is either understatement or else misses the point entirely. To put it in T. S. Eliot's by now old-fashioned terms, Anna's dancing—no matter how pregnant or naked she is, no matter how independent or how insulting her private ritual may seem to her husband Will—Anna's dancing simply will not correlate, objectively or subjectively, with Will's astonishing feeling that he is at the stake, burned alive, consumed, and obliterated.

Not—let me hurry to say it—*not* that I feel Lawrence should have found a better objective correlative for Will's reaction; *not* that I am unpersuaded by Will's response. As a matter of fact, in my view, no clear and present correlation between the objective situation of Anna's dancing and the fabulous "emotions" in Will's psyche ought to be more tightly demonstrated. What I do think is that to regard Will's response to Anna's dancing as somehow "emotional," in any conventional sense of the term, is mistaking Lawrence's point. Lawrence's brilliant contribution to the art of fiction—here as elsewhere —certainly has something to do with that genre's resources for painting the inward self. But his technique is not a matter of felt emotion merely. Considered as such, passages like this one (and they occur by the hundreds) are embarrassing hyperboles. Considered as emotion, such passages only produce sweeping emotional rejections and dismissals by otherwise sympathetic readers and critics.[43] Indeed, the history of the criticism of the English novel suggests that those novelists who lived by emotion perished by emotion. And what is imperishable in Lawrence, in this passage as elsewhere, is not his depiction of a heightened Man of Feeling but his deliberate attempt to get beyond feeling. To those readers and critics who feel, deeply and correctly, that every world of fiction is necessarily a generalization about reality, and who then cannot help complaining that such states of consciousness, if they exist, do not exist generally, we can admit this much: the states Lawrence depicts are not generally perceived; if perceived, they remain unrecognized; and even when recognized, they have no part in consciousness. And to those who would account for Lawrence's special contribution in terms of symbolism, poetry, timelessness, spacelessness, spontaneity, personal involvement, or sex, we must say that no such explanation can serve as an adequate analysis of Lawrence's technique—either its tools or its tensions—in such a passage as the one which follows—uniquely Lawrence, typically Lawrence:

> Sometimes, when his eyes met hers, a yellow flash from them caused a darkness to swoon over her consciousness, electric, and

a slight strange laugh came on his face. Her eyes would turn languidly, then close, as if hypnotized. And they lapsed into the same potent darkness. He had the quality of a young black cat, intent, unnoticeable, and yet his presence gradually made itself felt, stealthily and powerfully took hold of her. He called, not to her, but to something in her, which responded subtly, out of her unconscious darkness.

So they were together in a darkness, passionate, electric, forever haunting the back of the common day, never in the light. In the light, he seemed to sleep, unknowing. Only she knew him when the darkness set him free, and he could see with his gold-glowing eyes his intention and his desires in the dark. Then she was in a spell, then she answered his harsh, penetrating call with a soft leap of her soul, the darkness woke up, electric, bristling with an unknown, overwhelming imagination.

.   .   .

So they remained as separate in the light, and in the thick darkness, married. He supported her daytime authority, kept it inviolable at last. And she, in all the darkness, belonged to him, to his close, insinuating, hypnotic familiarity. (*R*, 202 f.)

It is Lawrence's method for treating "the thick darkness"—his technique—that needs clarification. The bare fact that he does indeed treat the shadows of the psyche is unmistakable, and it has always had a good deal of sympathetic notice and comment. In his introduction to Lawrence's letters, Aldous Huxley observes that "Lawrence could never forget, as most of us almost continuously forget, the dark presence of the otherness that lies beyond the boundaries of man's conscious mind." [44] And in his book on the novelist, F. R. Leavis writes at length of "Lawrence's preoccupation with relating the overt expression of personal life to the impersonal depths"; of "fields of force"; of "forces of the psyche of which the actors' wills have no cognizance, and which, consequently, do not seem to belong to their selves. . . ." [45] But Leavis gives us—and indeed everywhere we are invariably given—only illustrations of Lawrence's power to render "the impersonal depths"; not analyses of the nature and operation of the method. Lawrence, however, like Joyce, has contributed to the tradition of fiction an extraordinary method for rendering the self. Yet where Joyce's method, virtually in continuous operation through his fiction, has by now been amply clarified as a technique, Lawrence's own method, which is discontinuous—which blends and blurs kaleidoscopically with other, more conventional passages in his text—remains appreciated but unclarified.[43] In a way, this is as it should be, for as Huxley observes, "the mystery was always for him a *numen, divine.*" [47] Still, without attempting to close the mystery by clarifying the exact nature of Lawrence's *numen,* it may be possible to clarify the exact technical means by which he sets out to touch it.

We will see at once where the difficulty in explaining Lawrence's technique lies if we begin by trying to make a very simple statement: Lawrence attempts to render his characters' unconscious. The statement needs hasty qualification, if only because what we understand by the rendering of the unconscious in literature has been so thoroughly dominated by the artistry of Joyce. Joyce's inner ear for the varying levels of consciousness and unconsciousness in both *Ulysses* and *Finnegans Wake* assumes that the unconscious activity of the mind can best be heard by the reader as a distortion of conscious verbal activity.[48] The stream of consciousness, itself a distortion of conventional verbal structures, yields to a still greater distortion. And that maximal distortion, we are persuaded, corresponds maximally to the unconscious mental processes of the self (selves) beneath consciousness.

If now, for the moment, we rid our own consciousness of these assumptions, perhaps we can argue that unconscious mental life is not necessarily or even predominantly verbal at all (or to put it differently, that verbal activity is merely one of its principal manifestations to consciousness). If this is once granted or even assumed, then *nevertheless* a novelist will be compelled to render its existence verbally: in words; but not necessarily through their distortion. This is precisely what Lawrence is attempting. He is attempting to render the fluid, nonconscious, or as he would say, "dark" mental processes while at the same time remaining wholly within the region of conventional and conscious syntax.

How can he turn that trick? For will it not be objected that the word "unconscious" in this context is even inapt; if used to describe what Joyce creates, can it suitably be used to describe what Lawrence creates? It can be argued that to set down the living processes of the unconscious in the molds of conventional syntax is not to "render" the unconscious at all, but merely to admit its existence. It is as if a novelist were to tell us, of his character: He was experiencing hatred, but he did not know it. And in fact this is precisely what Lawrence seems to be doing from time to time.

> They fought an unknown battle, unconsciously. (*R*, 157)
>
> Gerald was held unconsciously by the other man. (*WL*, 65)
>
> Hermione writhed in her soul, knowing what she could **not** know. (*WL*, 103)

In passing, one may observe that Lawrence, at least, thinks that the word "unconscious" is appropriate to describe where he is heading: we need not turn to the essays which proliferate from the novels to be sure of that. But what sort of a *technique* of the unconscious is this (to parody Lawrence): They did not know that they were fighting. Gerald did not know that he was held by the other man. Hermione writhed in her soul, not knowing what she knew. This sort of thing, even done well, is surely not a method of making a great darkness visible but a technique of counting on the reader's goodwill.

And there are a number of passages which—quite openly—are less of an attempt to communicate, by any technique at all, the dynamic processes of the unconscious than to work toward an (always mysterious) definition of its content and nature:

> the darkness wheeled round about, with grey shadow-shapes of wild beasts, and also with dark shadow-shapes of the angels,

> whom the light fenced out, as it fenced out the more familiar
> beasts of darkness. (*R,* 413)

> But in reality each one was a dark, blind, eager wave urging
> blindly forward, dark with the same homogeneous desire. And
> all their talk and all their behaviour was sham, they were
> dressed-up creatures. She was reminded of the Invisible Man,
> who was a piece of darkness made visible only by his clothes.
> (*R,* 423)

Occasionally the unconscious that Lawrence names or imagines
bears a strong family resemblance to Freud's:[49]

> She seemed to run in the shadow of some dark, potent secret of
> which she would not, of whose existence even she dared not be-
> come conscious, it cast such a spell over her, and so darkened
> her mind. (*R,* 224)

> . . . it was as if he had had knowledge of her in the long red
> rent of her forearm, so silken and soft. He did not want to touch
> her. He would have to make himself touch her, deliberately.
> The long, shallow red rip seemed torn across his own brain,
> tearing the surface of his ultimate consciousness, letting through
> the forever unconscious, unthinkable red ether of the beyond,
> the obscene beyond. (*WL,* 275 f.)

More often than not, the unconscious that Lawrence treats seems to
have a content and a character all its own ("shadow-shapes of the
angels" do not wheel for Freud's unconscious).[50] But whether we call
it Freudian (or Lawrentian, for that matter), or emotional, or poetic,
or spontaneous, or physical, or sensual—however we name that
depth to which his narrative keeps diving, we have made barely a
start toward explaining either what Lawrence is attempting to
fathom, or his way of fathoming it, in such a characteristic passage
as this one:

> Behind her, there was so much unknown to him. When he
> approached her, he came to such a terrible painful unknown.
> How could he embrace it and fathom it? How could he close
> his arms round all this darkness and hold it to his breast and
> give himself to it? What might not happen to him? If he

> stretched and strained for ever he would never be able to grasp it all, and to yield himself naked of his own hands into the unknown power! How could a man be strong enough to take her, put his arms round her and have her, and be sure he could conquer this awful unknown next his heart? What was it then that she was, to which he must also deliver himself up, and which at the same time he must embrace, contain? (*R*, 50 f.)

To analyze the particular Lawrentian technique at work here—for it is a technique and not merely a sensibility[51]—we can be helped by glancing for comparison at a passage from Lawrence which evokes in another way the interior life of the same character, Tom Brangwen. It is a passage which has the special Lawrentian high flavor; we may even agree that only Lawrence could have written it. Nevertheless, the passage takes a perfectly conventional route toward rendering the inward self; its technique is familiar:

> For he was afraid of his wife. As she sat there with bent head, silent, working or reading, but so unutterably silent that his heart seemed under the millstone of it, she became herself like the upper millstone lying on him, crushing him, as sometimes a heavy sky lies on the earth. (*R*, 57)

The passage conveys Brangwen's emotions both by resort to the most explicit vocabulary of feeling ("afraid," "heart") and by resort to analogy—metaphor, simile—between the world of feeling, or psyche, and the world of objects, or physics. All of this is obvious. Still grinding our observations grossly after Eliot, we might say that the millstone serves as an objective correlative—or rather that the weight and grinding of the millstone *become* correlative, as does the heavy sky lying on the earth, with Brangwen's feelings of fear. Obvious; but (and it is a large *but*) this is not at all what Lawrence does in those passages where he attempts to touch the unconscious. There is, for example, not a single objective correlative in the excerpt from page fifty of *The Rainbow* quoted immediately above. When he does use conventional techniques, Lawrence *is* the novelist who can render emotional states with astonishing force. But from there he moves inexorably to render another state entirely, by a method which bears watching.

Farther down on the very same page we read another paragraph:

> She sank away again. The strange leaves beating in the wind on the wood had come nearer than she. The tension in the room was overpowering, it was difficult for him to move his head. He sat with every nerve, every vein, every fibre of muscle in his body stretched on a tension. He felt like a broken arch thrust sickeningly out from support. For her response was gone, he thrust at nothing. And he remained himself, he saved himself from crashing down into nothingness, from being squandered into fragments, by sheer tension, sheer backward resistance. (*R*, 57)

At first, this passage seems to proceed in a similar manner. Emotional (and even nervous or physical) states are rendered directly, and we are given besides an objective analogy for an inward situation: the broken arch. Indeed we are told explicitly that the object corresponds to a feeling: "he felt like a broken arch." And because his wife's feelings do not meet his, he "feels" as if he thrusts at nothing. But then we discover abruptly that what we have been reading are not precisely feelings at all:

> And he remained himself, he saved himself from crashing down into nothingness, from being squandered into fragments, by sheer tension, sheer backward resistance.

Whatever area of human existence that sentence refers to, it is not the area of mere feelings, it is broader than that. The paragraph begins with rapid brushstrokes which sketch in a character's interior emotional situation, and then quickly works its way around to something essentially and confusingly different in kind. Brangwen is now struggling against "being squandered into fragments," against "crashing down into nothingness." Clearly, although the passage does begin in quite the normal way, with references or objects which correlate with—or are correlatives for—emotions, it ends dizzyingly with emotions which are correlatives for something else entirely, and the effect is deliberately vertiginous.

Let us consider again another passage typical of Lawrence.

> They had passed through the doorway into the further space, where movement was so big, that it contained bonds and constraints and labours, and still was complete liberty. She was the doorway to him, he to her. At last they had thrown open the doors, each to the other, and had stood in the doorways facing each other, whilst the light flooded out from behind on to each of their faces, it was the transfiguration, the glorification, the admission. (*R, 87*)

Any analysis which regards these doors and doorways and the passage beyond as merely referring in some obscure way to states of feeling is reductive and misleading. We are not simply reading exceptionally vivid metaphors for the more effective portraiture of either consciousness *or* feelings. Only in the most superficial, easily granted, and breath-wasting sense (in the same sense as the letters d-o-o-r are signals for the concept of a portal) are these doors choice "objective correlatives" for fancy states of feeling. The characters' feelings about doors and doorways, their consciousness of passage and movement, are *themselves* meant as metaphors; the *feelings* are the analogies, or the signals, referring to something else.

To what? We can see Lawrence's goal—and his achievement— very precisely indeed by setting side by side two passages of, I think, equal excellence, one by Lawrence and the other by Hardy. The first, about Anna Lensky and Will Brangwen, is from *The Rainbow*.

> Into the rhythm of his work there came a pulse and a steadied purpose. He stooped, he lifted the weight, he heaved it towards her, setting it as in her, under the moonlit space. And he went back for more. Ever with increasing closeness he lifted the sheaves and swung striding to the centre with them, ever he drove her more nearly to the meeting, ever he did his share, and drew towards her, overtaking her. There was only the moving to and fro in the moonlight, engrossed, the swinging in the silence, that was marked only by the splash of sheaves, and silence, and

> the splash of sheaves. And ever the splash of his sheaves broke
> swifter, beating up to hers, and ever the splash of her sheaves re-
> curred monotonously, unchanging, and ever the splash of his
> sheaves beat nearer.
>
>   Till at last, they met at the shock, facing each other, sheaves
> in hand. (*R*, 113)

Within and beneath the apparent focus here, which is not at all on
the feelings but on the *actions* of characters, this description of the
activity of harvesting as a kind of rhythmic love-making is deliberately organized to convey the occurrence of an event trembling into
existence *neither* in action *nor* in feelings, but somewhere in the
"dark" unconscious.

The passage that follows is from *Tess of the d'Urbervilles*.

> Her binding proceeds with clock-like monotony. From the
> sheaf last finished she draws a handful of ears, patting their
> tips with her left palm to bring them even. Then, stooping low,
> she moves forward, gathering the corn with both hands against
> her knees, and pushing her left gloved hand under the bundle to
> meet the right on the other side, holding the corn in an embrace
> like that of a lover. She brings the ends of the bond together,
> and kneels on the sheaf while she ties it, beating back her skirts
> now and then when lifted by the breeze. A bit of her naked arm
> is visible between the buff leather of the gauntlet and the sleeve
> of her gown; and as the day wears on its feminine smoothness
> becomes scarified by the stubble, and bleeds. (Ch. XIV)

Hardy's symbolic technique, whose continuity in his work has not
been widely enough recognized,[52] is here manifestly in full operation.
Through outward description, Hardy is attempting to evoke or suggest a wide range of the interior matter of fiction: the demonic love
relation of Tess and Alec; the specific event of Tess's seduction by
Alec (indeed it is not too much to say that the passage is a *narrative*
of the moment of her seduction, which occurs a little earlier in the
text but is not, of course, described at all); Tess's personal qualities of
tenderness, innocence, and helplessness; her present manner, mood,
even physical misery: it is all there in the subtlest detail. The passage

will not easily be exhausted. But whatever excellence it may have, it is not different in kind from those of other novelists who work beneath the significance of events or activities for symbolic or emotional truths. But what such writing does not normally attempt directly—and what Lawrence normally sets out to do directly—is to *use* the activities described and the emotional situations evoked as correlatives for arriving at another region of existence.

With this method in mind, we can see what Lawrence is about in those passages which seem at first very improbable expressions of the interior life. In the first place we have to recognize that they are not hyperboles of emotion ("And he lay whipped, his soul whipped almost to death, yet unchanged"—R, 176); and in the second, that they are in no simple sense a direct rendering of actual emotional states. To assume either of these two things is what makes such passages seem bizarre, absurd, even embarrassing. But to see them as an attempt to find phrases and analogies in the conscious life for the nonverbal and nonapprehensible and imprisoned unconscious, renders their meaning far more comprehensible. In short, what we are reading are subjective correlatives:

> Her whole mind was a chaos, darkness breaking in upon it, and herself struggling to gain control with her will, as a swimmer struggles with the swirling water. But in spite of her efforts she was borne down, darkness seemed to break over her, she felt as if her heart was bursting. The terrible tension grew stronger and stronger, it was most fearful agony, like being walled up.
>
> And then she realised that his presence was the wall, his presence was destroying her. Unless she could break out, she must die most fearfully, walled up in horror. And he was the wall. She must break down the wall—she must break him down before her, the awful obstruction of him who obstructed her life to the last. It must be done, or she must perish most horribly.
>
> Terribly, shocks ran over her body, like shocks of electricity, as if many volts of electricity suddenly struck her down. She was aware of him sitting silently there, an unthinkable evil obstruction. Only this blotted out her mind, pressed out her very breathing, his silent, stooping back, the back of his head. (*WL*, 118)

Now by definition the unconscious content (nonverbal, as distinguished above, and non-"Freudian") which the subjective correlatives in the passage above are intended to convey is not available to
exegesis except by way of still other correlatives—other analogies,
other metaphors, other phrases and categories. As positive, "actual"
content it can only be touched; it is not graspable.[53] In Lawrence's
phrase, a bit altered here: That which it was, positively, was dark
and unrevealed, it could not come forth. (See R, 413.) Lawrence is
obliged to go about by indirections to find directions out. And that
which he is getting at remains necessarily unavailable—by definition
—to the verbal consciousness.

> They went towards the stackyard. There he saw, with some-
> thing like terror, the great new stacks of corn glistening and
> gleaming transfigured, silvery and present under the night-blue
> sky, throwing dark, substantial shadows, but themselves majes-
> tic and dimly present. She, like glimmering gossamer, seemed
> to burn among them, as they rose like cold fires to the silvery-
> bluish air. All was intangible, a burning of cold, glimmering,
> whitish-steely fires. He was afraid of the great moon-conflagration
> of the cornstacks rising above him. His heart grew smaller, and
> it began to fuse like a bead. He knew he would die. (R, 302)

The question—What does it all mean?—may be inescapable.[54] But it
cannot and, I would suggest, should not be answered. And in that
case the irony for critics of Lawrence's efforts (an irony which I
imagine he must have relished) is that if passages like these have
any validity, they evoke an "unconscious" correlative response, and
one which we cannot hope—by definition—to "explicate" any better
than Lawrence has already done, because it remains, and should remain, unconscious in ourselves.

Nevertheless, though Lawrence constantly recurs to such passages,
to central rhythms or events in the unconscious life of his characters,
what makes his novels readable as novels and not as dreams or
nightmares is that he is at the same time very busy with all the
normal material of storytelling: perceptible character, crystal-clear

places, public and personal events, palpable objects, and feelings *per se*. Yet he circles back inexorably, and passages like those we have cited act as cores or nodes on which the entire meaning of very extended passages is ultimately apt to condense. The reader is likely to slip almost imperceptibly from some other region of narrative—description, meditation, or desire—into one of these nodal passages: which then takes him unawares, comes upon him half-disguised as conventional, though heightened, awareness.

> His wife and he! With a pang of anguish he realized what uncertainties they both were. He was a man of forty-five. Forty-five! In five more years fifty. Then sixty—then seventy—then it was finished. My God—and one still was so unestablished!
>
> How did one grow old—how could one become confident? He wished he felt older. Why, what difference was there, as far as he felt matured or completed, between him now and him at his own wedding? He might be getting married over again— he and his wife. He felt himself tiny, a little, upright figure on a plain circled round with the immense, roaring sky: he and his wife, two little, upright figures walking across this plain, whilst the heavens shimmered and roared about them. When did one come to an end? In which direction was it finished? There was no end, no finish, only this roaring vast space. Did one never get old, never die? That was the clue. He exulted strangely, with torture. He would go on with his wife, he and she like two children camping in the plains. What was sure but the endless sky? But that was so sure, so boundless.
>
> Still the royal blue colour burned and blazed and sported itself in the web of darkness before him, unwearyingly rich and splendid. How rich and splendid his own life was, red and burning and blazing and sporting itself in the dark meshes of his body: and his wife, how she glowed and burned dark within her meshes! Always it was so unfinished and unformed! (*R*, 124 f.)

The writing slips in the easiest and most sinuous fashion from exterior fact to the interior and impalpable unconscious. We move from the bustle of a wedding scene and from other characters who are *outside* Brangwen (for brevity's sake, I have not quoted much of the earlier material: "Anna bent her head and smiled in her veil.

How absurd he was! Brangwen was staring away at the . . .") to a position *inside* Brangwen's head. And once inside, we move from the convention in which phrases stand for thoughts and feelings, to a new convention in which subjective states of awareness stand for something still further "inside." The whole then moves, as so often and inexorably it does in *The Rainbow,* to a dazzling focus on prismatic colors trembling against a dark background (to which the book as a whole moves in its last two paragraphs). And then we are led back to the wedding. "There was a loud noise of the organ." The deception in this sliding effect is that we are likely to fail to distinguish, once we are inside Brangwen's head, between subjective statements and subjective correlatives. And the distinction is imperative if we are not to distort Lawrence's intentions: that is, if we are not to mistake Lawrence's crucial passages as forms of distorted feeling. "How did one grow old—how could one become confident?"—here we are on the sure grounds of awareness. But there is a good deal in the passage that has simply nothing to do with the conventional region of thought or feeling, nothing whatever: "He exulted strangely, with torture. . . . What was sure but the endless sky? . . . and his wife, how she glowed and burned dark within her meshes!" When we are on these uneasy grounds, we are moving, or being pushed, into "the web of darkness."

When all of these modes for treating the inward self of character are working together, they produce an astonishing flow of prose which bears the same relation to the normal novelistic expression of interior life as James Joyce's distortion of syntax to render consciousness bears to the conventional syntax of awareness. If Joyce's technique is the stream of consciousness, Lawrence's technique is, and ought to be clearly recognized as, a stream of the unconscious. The trouble, the obstacle, is that Joyce has so pre-empted by a single technique the entire field of the literary unconscious that other approaches to it are not recognizable for what they are. Indeed, they seem to be going astray. But let us be clear about the boundary lines when we recognize Joyce's annexation of the unconscious: his technique for conveying unconscious material—and an excellent technique it is for the purpose—involves the pulverization of the verbal consciousness. The deep unconscious infiltrates the stream of distorted verbal consciousness. Lawrence's technique for conveying unconscious material (and as the technique varies, so does the kind of unconscious material conveyed) involves another distortion: the distortion of emotional consciousness. The deep unconscious intrudes through a tissue of correlative feelings and perceptions. And the flow of correlatives is quite literally an energetic, ceaseless, and serpentine stream of the unconscious.

> As he drew nearer to her, he plunged deeper into her enveloping soft warmth, a wonderful creative heat that penetrated his veins and gave him life again. He felt himself dissolving and sinking to rest in the bath of her living strength. It seemed as if her heart in her breast were a second unconquerable sun, into the glow and creative strength of which he plunged further and further. All his veins, that were murdered and lacerated, healed softly as life came pulsing in, stealing invisibly in to him as if it were the all-powerful effluence of the sun. His blood, which seemed to have been drawn back into death, came ebbing on the return, surely, beautifully, powerfully.
>
> He felt his limbs growing fuller and flexible with life, his body gained an unknown strength. He was a man again, strong and rounded. And he was a child, so soothed and restored and full of gratitude.
>
> And she, she was the great bath of life, he worshipped her. Mother and substance of all life she was. And he, child and man, received of her and was made whole. His pure body was almost killed. But the miraculous, soft effluence of her breast suffused over him, over his seared, damaged brain, like a healing lymph, like a soft, soothing flow of life itself, perfect as if he were bathed in the womb again.
>
> His brain was hurt, seared, the tissue was as if destroyed. He had not known how hurt he was, how his tissue, the very tissue of his brain was damaged by the corrosive flood of death. Now, as the healing lymph of her effluence flowed through him, he knew how destroyed he was, like a plant whose tissue is burst from inwards by a frost.

. . .

> She was exhausted, wearied. Yet she must continue in this
> state of violent active super consciousness. She was conscious of
> everything—her childhood, her girlhood, all the forgotten inci-
> dents, all the unrealised influences and all the happenings she
> had not understood, pertaining to herself, to her family, to her
> friends, her lovers, her acquaintances, everybody. It was as if she
> drew a glittering rope of knowledge out of the sea of darkness,
> drew and drew and drew it out of the fathomless depths of the
> past, and still it did not come to an end, there was no end to it.
> She must haul and haul at the rope of glittering consciousness,
> pull it out phosphorescent from the endless depths of the uncon-
> sciousness, till she was weary, aching, exhausted, and fit to break,
> and yet she had not done. (*WL,* 394 ff.)

Now the extensive quotation from Lawrence will at least have
served to make sharp and obvious the fact that we are not dealing
merely with a method. Though it is method, yet there is madness in
it, a kind of holy rage for value. When Lawrence tries to commit to
paper the subterranean voice, he is engaged in an active moral struggle. "This struggle for verbal consciousness should not be left out in
art. It is a very great part of life. It is not superimposition of a theory.
It is the passionate struggle into conscious being." (Lawrence's Foreword to *Women in Love,* p. x.) But we need not necessarily concern
ourselves here with what Lawrence says about his technique. Inevitably, that technique *itself* makes ceaseless and fluent assumptions
about value. An analogy here may help to clarify the nature of those
assumptions. The unique syntactical refinement of the sensibility of
his characters in Henry James's fiction is not merely a mode of rendering consciousness in prose. The play of moral intelligence over
the surface of events—polishing perceptions, perceiving values, eval-
uating feelings, and feeling polished—takes on the character of the
highest form of conscience. The tissue of fine, grammatical, moral
perception, forever strenuous, forever in tune, becomes both a technique in fiction and a *desideratum,* a way for existence. Similarly,
Lawrence's opening and exploration of the channels, and even more

importantly his deliberate preservation of open tensions between consciousness and the unconscious, becomes in his work both a driven mode for fiction and an ultimately desirable mode for existence. Perhaps I may suggest—playfully, but not on that account without seriousness—that we can usefully understand the art and the achievement of the three greatest masters of modern English fiction by recognizing that James writes a stream of conscience, Joyce a stream of consciousness, and Lawrence a stream of the unconscious.

From here it is barely a step to show how the flow of the unconscious in Lawrence's fiction works with—indeed, is crucial to—the structure of events in the finally unstable form he creates. We have here examined the unconscious events of the inward self and, earlier, the process of interaction between the self and the outer world. The stream of experience so produced leads the reader forward through a structure in which the parts fit together like the parts of a Chinese box. First, at the simplest level, there is the movement which carries the narrative from the low-lying Marsh enclosed by the canal embankment to the rainbow, and beyond to the peaks of the Alps, and again beyond. There is secondly the inexorable narrative of the events of generations and couples which all along and insistently rejects marriage, death, or any other final event which may lead to a closed ending (the damned reach inconclusive conclusions, the saved move continually "beyond"). And these unstable forms are both related to a third, to the transcendence of the stable ego or the closed self, a transcending of the technique of finished internal portraiture that dominates nineteenth-century fiction. "You mustn't look in my novel for the old stable *ego* of the character." By finding subjective correlatives within perception for the unknown regions beyond, Lawrence has produced a trapdoor which in his fiction is likely to open at any moment into the unconscious. Whatever that "dark" region may be for which he adduces his correlatives, it is fathomless—it is not to be explained—and this is of the utmost importance to him, since an explanation would, of course, close the door. So the sweep of Lawrence's narrative does not simply move limitlessly forward to and through his endings; it also expands limitlessly in depth at points all along.

> Waves of delirious darkness ran through her soul. She wanted to let go. She wanted to reach and be amongst the flashing stars, she wanted to race with her feet and be beyond the confines of this earth. She was made to be gone. It was as if a hound were straining on the leash, ready to hurl itself after a nameless quarry into the dark. And she was the quarry, and she was also the hound. The darkness was passionate and breathing with immense, unperceived heaving. It was waiting to receive her in her flight. And how could she start—and how could she let go? She must leap from the known into the unknown. Her feet and hands beat like a madness, her breast strained as if in bonds. (*R,* 298 f.)

Only becoming, process, promise, transcendence, has value in Lawrence's stream of life; in conclusion, may I add, lies corruption.

7

The Myth of Openness: "No End, No Finish, Only This Roaring Vast Space"

What happened to the novel after Lawrence I have already discussed briefly in Chapter Two, where the two opposed forms, open and closed, were set in contrast. I suggested there that in the work of James Joyce, Virginia Woolf, Aldous Huxley, F. Scott Fitzgerald, and Ernest Hemingway the novel turned to a new structure, to a flux of conscience that finished in the experience of incompletion. Further discussion of these writers in greater detail is outside the province of this work; my attempt has been to make visible the efforts of novelists at about the turn of the century to alter the shape of fictional experience which they had inherited. But I believe it is fair to say, and I should like to suggest briefly here, that the novelists I have discussed created a new pattern not just for their own time, but for ours.

Whether culture produced the new pattern of the novel, or whether the new pattern of the novel produced a new culture, is a question to which I should certainly answer: culture came first. Nevertheless, we are dealing with a circular process. The new pattern, wherever it came from, once it had been successfully created and fixed in our novels, acquired a peculiar energy in our culture. If the new novel is open, it is open, one can agree, *not* because Lawrence or Hardy left it that way. It is open presumably because the new novelist conceives that experience in life itself is open. But among other forces and influences, the shape of life imagined in our novels has so often been reflected back on our actual lives that our novels have helped us see—or imagine we see—ourselves. And one must conclude that, in the circular process, the new pattern has developed the power of a myth: an underlying and organizing vision of experience.

To put the energy behind that pattern in general terms, the modern novelist exposes innocence to an essentially unlimited experience. And when he does that most uncompromisingly, he gives us our special sense that in *his* vision of life something is intangibly but forcefully modern. Whereas older novelists, under conditions of difficulty deliberately provided by their stories, once worked to achieve endings which closed their novels, the new novelist works hard to achieve the reverse effect: to keep the fictional experience unclosed. But the new turn toward openness invariably leads him along the two horns of a dilemma. How can he suggest at the end of his novel that these are the final pages of this particular rendering of experience—for practical necessity dictates that he must end—while at the same time he suggests that there is never a close to experience—as mythic necessity dictates, for there is no end, really, is there? In short, how can he end without closing?

Solutions are as various and intricate as novels. (The choice of a few novels and novelists here is necessarily arbitrary but will, I hope, be suggestive of the influence of the newer pattern.) Lawrence Durrell prefaces this cautionary note to the last volume of his four-volume *Alexandria Quartet:*

> Among the workpoints at the end of this volume I have sketched a number of possible ways of continuing to deploy these characters and situations in further instalments—but this is only to suggest that even if the series were extended indefinitely the result . . . would remain strictly part of the present word-continuum. . . . But to all intents and purposes the present set of four volumes may be judged as a completed whole.

(The echo of André Gide is significant: " 'Might be continued'—
these are the words with which I should like to conclude my *Counterfeiters.*")[1]

The gymnastic poise with which the gangplank can be walked is
astonishing. Instead of "The End," "Terminal" is the last word of
John Barth's *End of the Road,* but the terminal word is also a railroad terminal, which is also the place (another railroad terminal) in
which the chronological action of the novel started. The last three
pages insist explicitly on the incompleteness which the entire novel
has rendered:

> Lord, the raggedness of it; the incompleteness! . . . I was fran-
> tic. Half a dozen letters I started—to Joe, to the police, to Peggy,
> to Joe again—and none could I finish. . . . The terrific incom-
> pleteness made me volatile; my muscles screamed to act; but my
> limbs were bound like Laocoön's. . . .

On the last page of Flannery O'Connor's *The Violent Bear It Away*
the terrifying central experience is still in violent motion:

> By midnight he had left the road and the burning woods behind
> him and had come out on the highway once more. . . . His
> singed eyes, black in their deep sockets, seemed already to en-
> vision the fate that awaited him but he moved steadily on, his
> face set toward the dark city, where the children of God lay
> sleeping.

Yossarian, in Joseph Heller's *Catch-22,* ends his experience in this
way:

> "How do you feel, Yossarian?"
> "Fine. No, I'm very frightened."
> "That's good," said Major Danby. "It proves you're still alive.
> It won't be fun."
> Yossarian started out. "Yes it will."
>
>   •   •   •
>
> "Jump!" Major Danby cried.
> Yossarian jumped. Nately's whore was hiding just outside the

door. The knife came down, missing him by inches, and he took off.

And one can only marvel at the resolute skill with which Saul Bellow manages to bring the flux of experience in his novels to a balanced irresolution: the memorable funeral at the end of *Seize the Day* comes to mind, that hallucinatory death-in-life; or one thinks of Moses E. Herzog, poised at the end between two (or three) worlds, the latest still powerless to be born.

The impulse toward an open flux of conscience in the unfolding and finishing of a story cannot be considered an aberration peculiar to the temperament of particular novelists or to the meaning of a particular novel. It is a literary current which made itself felt in sporadic eddies before Hardy and has continued with force after Lawrence. The design of life in that open form is presented as an endlessly expanding process, a design in which protagonists are forced by the organization of events to attempt to resolve experiences which cannot finally be resolved. But the protagonist's disturbance becomes the reader's. The internal force that rises through the twentieth-century novel leads the *reader* to a powerful ebb tide of the narrative, which carries the central experience—his own—not back to a resting place (there is no resting place for conscience), but inexorably farther out. The current, the movement, is strenuous, even frightening. Readers who are carried, some willingly, some very unwillingly, along that sort of a bend in the stream of conscience, have themselves been subjected to the bending of a myth. As they turn the last page, "The End" turns out to be only another opening.

Naturally, there has been congratulation:

> the end of experience, in the modern world, is only the beginning of selfhood. . . . Such a [Lawrentian] view of experience has influenced a writer like Hemingway. . . . Certainly the ending of *The Old Man and the Sea* owes something in spirit to that of [Lawrence's] *The Rainbow*.[2]

This is the view of Edward Engelberg in a study which, concentrating attention on Lawrence, asserts the existence of a new, more modern *Bildungsroman*. But if literature, as Engelberg asserts, is prepared to arrive at the beginning of selfhood as an end in itself, it must also be prepared to meet with a more guarded species of congratulation, a mixture of skepticism, appreciation, and caution:

> for reasons which, at least here, must defy speculation, the ideal of pleasure has exhausted itself, almost as if it had been actually realized and had issued in satiety and *ennui*. In its place, or, at least, beside it, there is developing—conceivably at the behest of literature!—an ideal of the experience of those psychic energies which are linked with unpleasure and which are directed toward self-definition and self-affirmation.

> But before we conclude . . . that the tendencies in our literature which we have remarked on are nothing but perverse and morbid, let us recall that although Freud did indeed say that "the aim of all life is death," the course of his argument leads him to the statement that "the organism wishes to die only in its own fashion," only through the complex fullness of its appropriate life.[3]

These are the views of Lionel Trilling in a study that traces the complex "fate of pleasure" in literature and even contemplates the possibility of a "mutation" in culture.

And naturally there have been outright complaints:

> Not only do the "endings" fail to resolve most of the tensions generated by the novels but they often provide new ones.[4]

This is the complaint of Walter Slatoff in a strikingly documented study of William Faulkner. Slatoff's conclusions are instructive. He writes that Faulkner's "books are all governed at bottom . . . by the desire to create and maintain highly complex and largely irresolvable suspensions"; that "every technique of [Faulkner's] is a movement away from coherence and resolution"; that "the endings of all his novels . . . seem carefully designed to prevent such resolution." [5] If all this is true, and I have no doubt that it is, then surely Faulkner is the inheritor—and a still more uncompromising exponent than is Lawrence—of the tradition of fictional form I have been tracing. If that form, which in Faulkner leads by design from internally expanding disorder and irresolution to *still* finally expanding disorder and irresolution, is part of a developing tradition, it is a development that surely contributes to temperament. I think then that one is obliged to question sharply Slatoff's temperamental conclusion:

> Finally, however, I do not think we can adequately explain the kinds of tensions and suspensions we find in Faulkner's work except in terms of [his] temperament. (p. 253)

And I think one has to attribute the critic's final "irritation"

> that Faulkner's fictional world is in many respects even more ambiguous and complex than the real one (p. 264)

to a critical sense of "the real world" which has another strong literary basis in another tradition, in another ordering of the materials of experience, in another mythic assumption.

From the viewpoint of that other myth—the myth that somehow in life and in literature it must be possible to bring to a reasonable "close" the pressures and flux of conscience—work conceived in Faulkner's vision must inevitably, I suppose, seem both temperamental and irritating. From that viewpoint or that assumption, the opposed tradition of an increasing final "disorder" from Hardy to Lawrence to Faulkner and beyond (one might suggest, according to taste, Vladimir Nabokov, Samuel Beckett, or William Burroughs), will in its most extreme cases also seem anti-rational and anti-moral. For what is one who shares that assumption to make of a work which, with integrity, most completely "fails" to resolve moral ambiguities; which, with that new integration of structure and ending, leaves them most completely in a state of irresolvable suspension? But if the view of the matter I have all along advanced is valid, then the deliberate avoidance, in the depiction of an experience, of any resolution of an experience anywhere is not only a narrative sequence; it is an ethical statement in its own right. The flux of conscience remains unclosed: experience *is* not closed. If in certain extreme cases—Lawrence, Joyce, Faulkner, and beyond—the expanding process of conscience remains not merely unclosed but unclosable, that information is a more extreme mythic statement: experience *cannot* be closed.

When, therefore, Wayne Booth in his brilliantly elaborated study of ethical unreliability in modern fiction complains that

> the novelist cannot be excused from providing the judgment upon his own materials which alone can lift them from being what Faulkner has called the mere "record of man" and turn them into the "pillars" that can help him be fully man,[6]

one wonders. One wonders whether in fact Booth is—as he supposes—raising fundamental issues about judgment, clarity, and responsibility in the novel, or whether he is not looking for the old judgment, clarity, and responsibility in the newer form, worriedly searching in the newer pattern of the novel for the specific ethical process embodied in the older pattern. The antinomies of ambiguous and even rationally contradictory ethics in modern fiction are themselves, strictly speaking, a "judgment"—a judgment that implicitly asserts that it alone can help man be fully man. No doubt such fictions create and embody ethical positions which Booth's ethics cause him to see as unacceptable moral confusions, ethical irresponsibilities so extraordinarily contradictory as to be ultimately anti-aesthetic. Commenting on the final section of Joyce's *A Portrait of the Artist as a Young Man,* Booth wonders effectively

> Well, which *Portrait* do we choose, that of the artistic soul battling through successfully to his necessary freedom, or that of the child of God, choosing, like Lucifer, his own damnation? No two books could be further from each other than the two we envision here. There may be sufficient core of what is simply interesting to salvage the book as a great work of the sensibility, but unless we are willing to retreat into babbling and incommunicable relativism, we cannot believe that it is *both* a portrait of the prisoner freed *and* a portrait of the soul placing itself in chains. (pp. 327 f)

One cannot avoid noticing here the rhetoric of criticism—"babbling and incommunicable relativism"—or again, on Vladimir Nabokov's *Lolita:*

> In short, we have looked for so long at foggy landscapes reflected in misty mirrors, that we have come to *like* fog. (p. 372)

But it is evident that in fiction the clarity of ethical solutions cannot long be separated from the failing certainty of narrative resolutions. The open experience which is unsolved leads to the form which is anti-soluble: that deliberate twirling of the ethical compass which Booth regards with discomfort as "incommunicable relativism" or "fog." For there is a stage in the development of the novel at which last-page ethical nonsolution, which is one possible pattern for an open fiction, leads to page-by-page ethical dissolution or insolubleness (even anti-solubleness) at all points. And though I think my point is open to debate, I take it that a fictional structure (see Booth's discussion of *Lolita,* pp. 371 f and 390 f) which both internally *and* in conclusion defies moral clarity through its subtleties of indirection and through its irreconcilable moral contradictions, is neither irresponsible nor unclear. Neither unaesthetic nor anaesthetic. It is *anti*-aesthetic—and it is *anti*-ethical—but only in this sense, that it goes about to subvert the aesthetic and ethical form of human narrative and human life which it opposes. As I see it, the development of that subversion leads in a direct line from an emphasis on the unacceptable indignity of a closed stream of conscience (in late Hardy and Conrad) to an emphasis on the crucial dignity of an open stream of conscience (in late Forster and early Lawrence) and ultimately to the elimination from discussion (from Joyce to Faulkner) of the possibility of resolving the central ethical experience when the novel "closes." That tradition of openness, from its more moderate to its more extreme impulse, is an ethical vision of the process of experience in life; and it is what defines the distinctively modern vision in the modern novel.

That tradition makes an unmistakable ethical statement. It tells us, the tradition as a whole tells us and every step of the way tells us, that whether our heroes or anti-heroes perish or flourish (for it simply doesn't matter in *this* respect), they must continually attempt to transcend—to order finally, finally make sense of, finally limit, and hence transcend—their disturbing, expanding experiences which *in fact* cannot be transcended, can never be transcended.

That change reflects a profound movement in our way of seeing ourselves in the world and through time. The new way is inconsistent. It is on its face an impossible vision, though it can be understood as a possible (and desperate) attitude. Still, as an ethical statement, it is so utterly paradoxical as to be irrational—as irrational as a good myth ought to be—and certainly no more irrational (I submit) than its opposite: that anyone's disturbing, expanding experience can ever be ordered finally, finally made sense of, finally limited, and hence transcended. Still, some people do prefer that latter myth, the old myth, find it comfortable and even rational. And though it too is on its face an impossible vision, one can understand it as a possible (and desperate) attitude.

The new myth of continual openness in the flux of experience has provided us with a new tradition. Early novels written in the open pattern do not now seem to us to be inconsistent as we look back from our present vantage point; to audiences contemporary with those novels, the form seemed inconsistent with "reality." But about our own contemporary novelists we are less certain. I would suggest that when writers of all moods and methods feel compelled—and it seems virtually a compulsion—to structure their imagination of the progress of the innocent self through the world of experience into a form which, by now, seems to have become a coherent pattern of growing inconsistencies, we can at least credit the consistency of their inconsistency. We can credit it as a new myth, already substantially created. Our novel "enlarges the views" (Hardy), it never "narrows the views." Although it comes to "the end, such as it is" (Conrad), it is "not final." It prefers "expansion" (Forster), it is wary of completion. There is "no end, no finish, only this roaring vast space" (Lawrence); if "it is finished," then "it has been a failure." In the mythic journey it traces from innocence to experience, the modern novel offers to take the self of the reader along, and to structure and inform that self by its truer ending, either an ever-widening disorder or a finally open "order" which embraces all the opposed directions on whatever ethical compass it has brought along for the trip. Like the modern cosmos, the modern novel is ever expanding, and it is racing away fastest at its outermost reaches.

Notes

Chapter 1

1. Daisy Ashford, *The Young Visiters* (London, 1919). The various passages given here are quoted from the first fifty pages of the London. 1060, edition.

2. John Cleland, *Memoirs of a Woman of Pleasure* (New York, 1963), p. 30. Subsequent page references are also to the 1963 edition.

3. Mark Schorer, "Foreword: Self and Society," *Society and Self in the Novel, English Institute Essays, 1955,* ed. Mark Schorer (New York, 1956), p. ix.

4. Nevertheless, with the analysis given here one should compare Ronald S. Crane's analysis of the "working or power" of the novel, in an essay which considerably extends the concept of plot by viewing it as a "dynamic whole which affects our emotions in a certain way through the functioning together of its elements in subordination to a determinate poetic form."— "The Concept of Plot and the Plot of *Tom Jones,*" in *Critics and Criticism,* ed. by Ronald S. Crane, abridged ed. (Chicago, 1957), p. 91.

5. Compare the following definitions: "The unit of fiction is the event. . . . We may define a fictional event as the representation in language of any psychic or psychological phenomenon which is observed as a process rather than as an entity"—Marvin Mudrick, "Character and Event in Fiction," *Yale Review,* L (Winter 1961), pp. 210 and 207. (The two passages have been excerpted in reversed order.) "The surface of a novel is made up of items concretely represented and temporally arranged (the temporal arrangement includes plot and other kinds of pattern), enabling us to perceive the immediately felt qualities of a human 'world,' experiences in the imagination, not through any one sense"—Joseph E. Baker, "Aesthetic Surface in the Novel," *The Trollopian,* II (September 1947), p. 98. "Most

novels develop their meaning through a communication to the reader of
the imagined adventures (psychological and physical, occasionally only one
or the other of these two kinds) of imaginary characters"—David Daiches,
"Problems for Modern Novelists," in *Accent Anthology* (New York),
p. 549.

6. Compare Lionel Trilling's emphasis: "For our time the most effective
agent of the moral imagination has been the novel of the last two hundred
years. It was never, either aesthetically or morally, a perfect form and its
faults and failures can be quickly enumerated. But its greatness and its
practical usefulness lay in its unremitting work of involving the reader
himself in the moral life, inviting him to put his own motives under
examination, suggesting that reality is not as his conventional education
has led him to see it. It taught us, as no other genre ever did, the extent
of human variety and the value of this variety. It was the literary form
to which the emotions of understanding and forgiveness were indigenous,
as if by definition of the form itself."—"Manners, Morals, and the Novel,"
The Liberal Imagination (London, 1951), p. 222.

Chapter 2

1. By myth I mean a "solemn narrative being played out conformably to an
immemorial pattern." A more extended definition follows: "Myths are the
instruments by which we continually struggle to make our experience in-
telligible to ourselves. A myth is a large, controlling image that gives
philosophical meaning to the facts of ordinary life; that is, which has
organizing value for experience." The first of the two quotations above
is by Thomas Mann, from "Freud and the Future," in *Essays of Three
Decades* (New York, 1937). The second is by Mark Schorer, from *William
Blake: The Politics of Vision* (New York, 1946). Both definitions can be
found, quoted in a far more extended form, in *Myth and Mythmaking,*
ed. by Henry A. Murray (New York, 1960), pp. 371-5 and pp. 354-8.

2. To avoid confusion, it seems advisable to remind the reader here that since
I use "closed" and "open" to refer directly to fictional experience itself as
a form, rather than to its "meanings," I use the terms in a sense different
from (and more limited than) the sense adopted by Robert M. Adams in
Strains of Discord: Studies in Literary Openness (Ithaca, N. Y., 1958).
Later in this chapter, the difference is discussed at greater length.

3. Perhaps a few words might be devoted here, beyond what has already
been said in the Introduction, to the relation between the terms flux
or stream of conscience and stream of consciousness. Both "streams" are

metaphors and both refer to processes or currents in fiction, but there the parallel stops. Indeed, the flux or stream of conscience, insofar as it is designed as a term to include every mode by which the self responds to the world, would include the stream of consciousness as one such mode.

The stream of consciousness is a technique (or a variety of such techniques) for rendering consciousness in fiction. The stream of conscience is not a technique. Whereas evidently novels can exist without rendering a stream of consciousness, no novel can exist without rendering a stream of conscience. The latter is the moral *movement* of fiction itself (not merely the moral movement of character, which it *includes*); it is the evolution of the full moral complexity of a work of fiction, developed and elaborated as a process (not as a meaning or meanings, merely) through the structure of events.

It may be helpful, too, to consider the relationships among the three terms: the flux of experience, the stream of events, and the stream (or flux) of conscience. The old analogy with "convex" and "concave" will serve. Viewed from the inside, an arc or dome is concave; viewed from the outside, it is convex: although the two words are not interchangeable, they refer to precisely the same arc, differently viewed. The stream of events in a novel is the flux of experience viewed from the outside: an architectural view. The stream (or flux) of conscience is an inside view: it is the flux of experience viewed morally.

4. Clearly, since the nature of innocence is invariably established in relation to the nature of the experience to follow, the particular limitations of character conveyed by early events are in each case different.

5. For a detailed presentation and analysis of a whole novel composed in the closed form of experience, the reader is referred to the consideration of Thomas Hardy's *Far from the Madding Crowd,* at the beginning of Chapter Three.

6. Compare: "In Sterne's deceptively frivolous, deceptively ingenuous novel *Tristram Shandy,* a new type of structure makes its appearance, a type that is of singular importance for the development of the modern novel." —Dorothy Van Ghent, *The English Novel: Form and Function* (New York, 1961), p. 83.

"The dislocation of values is far from being a twentieth-century invention, and *Wuthering Heights* or *Tristram Shandy* could easily be used to illustrate many aspects of fiction."—Earl H. Rovit, "The Ambiguous Modern Novel," *Yale Review,* XLIX (Spring 1960), p. 420

7. Wayne Booth, "Did Sterne Complete *Tristram Shandy?,*" *Modern Philology,* XLVII (February 1951), 172-83.

8. In "Technique as Discovery," *Hudson Review*, I (Spring 1948), 67-87. Reprinted in *Forms of Modern Fiction*, ed. William Van O'Connor (Minneapolis, Minn., 1948), pp. 9-29; see esp. pp. 13-14.

9. David Daiches, *The Novel and the Modern World*, rev. ed. (Chicago, 1960), p. 138.

10. Henry James, "Preface to *Roderick Hudson*," in *The Art of the Novel*, ed. R. P. Blackmur (New York, 1947), p. 5.

11. Frederick R. Karl, "*The Mayor of Casterbridge:* A New Fiction Defined," *Modern Fiction Studies*, VI (Autumn 1960), p. 195. But compare: "*The Mayor of Casterbridge* is not, however, any more than *Lear* and *Oedipus*, a study in the impulse to self-destruction"—John Paterson, "*The Mayor of Casterbridge* as Tragedy," *Victorian Studies*, III (December 1959), p. 158.

12. Robert M. Adams, *Strains of Discord: Studies in Literary Openness* (Ithaca, N. Y., 1958).

13. Schorer, "Technique as Discovery," in O'Connor, p. 18.

Chapter 3

1. Henry James, "Hardy's *Far from the Madding Crowd*," *The Nation* (December 24, 1874). Reprinted in *Literary Reviews and Essays by Henry James,* ed. by Albert Mordell (New York, 1957), p. 296.

2. *Jude the Obscure* (New York, 1920, Anniversary Edition), p. 32. All future citations of page numbers in the novels of Hardy will be incorporated in the present text and will refer to the Anniversary Edition. Any quotation for which no page number is given will be found on the page cited for the preceding quotation.

3. Against the incisive style—personal style and prose style—of Bathsheba's remark one might set the crispness of Ursula's:

> "But really imagine it: imagine any man one knows, imagine him coming home to one every evening, and giving one a kiss—"
> There was a blank pause.
> "Yes," said Gudrun, in a narrowed voice. "It's just impossible. The man makes it impossible."—*Women in Love* (New York, 1922), p. 9

Or again, compare Bathsheba's remarkable reason for not taking a husband:

> "Why, he'd always be there . . . ; whenever I looked up, there he'd be." (33)

The specific sequence of heroines from Bathsheba Everdene and Sue Bridehead to Ursula Brangwen and Constance Chatterley has some relevance to a study of the shaping of experience by a sequence of novelists from Thomas Hardy to D. H. Lawrence. All four heroines are carefully shown to pass from their virginal innocence to the experience of a wider and threatening sexual morality. But the first two are finally guided or beaten into a retreat, while the latter two are encouraged to persist.

4. *Colby Notes on* Far from the Madding Crowd, ed. by Carl J. Weber (Waterville, Maine, 1935), p. 41.

5. Watch-dog modifications in Hardy's text were usually made in the opposite way: "offensive" passages deleted in advance from magazine versions were regularly restored in the volume publication. Perhaps the most astonishing instance of this procedure—involving the use of varicolored inks for planned deletions of whole sections of *Tess of the d'Urbervilles*— is explained in some detail on page 291 of F. E. Hardy, *The Early Life of Thomas Hardy* (London, 1928).

6. As the installments were coming out in serial form, a friend (Mrs. Proctor) wrote Hardy: "You would be gratified to know what a shock the marriage of Bathsheba was. I resembled Mr. Boldwood—and to deceive such an old novel-reader as myself is a triumph. We are always looking out for traps, and scent a long way off a surprise. . . ."—F. E. Hardy, *The Early Life,* p. 133.

7. Against this, one is tempted to set the more extreme innocence of Lawrence's Constance Chatterley: "being a girl, one's whole dignity and meaning in life consisted in the achievement of an absolute, a pure and noble freedom. What else did a girl's life mean? To shake off the old and sordid connections and subjections."—*Lady Chatterley's Lover* (New York, 1959), p. 4. See note 3, above.

8. A marriage whose validity is questionable either legally or morally is, of course, the fate or near-fate of a distinguished line of Hardy heroines: Cytherea, Lucetta, Grace Melbury, Tess, Sue.

9. J. O. Bailey, "Hardy's 'Mephistophelian Visitants,'" *PMLA*, LXI (December 1946), p. 1149.

10. "What raises [*Far from the Madding Crowd*] above the commonplace of Victorian fiction is the way in which its episodes of passion and violence are so implicated with the life of the fields that they take their place as only one aspect of a universe elsewhere deeply ordered and composed" —J. I. M. Stewart, *Eight Modern Writers,* The Oxford History of English Literature, Vol. XII (Oxford, 1963), pp. 29-30.

11. For an elaborate comparison of *Tess* and *Paradise Lost,* see Allan Brick,

"Paradise and Consciousness in Hardy's *Tess*," *Nineteenth-Century Fiction*, XVII (September 1962), pp. 115-34.

12. This is the view (though the details given here are mine) of Horace E. Hamilton, "A Reading of *Tess of the d'Urbervilles*," in *Essays in Literary History Presented to J. Milton French* (New Brunswick, N. J., 1960), p. 216, fn. 3. See also his fn. 5.

13. F. E. Hardy, *The Early Life*, p. 234.

14. For a different attempt to suggest the significance of Saint Teresa in the naming of Tess, see Hamilton, p. 216.

15. With the view taken here one might compare what seems to me a curiously wrongheaded view: "we feel the decline and fall of Michael Henchard, because we can believe that things could have continued to go well with him, whereas Tess, with whom nothing could ever have gone right, fails to move us so greatly."—Robert Liddell, *Some Principles of Fiction* (London, 1953), p. 61.

16. For a tabular listing of recurrent episodes in Hardy, see the unpublished dissertation (University of California, Berkeley, 1941) by Philip F. Farley, "Pattern, Structure, and Form in the Novels of Thomas Hardy," pp. 242-8.

17. Cf. Hardy's note of January 1887: "I want to see the deeper reality underlying the scenic, the expression of what are sometimes called abstract imaginings"—F. E. Hardy, *The Early Life*, p. 242.

18. Lascelles Abercrombie was moved to cry in outrage: "no decent person, knowing Angel's history, would house with him or, if possible, talk with him"—*Thomas Hardy: A Critical Study* (New York, 1912), p. 149.

19. Significantly, by the time of Hardy's late fiction a narrowing conclusion has become inappropriate, aesthetically and ethically; whereas the ending Hardy was obliged to tack onto the body of *The Return of the Native* is not entirely "inapposite," as John Paterson points out, to the book that has gone before. "As Hardy was himself to confess in the celebrated footnote on p. 473 of the British Wessex edition (1912), he was forced, by editorial pressure and the necessities of serial publication, to provide for a happy ending. The allegedly extraneous sixth book of *The Return of the Native* is less inapposite, however, than Hardy and some of his critics would lead one to believe. His attitude to Eustacia's romantic revolt, to the extraordinary and the tragic in human experience, is not after all wholly uncritical. Hence the celebration of the ordinary and the comic in human experience which is the domesticating effect of the sixth book is not altogether foreign to the novel as originally conceived. The implications of his footnote notwithstanding, in other words, Hardy in effect converted editorial necessity into artistic virtue"—John Paterson, *"The Mayor of*

Casterbridge as Tragedy," *Victorian Studies,* III (December 1959), fn. to p. 152.

20. Compare Albert Guerard: "What appears to be surrender to fatigue may actually be surrender to what the public presumably wanted in the way of a theatrical or consoling ending. We know that Hardy altered his original plan for *The Return of the Native* (which would have left Diggory Venn isolated and 'mysterious') in deference to his tender-minded public; the same cynicism was responsible for the ending of *The Woodlanders* and may have been responsible for the ending of *Far from the Madding Crowd.* The conclusions of Victorian novels so often have nothing to do with the novels themselves that we must look to earlier chapters for significant instances of abandoned or perverted impulse [of composition]"—*Thomas Hardy* (Cambridge, Mass., 1949), p. 52.

21. His plot, Hardy writes, is "almost geometrically constructed," but then he hastily adds by way of qualification: "beyond a certain point, the characters necessitated it, and I simply let it come."—F. E. Hardy, *The Later Years of Thomas Hardy* (New York, 1930), p. 40. These comments suggest that the ending, at least, may have been intuitive; but Hardy tells another reviewer: "in writing *Jude* my mind was fixed on the ending" (ibid., p. 43). The mixture of both kinds of awareness (deliberate and intuitive) in his manipulation of the approaching resolution of the novel can perhaps best be suggested by a remark from the notebooks: "Get it done and let them howl!" (ibid., p. 38). The Lawrentian ring is authentic. (Hardy claims he is quoting an anonymous friend of Jowett's, but the satisfaction with which he records the remark is illuminating.)

22. Kathleen R. Hoopes, "Illusion and Reality in *Jude the Obscure,*" *Nineteenth-Century Fiction,* XII (September 1957), 157.

23. Hardy's approach to *Jude,* J. I. M. Stewart writes, suggests that he may have "felt that in *Tess* he had not got far enough away from literary conventions and the lure of art. Tess herself has great stature, and may have seemed to him to render a final impression more in the grand manner of tragedy than his present sense of the mere desperation of the human situation warranted"—*Eight Modern Writers,* p. 44.

24. F. E. Hardy, *The Early Life,* p. 289.

25. F. E. Hardy, *The Later Years,* p. 6; and Thomas Hardy's own postscript to *Jude,* p. viii.

Chapter 4

1. Joseph Conrad, *Almayer's Folly* (New York, 1924), p. 33 (see also p. 37).
   All subsequent references to Conrad's fiction will be to the same edition
   by Doubleday, Page, & Company.
2. H. E. Bates, "Joseph Conrad and Thomas Hardy," in Derek Verschoyle,
   ed., *The English Novelists* (London, 1936), p. 231.
3. Joseph Conrad, "Henry James, An Appreciation," in *Notes on Life and
   Letters* (London, 1924), pp. 18-19.
4. Robert Penn Warren, "On *Nostromo,*" in R. W. Stallman, *The Art of
   Joseph Conrad: A Critical Symposium* (Ann Arbor, Mich., 1960), p. 216.
   First published as the Introduction to the Modern Library edition of
   Nostromo (New York, 1951).
5. F. R. Leavis, *The Great Tradition* (London, 1948), p. 199.
6. Albert J. Guerard, *Conrad the Novelist* (Cambridge, Mass., 1958), p. 204.
7. Graham Hough, *Image and Experience: Studies in a Literary Revolution*
   (London, 1960), p. 216.
8. "Our lack of identification with Nostromo" is due, among other causes,
   to "the detachment with which Conrad himself seems to view him" and
   to Conrad's characterization of the "hero" as "too simple in intellect and
   too consistent in behavior." This is the opinion of Claire Rosenfield, who
   further suggests that "the final reason for Nostromo's failure as a hero
   [that is, as an archetypal hero] is that he simply lacks status. . . . He is
   only a sailor and the men he dominates are mainly Negroes . . . traditionally symbols of the unknown—and by extension, evil. . . ."—Claire
   Rosenfield, "An Archetypal Analysis of Conrad's *Nostromo,*" *Texas Studies
   in Literature and Language,* III (Winter 1962), 529-30.
9. Conrad, "Henry James," p. 17.
10. Leavis, pp. 190, 196, and 200.
11. The book is identified as *"On Many Seas: The Life and Exploits of a
    Yankee Sailor,* by Frederick Benton Williams, edited by his friend William
    Stone Booth, New York: the Macmillan Company, 1897" in "The Orig-
    inal Nostromo: Conrad's Source," by John Halverson and Ian Watt in
    The Review of English Studies (New Series), X (1959), p. 45.

    Another source, G. F. Masterson's *Seven Eventful Years in Paraguay,*
    1869, is cited by Ivo Vidan in "One Source of Conrad's *Nostromo,*" *The
    Review of English Studies* (New Series), VII (1956), 288-9.

    A third source for some of the material in *Nostromo,* the autobiography
    of Giuseppe Garibaldi (*Mémoires de Garibaldi,* 2 vols., trans. Alexander

Dumas, Paris, 1860) is suggested by Rosemary Freeman in "Conrad's *Nostromo:* A Source and Its Use," *Modern Fiction Studies,* VII (1961), 317-26.

Halverson and Watt also treat, in a manner different from the treatment of the subject given in the present study, the meaning and relation of "Nostromo" (as word, as character) to the book and its title: "What was needed, therefore, was a character who would be worthy of the larger paradoxes implicit in Nicolo's act; worthy, that is, of its moral essence, the irony of misplaced trust; what was needed, in fact, was someone who could be legitimately taken as 'our man'; and so, as he wrote to Galsworthy, Conrad began his novel by writing the single word of the title—*Nostromo.* [Footnote:] G. Jean-Aubry, *Joseph Conrad: Life and Letters,* i. 308. [Their footnote continues:] . . . Some critics—as most recently Richard Curle in his introduction to the Everyman's Library *Nostromo* (p. xii)—have pointed out that the title is not wholly felicitous, since it refers to only one of the novel's many elements; the reason is presumably that the title is essentially a relic of the novel's germinal inspiration."—Halverson and Watt, p. 52 and fn. 1.

12. Frederick R. Karl explains the confusion as a deliberate result of Conrad's and Ford Madox Ford's theory of fiction, in "Joseph Conrad's Literary Theory," *Criticism,* II (Fall 1960), 317-35, see especially p. 320.

13. Letter to R. B. Cunninghame Graham (May 9, 1903) in G. Jean-Aubry, *Joseph Conrad: Life and Letters* (Garden City, N. Y., 1927), Vol. I, p. 315.

14. Letter to R. B. Cunninghame Graham (July 8, 1903) in Jean-Aubry, p. 315.

15. Letter to John Galsworthy (September 1, 1904) in Jean-Aubry, pp. 332 ff.

16. Letter to William Rothenstein (September 3, 1904) in Jean-Aubry, p. 336.

17. Letter to R. B. Cunninghame Graham (October 7, 1904) in Jean-Aubry, p. 337.

18. Letter to R. B. Cunninghame Graham (October 31, 1904) in Jean-Aubry, p. 337.

19. See fn. 11 above.

20. Karl, p. 320.

21. This is the position in which Garibaldi was tortured. See Rosemary Freeman, fn. 11 above.

22. The enmity between Nostromo and Monygham is dramatically represented as resembling that between a sinner and the devil: see such phrases as, "The priests say he is a tempter" and "the engine-driver says you have an evil eye" (462 f.). See also Monygham's disappointment at Nostromo's deathbed (560).

23. This is not to say that the final treatment of Nostromo is well done, but

only that it is done deliberately and appropriately. Compare Albert Guerard's objection that the final section surrenders to "a relaxed method and a much more popular story."—*Conrad the Novelist*, p. 216.

24. Conrad's difficulties in treating the kind of subject matter he here attempts are discussed in Thomas Moser, "Joseph Conrad and the Uncongenial Subject," in his *Joseph Conrad: Achievement and Decline* (Cambridge, Mass., 1957); see especially pp. 87-90.

25. Leavis, p. 192.

26. Guerard, p. 204.

27. Ibid., p. 204.

28. There are, of course, other individuals whose fate conditions the process of experience in the novel. To make our picture complete, we can hardly do better than to quote Jocelyn Baines: "The fate of the individuals with whom *Nostromo* has been particularly concerned and of Costaguana as a whole are equally hopeless. Antonia Avellanos and Linda Viola both have the men they love taken away by death. Mrs. Gould virtually loses her husband to the mine and is in the end disillusioned: 'She resembled a good fairy, weary with a long career of well-doing, touched by the withering suspicion of the uselessness of her labours, the powerlessness of her magic.' [p. 520] She is engulfed by 'an immense desolation, the dread of her own continued life.' [p. 522]" Jocelyn Baines, *Joseph Conrad: A Critical Biography* (London, 1959), p. 310.

With respect to the book's structure, the following observations may be pertinent: Emilia Gould's repudiation of "material interest" by refusing even to listen to Nostromo's offer to tell her the whereabouts of the treasure is a moment of affirmation; but it hardly serves as a containment of her disintegrating experience (see p. 511 f.) with Charles Gould or his mine. If one is disposed to consider the event as a reversal—which I do not believe it is—then it is a vestige of the more conventional form. But in any case, it does not serve to reverse the entire book's stream of conscience, which is irreversible on a grand national scale as well as in Nostromo's life (again see p. 511 f.).

As for the other experience of affirmation in the book, Dr. Monygham's, his personal redemption can hardly be regarded as a tapering moral reorganization of his experience *after* a disintegrating climax: on the contrary, Monygham begins the book morally and spiritually shattered. (His torture by Father Beron—see pp. 372 ff.—precedes the events of the story.) And his entire story is a movement of expanding moral integration and salvation: *up to* the climax in the events of the revolution (where his behavior is heroic) and *continuing after* the climax. His experience, like

Nostromo's, is exclusively an expanding form. Of course their consciences, like their experiences, expand in reverse directions. But neither of their contrary directions of experience shows the *conventional* pattern of a narrowing movement to arrive at a "conclusion" after the climax. As Rosemary Freeman puts it: "The two change places morally."—Freeman, p. 325.

29. J. I. M. Stewart, *Eight Modern Writers,* The Oxford History of English Literature, Vol. XII (Oxford, 1963), p. 205.
30. Kenneth Burke, *Counter-Statement* (New York, 1931), p. 157.
31. Letter to Richard Curle (July 14, 1923) in Jean-Aubry, II, p. 317.
32. That Pound was aware of following in Conrad's footsteps (Ezra Pound, *Polite Essays* [London, 1937], pp. 50-57) is pointed out by Frederick R. Karl in "Joseph Conrad's Literary Theory," p. 318. My own remarks on Conrad's theory are based on Karl's discussion, which quotes the letter to Curle.
33. Ford Madox Ford, *Joseph Conrad: A Personal Remembrance* (Boston, 1925), p. 185.
34. Ibid., p. 225.
35. Conrad, *Letters from Conrad, 1895 to 1924,* ed. Edward Garnett (London, 1928), p. 61.
36. Conrad, *Notes on Life and Letters* (London, 1949), p. 55. I am indebted to John Paterson for calling my attention to both this remark of Conrad's and the letter cited in the last footnote.
37. Ford, *Joseph Conrad,* p. 185.
38. Leavis, p. 208.
39. Robert F. Haugh, *Joseph Conrad: Discovery in Design* (Norman, Okla., 1957), p. 116.
40. Kingsley Widmer, "Conrad's Pyrrhic *Victory,*" *Twentieth Century Literature,* V (October 1959), p. 129.
41. V. S. Pritchett, *The Living Novel* (London, 1946), p. 144.

Chapter 5

1. E. M. Forster, *Aspects of the Novel* (New York, 1958), pp. 241 f.
2. Critics who have applied Forster's notion about "expansion" to his own work have, of course, done so in the context of meaning established by the novelist, observing in his novels an expansion produced by "rhythmic" relationships: "But to read a novel of Forster's is like listening to a symphony. The novel expands; what we have read indeed melts into the past, for new vistas are continually opening before us. Yet the slightest hints

are often of importance to the plot, and the quietest phrases may develop into 'rhythms.'" J. K. Johnstone, *The Bloomsbury Group: A Study of E. M. Forster, Lytton Strachey, Virginia Woolf, and Their Circle* (New York, 1954), p. 160.

This is, of course, the approach taken elaborately throughout E. K. Brown's *Rhythm in the Novel* (Toronto, 1950), but see especially pp. 63-64 and 92.

3. Forster, *Aspects,* p. 242.

4. George Eliot, *Daniel Deronda,* Ch. LXV.

5. Page references to *A Room with a View* will be to the New Directions edition (Norfolk, Conn., n.d.) and will be incorporated in the text. All quotations from this and other novels of Forster's not identified by page numbers will be found on the page of the last preceding citation.

6. An ending which unleashes, rather than contains, is carried to more extreme lengths in *Howards End.* After the book's climax in the death of Leonard Bast, the last chapter unites under one roof (Howards End) Henry Wilcox, in his athletic commercialism, Margaret Schlegel, in her poetic compassion, and Margaret's sister Helen (who has brought a "Bast" child into the world)—a three-way union whose extra-marital threads (both Helen and Henry have had "Bast" affairs) strain their expanded consciences and the reader's credulity.

7. *Where Angels Fear to Tread* was published in 1905, before *A Room with a View* (1908). Of the latter novel, Rose Macaulay writes that "its embryo was conceived several years earlier."—*The Writings of E. M. Forster* (New York, n.d., first published 1938), p. 36.

8. Page references, incorporated in the text, refer to the Vintage Books edition of *Where Angels Fear to Tread* (New York, 1958).

9. See Frederick C. Crews, *E. M. Forster: The Perils of Humanism* (Princeton, 1962), p. 74.

10. Lionel Trilling, *E. M. Forster* (London, 1944), p. 66.

11. Compare: "Forster seems to be saying, in what constitutes a kind of epilogue to his book, that Philip and Caroline, despite their growth, have not been able to attain full stature, that the most difficult thing to achieve —true and lasting relationships, and through them complete involvement in life—is not yet, perhaps never will be, within their grasp."—Alan Wilde, "The Aesthetic View of Life: *Where Angels Fear to Tread,*" *Modern Fiction Studies,* VII, 3 (Autumn 1961), p. 215.

12. Macaulay, p. 198.

13. J. B. Beer, *The Achievement of E. M. Forster* (London, 1962), p. 132.

14. Trilling, p. 136 f.

15. *Writers at Work, The Paris Review Interviews* [1953] (New York, 1958), p. 28.

16. Beer, p. 133.

17. Ibid., p. 162.

18. Gertrude M. White, *"A Passage to India:* Analysis and Revaluation," *PMLA,* LXVIII (Sept. 1953), p. 641 and fn. 1, loc. cit.

19. Ibid., p. 644.

20. Glen O. Allen, "Structure, Symbol, and Theme in E. M. Forster's *A Passage to India,"* *PMLA,* LXX (Dec. 1955), p. 935.

21. Allen, pp. 952 and 953 f.

22. Glenn Pederson, "Forster's Symbolic Form," *Kenyon Review,* XXI (Spring 1959), p. 239.

23. David Shusterman, "The Curious Case of Professor Godbole: *A Passage to India* Re-examined," *PMLA,* LXXVI (Sept. 1961), p. 435.

24. Crews, p. 142.

25. Page references to *A Passage to India* will be to the Harcourt, Brace and Company edition (New York, 1924) and will be incorporated in the text.

26. Johnstone, p. 264.

27. "What, then, did happen in the cave? Nothing. And everything."—Louise Dauner, "What Happened in the Cave? Reflections on *A Passage to India,"* *Modern Fiction Studies,* VII (Autumn 1961), p. 270.

28. *Writers at Work,* p. 28.

29. Beer, p. 133.

30. Reuben Brower, "The Twilight of the Double Vision: Symbol and Irony in *A Passage to India,"* in his *The Fields of Light* (New York, 1948), p. 198.

Chapter 6

I

1. D. H. Lawrence, *The Letters of D. H. Lawrence,* ed. Aldous Huxley (New York, 1932), pp. 199 f.

2. Virginia Woolf, "Notes on D. H. Lawrence," in *The Moment and Other Essays* (New York, 1948), p. 96.

3. Since the letter does not name *The Rainbow* (although the letter's date makes that novel the most likely one), a very small degree of uncertainty exists about which novel, if any one in particular, Lawrence meant. Most critics assume it was *The Rainbow;* no one has denied that it was. Fortunately, the present argument does not really depend on a certain identification.

4. ". . . Leavis writes entirely from Lawrence's point of view, as though he were himself Lawrence."—David Daiches, *The Novel and the Modern World,* rev. ed. (Chicago, 1960), p. 185.

5. F. R. Leavis, *D. H. Lawrence: Novelist* (New York, 1956), p. 172.

6. Ibid., p. 170.

7. Mark Schorer, "Technique as Discovery," *Hudson Review,* I (Spring 1948); reprinted in *Myth and Method: Modern Theories of Fiction,* ed. James E. Miller, Jr. (Lincoln, Nebr., 1960), p. 96.

8. *The Letters,* ed. Huxley, p. 78.

9. Ibid., p. 79.

10. Louis Fraiberg, "The Unattainable Self: D. H. Lawrence's *Sons and Lovers,*" in *Twelve Original Essays on Great English Novels,* ed. Charles Shapiro (Detroit, Mich., 1960), p. 199.

11. Compare F. R. Leavis' observation quoted above (see n. 6).

12. Fraiberg, p. 199.

13. Herbert Lindenberger, "Lawrence and the Romantic Tradition," in *A D. H. Lawrence Miscellany,* ed. Harry T. Moore (Carbondale, Ill., 1959), p. 340.

14. Graham Hough, *The Dark Sun: A Study of D. H. Lawrence* (New York, 1957), p. 103.

15. Daiches, p. 166.

16. Hough, p. 71.

17. Roger Sale, "The Narrative Technique of *The Rainbow,*" *Modern Fiction Studies,* V (Spring 1959), p. 38.

18. Mark Spilka, "The Shape of an Arch: A Study of Lawrence's *The Rainbow,*" *Modern Fiction Studies,* I (May 1955), p. 38; a slightly altered version of these remarks appears in Mark Spilka, *The Love Ethic of D. H. Lawrence* (Bloomington, Ind., 1955), p. 115.

19. Hough, p. 85.

20. Daiches, pp. 168 f.

21. Leavis, p. 19.

22. Edward Engelberg, "Escape from the Circles of Experience: D. H. Lawrence's *The Rainbow* as a Modern *Bildungsroman,*" *PMLA,* LXXVIII (March 1963), p. 112.

23. Marvin Mudrick, earlier than Engelberg, suggested briefly that Lawrence's form was an achievement, not a failure: "Still, *The Rainbow* is, finally, not about consummation but about promise."—"The Originality of *The Rainbow,*" in *A D. H. Lawrence Miscellany,* ed. Moore, p. 77.

But one should compare with these views the continuing "difficulty" critics face in seeing Lawrence's form as an achievement. Eugene Goodheart refers to "Lawrence's vision of the ritual movement of life itself . . . the cycle of fulfilment, dissatisfaction, fulfilment, etc. This is why, one might argue, none of the novels is 'resolved.' Every resolution precedes another dissatisfaction, another urge to make forays into the unknown. The difficulty with this explanation, however, is [that the] failure of each relationship is particular, arising from the failures in the characters themselves."—*The Utopian Vision of D. H. Lawrence* (Chicago, 1963), p. 119. One might comment that such particularity in characterization seems hardly a "difficulty" but a blessing and an aid in seeing Lawrence's achievement of his "vision of the ritual movement of life itself" in fiction.

24. Robert M. Adams writes that for all Lawrence's "modern romantic openness," in fact "the structure of his novels is not, ordinarily, open to any notable degree."—*Strains of Discord: Studies in Literary Openness* (Ithaca, N. Y., 1958), p. 188. A discussion of the difference between Adams' concept of an "open" structure and my own will be found in Chapter Two of the present work.

25. Engelberg, p. 112.

26. D. H. Lawrence, *Phoenix: The Posthumous Papers of D. H. Lawrence* (New York, 1936), p. 308.

27. D. H. Lawrence, *Women in Love,* Modern Library edition (New York, n.d.), p. 475.

II

28. Both renewals of experience—in a nonterminating novel (*Women in Love*) and in an unfathomable marriage—have the same form as the renewal of society prophesied in the novel's last paragraph under the sign of the rainbow. Compare Lawrence's phrases in *Fantasia of the Unconscious:* ". . . the human potentiality to evolve something magnificent out of a renewed chaos . . . the strangeness and rainbow-change of ever-renewed creative civilizations."—(London, 1961, p. 8. First published in 1923.)

29. See p. 42 of the Random House, Modern Library edition. All future page references in the present work to *The Rainbow* and *Women in Love* (referred to as *R* and *WL*) will be to the Modern Library editions; the page numbers will be incorporated in the text. A quotation not identified by page number will be found on the same page as that of the preceding citation.

30. Edward Engelberg finds this change significant; see "Escape from the Circles of Experience," p. 107.

31. The last paragraph of *The Rainbow* has annoyed almost everyone. This is understandable, but Lawrence's intention in that conclusion, let us insist, cannot be exhausted by criticizing its abrupt, undue, and irrelevant social optimism. ("She saw in the rainbow the earth's new architecture, the old, brittle corruption of houses and factories swept away. . . .") Taken as a burst of rhetoric, this is unsatisfying. Like the vision of Paul Morel, who also saw a glow over a town and hurried toward it in a burst of personal optimism, Ursula's glowing vision remains, as social optimism, unpersuasive. But Ursula's vision is more than that: it is a vision of light in the darkness of her self. Indeed, the explicit social prophecy—"the old, brittle corruption of houses and factories swept away, the world built up in a living fabric of Truth, fitting to the over-arching heaven"—cannot be understood (or not merely) as a simplified prediction for the world; it must also be understood as a predication of the self. That is, Ursula's "vision" of the town can and ought to be taken in the same sense that her earlier "vision" of the wild horses is commonly taken. Both are symbols for an inner process: natural movement and historical movement, respectively, help convey a movement in the soul.

III

32. Mark Schorer, *"Women in Love* and Death," in *D. H. Lawrence: A Collection of Critical Essays,* ed. Mark Spilka (Englewood Cliffs, N. J., 1963), p. 56. First published in *The Hudson Review,* VI (Spring 1953).
33. Compare *The Rainbow,* pp. 456-8, discussed above.
34. The theoretical comments on the novel in chapter nine of *Lady Chatterley's Lover* provide another instance in another novel.
35. Graham Hough, *The Dark Sun,* p. 85.
36. David Daiches, *The Novel and the Modern World,* p. 169.
37. Wallace Stevens, "An Ordinary Evening in New Haven," *The Collected Poems of Wallace Stevens* (New York, 1961), p. 486.

IV

38. D. H. Lawrence, *Psychoanalysis and the Unconscious* (reprinted in *Fantasia of the Unconscious* and *Psychoanalysis and the Unconscious,* London, 1961), p. 199. First published in 1923.
39. "Joyce and Lawrence, violently unlike though they are, were writers of very formidable original genius. It sometimes seems that no literary form can afford genius of extreme revolutionary talent too often. . . . It is plain that after thirty years Lawrence and Joyce are still well ahead of any Eng-

lish novelist writing today. They are as advanced now as they were then."
—Walter Allen, *The English Novel* (New York, 1954), p. 412.

"In his mature novels Lawrence was at least as revolutionary as Joyce in the conception of prose fiction which he was acting out. . . . [He put] the novel form to genuinely new uses and broke out of the limits imposed on storytelling by two hundred years of prose fiction. . . ."—David Daiches, *The Novel and the Modern World*, pp. 139 f.

"*Women in Love* has perhaps a better claim than either *Ulysses* or *Finnegans Wake* to be the radically original English novel of the age."—J. I. M. Stewart, *Eight Modern Writers*, The Oxford History of English Literature, Vol. XII (Oxford, 1963), p. 513.

40. On Lawrence's "daimon," see Aldous Huxley, Introduction to *The Letters of D. H. Lawrence*, ed. Huxley, pp. xvi-xvii. On his personal involvement in the novel, see Daiches, pp. 141-2. For Lawrence's reliance on symbolic scenes, see Raney Stanford, "Thomas Hardy and Lawrence's *The White Peacock*," *Modern Fiction Studies*, V (Spring 1959), 20-23. For his recourse to a timeless and spaceless narration, see Roger Sale, "The Narrative Technique of *The Rainbow*," pp. 29-38. For the significance of sexual realization, see Marvin Mudrick, "The Originality of *The Rainbow*," in *A D. H. Lawrence Miscellany*, ed. Moore, p. 70.

41. The first quotation is from Eliseo Vivas, *D. H. Lawrence: The Failure and the Triumph of Art* (Evanston, Ill., 1960), p. 203. The second quotation is from Harry T. Moore, "*The Rainbow*," in *The Achievement of D. H. Lawrence*, ed. Frederick J. Hoffman and Harry T. Moore (Norman, Okla., 1953), p. 145.

42. Stewart, *Eight Modern Writers*, p. 502.

43. "[Lawrence] has also been criticized for attempting the impossible by seeking to give us the felt quality of an experience by direct presentation in words. The truth is that when he makes such attempts he sometimes falls into incoherence, straining the language and piling metaphor on image, with disastrous results."—Vivas, p. 198.

44. Huxley, Introduction to *The Letters*, pp. xi f.

45. F. R. Leavis, *D. H. Lawrence: Novelist* (New York, 1956), pp. 235, 232, and 236.

46. Father Tiverton, too, recognizes that Lawrence "explored regions of consciousness that could never be described by a method which he here devises," but the critic does not offer to treat the novelist's method. Father William Tiverton [pseud. of William Robert Jarrett-Kerr], *D. H. Lawrence and Human Existence* (London, 1951), p. 35.

One ought to mention that Max Wildi, in his excellent early study of Lawrence, recognized in the novelist's "treatment of character" the rise of "a subtle conflict between intuitive, unconscious truth and conscious interpretation."—in "The Birth of Expressionism in the Work of D. H. Lawrence," *English Studies,* XIX (December 1937), 244.

47. Huxley, loc. cit.

48. Compare: "There are, however, two levels of consciousness which can be rather simply distinguished: the 'speech level' and the 'prespeech level.' There is a point at which they overlap, but otherwise the distinction is quite clear. The prespeech level, which is the concern of most of the literature under consideration in this study, involves no communicative basis as does the speech level (whether spoken or written). This is its salient distinguishing characteristic. . . . With such a concept of consciousness, we may define stream-of-consciousness fiction as a type of fiction in which the basic emphasis is placed on exploration of the prespeech levels of consciousness for the purpose, primarily, of revealing the psychic being of the characters."—Robert Humphrey, *Stream of Consciousness in the Modern Novel* (Berkeley and Los Angeles, Cal., 1955), pp. 3 f.

49. *Per contra:* ". . . the nature of the true, pristine unconscious, in which all our genuine impulse arises [is] a very different affair from that sack of horrors which psychoanalysts would have us believe is [the] source of motivity."—D. H. Lawrence, *Psychoanalysis and the Unconscious,* p. 204. See also Frederick J. Hoffman, "Lawrence's Quarrel with Freud," in Hoffman and Moore (eds.), *The Achievement of D. H. Lawrence:* Freud and Lawrence "go their own ways, and it is perhaps unwise to measure the one by the standards of the other, for their development of the idea of consciousness becomes widely separate" (pp. 126 f.). And see Philip Rieff, "A Modern Mythmaker," in *Myth and Mythmaking,* ed. Henry A. Murray (New York, 1960): "Freud, the intellectualist, trusts reason. To Lawrence, therefore, Freud is the great enemy spokesman, engaged to the analysis but not the advocacy of the Unconscious" (p. 274).

50. "The Freudian unconscious is the cellar in which the mind keeps its own bastard spawn."—Lawrence, *Psychoanalysis,* p. 204.

51. Compare Francis Fergusson, "D. H. Lawrence's Sensibility," in *Forms of Modern Fiction,* ed. William Van O'Connor (Minneapolis, Minn., 1948), pp. 72-9.

52. Compare: "The importance of symbolic scenes for dramatizing Hardy's fictional meanings has been noted by most of his modern critics but has been investigated in detail by few."—Raney Stanford, "Thomas Hardy

and Lawrence's *The White Peacock*," p. 20. Stanford supplies a footnote which lists three brief discussions of the technique.

53. In his book on Lawrence, Daniel A. Weiss makes a related point, asserting that the artist himself must—by definition—"pursue his unconscious bents in blindness." See *Oedipus in Nottingham* (Seattle, Wash., 1962), pp. 10-11.

54. See the "common-sense questions" of David Daiches, *The Novel and the Modern World*, pp. 164-6.

Chapter 7

1. André Gide, *The Counterfeiters*, trans. Justin O'Brien (New York, 1959), p. 310.

2. Edward Engelberg, "Escape from the Circles of Experience: D. H. Lawrence's *The Rainbow* as a Modern *Bildungsroman*," *PMLA*, LXXVIII (March 1963), pp. 112 f.

3. Lionel Trilling, "The Fate of Pleasure," in *Beyond Culture: Essays in Literature and Learning* (New York, 1965), pp. 85 ff.

4. Walter Slatoff, *Quest for Failure: A Study of William Faulkner* (Ithaca, N. Y., 1960), p. 136.

5. Ibid., pp. 203, 264, and 149.

6. Wayne C. Booth, *The Rhetoric of Fiction* (Chicago, 1961), p. 397.

Index

The principal references for authors and titles are shown in italic numbers.